OECD Rural Policy Reviews

Mexico

OECD

ORGANISATION FOR ECONOMIC CO-OPERATION AND DEVELOPMENT

ORGANISATION FOR ECONOMIC CO-OPERATION AND DEVELOPMENT

The OECD is a unique forum where the governments of 30 democracies work together to address the economic, social and environmental challenges of globalisation. The OECD is also at the forefront of efforts to understand and to help governments respond to new developments and concerns, such as corporate governance, the information economy and the challenges of an ageing population. The Organisation provides a setting where governments can compare policy experiences, seek answers to common problems, identify good practice and work to co-ordinate domestic and international policies.

The OECD member countries are: Australia, Austria, Belgium, Canada, the Czech Republic, Denmark, Finland, France, Germany, Greece, Hungary, Iceland, Ireland, Italy, Japan, Korea, Luxembourg, Mexico, the Netherlands, New Zealand, Norway, Poland, Portugal, the Slovak Republic, Spain, Sweden, Switzerland, Turkey, the United Kingdom and the United States. The Commission of the European Communities takes part in the work of the OECD.

OECD Publishing disseminates widely the results of the Organisation's statistics gathering and research on economic, social and environmental issues, as well as the conventions, guidelines and standards agreed by its members.

This work is published on the responsibility of the Secretary-General of the OECD. The opinions expressed and arguments employed herein do not necessarily reflect the official views of the Organisation or of the governments of its member countries.

Foreword

With gains in agricultural productivity leading to a dramatic reduction in farm employment, rural regions across the OECD now depend on a wide range of economic engines for growth. Increasing globalisation, improved communications and reduced transportation costs are additional drivers of economic change in rural areas. Traditional policies to subsidise farming have not been able to harness the potential of these economic engines. In 2006 the OECD published a thematic report The New Rural Paradigm: Policies and Governance, which seek to explain the shift in rural development policies to account for these important economic changes and the new approach to governance that these policy approaches require.

Policies to develop rural places are beginning to take into account the diversity of economic engines as well as the diversity of rural region types. On the aggregate, rural regions face problems of decline with out-migration, ageing, a lower skill base and lower average labour productivity that then reduce the critical mass needed for effective public services, infrastructure and business development, thereby creating a vicious circle. However, there are many other rural regions that have seized opportunities and built on their existing assets, such as location, natural and cultural amenities, and social capital. The success of such dynamic rural regions is evident in regional statistics.

Promoting rural development poses numerous policy and governance challenges because it requires co-ordination across sectors, across levels of government, and between public and private actors. OECD countries have therefore been undergoing a paradigm shift in their approaches to accommodate such important challenges. The most defining characteristics of this shift are a focus on places rather than sectors and an emphasis on investments rather than subsidies.

The multi-disciplinary nature of rural development has contributed to the lack of comprehensive analytic frameworks to analyse and evaluate multi-sectoral, place-based approaches. The OECD will continue to work with other stakeholders worldwide to fill this knowledge gap. The OECD's work on rural development through the Group of the Council on Rural Development, created in 1990, was intensified with the creation in 1999 of the Territorial Development Policy Committee (TDPC) and its Working Party on Territorial Policy in Rural Areas. These bodies provide governments with a forum for discussing regional and rural development. In early 2006, under TDPC's guidance the Directorate of Public Governance and Territorial Development (GOV) launched a series of national rural policy reviews, such as this one, to deepen international knowledge in this field.

Acknowledgements

This review was elaborated by the Directorate of Public Governance and Territorial Development (GOV) of the OECD. The OECD Secretariat would like to thank the Mexican authorities for their co-operation and support. Peer reviewers in this process were Italy and Spain.

The Review was directed by Mr. Mario Pezzini, Head of the Territorial Reviews and Governance Division, co-ordinated and drafted respectively by Mr. Nicola Crosta and Mr. José Antonio Ardavín of the OECD Secretariat. Individual contributions were provided by Mr. Brian McCauley and Ms. Karen Maguire of the OECD Secretariat. External contributors were Mr. Pablo Rodas-Martini (ASIES/IDRC) and Mr. Yancy Vaillant (Barcelona Autonomous University). Mrs. Erin Byrne and Miss. Suzanna Grant prepared the Review for publication.

Table of Contents

OECD RURAL POLICY REVIEWS: MEXICO – ISBN 978-92-64-01152-6 – © OECD 2007

List of figures

List of Acronyms*

Acronym	Spanish/English Translation
CCA(s)	Centros Comunitarios de Aprendizaje *Learning Community Centres*
CDRS	Consejos de Desarrollo Rural Sustentable (Nacional, Estatal, Districtal, Municipal) *Councils for Sustainable Rural Development (National, State, District and Municipal)*
CEC(s)	Centros Estratégicos Comunitarios (de la Estrategia Microrregiones) *Strategic Community Centres (of the Micro-Regions Strategy)*
CECADER	Centros de Calidad para el Desarrollo Rural *Centres for Quality in Rural Development*
CIDRS	Comisión Intersecretarial para el Desarrollo Rural Sustentable *Inter-Ministerial Commission for Sustainable Rural Development*
CNA	Comisión Nacional del Agua *National Water Commission*
CONADEPI	Comisión Nacional para el Desarrollo de los Pueblos Indígenas *National Commission for the Development of Indigenous Towns*
CONAFOR	Comisión Nacional Forestal *National Forest Commission*
CONAPO	Consejo Nacional de Población *National Council of Population*
COPLADE	Comité(s) de Planeación y Desarrollo Estatal *Committee(s) for State Planning and Development*
COPLADEMUN	Comité(s) de Planeación y Desarrollo Municipal *Committee(s) for Municipal Planning and Development*
ENHRUM	Encuesta Nacional a Hogares Rurales de México *National Survey of Rural Households of Mexico*
ENIGH	Encuesta Nacional de Ingreso-Gasto de los Hogares *National Survey of Household's Income-Expenditure*

* The acronym in full in its original language appears in roman characters with the translation in italics.

FISM	Fondo para Infraestructura Social Municipal
	Municipal Fund for Social Infrastructure
FAO	Organización de las Naciones Unidas para la Agricultura y la Alimentación
	Food and Agriculture Organisation
GATT	Acuerdo General sobre Tarifas y Comercio
	General Agreement on Tariffs and Trade
HDI	Índice de Desarrollo Humano
	Human Development Index
IMSS	Instituto Mexicano del Seguro Social
	Mexican Institute of Social Security
IN	Intermediate Regions (OECD Regional Typology)
INAFED	Instituto Nacional para el Federalismo y el Desarrollo Municipal
	National Institute for Federalism and Municipal Development
INCA-Rural	Instituto Nacional para el Desarrollo de Capacidades del Sector Rural
	National Institute for the Development of Rural Capacities
INEGI	Instituto Nacional de Estadística, Geografía e Informática
	National Institute of Statistics, Geography and Informatics
LDRS	Ley de Desarrollo Rural Sustentable
	Law of Sustainable Rural Development
NAFTA	Tratado de Libre Comercio de América del Norte
	North American Free Trade Agreement
PAPIR	Programa de Apoyo a Proyectos de Inversión Rural
	Programme of support to rural investment projects
PDR	Programa de Desarrollo Rural
	Programme of Rural Development
PEC	Programa Especial Concurrente para el Desarrollo Rural Sustentable
	Special Concerted Programme for Sustainable Rural Development
PR	Predominantly Rural (OECD regional typology)
PROCAMPO	Programa de Apoyo Directos al Campo
	Programme of Direct Payments to the Countryside
PROCEDE	Programa de Certificación de Derechos Ejidales y Titulación de Solares
	Programme of Certification of Ejido Property Rights and Entitling of Parcels
PRODESCA	Programa de Desarrollo de Capacidades en el Medio Rural
	Programme of development of rural capacities
PROFEMOR	Programa para el Fortalecimiento de Empresas y Organización Rural
	Programme for strengthening rural enterprises and organisation

OECD RURAL POLICY REVIEWS: MEXICO – ISBN 978-92-64-01152-6 – © OECD 2007

PROFEPA	Procuraduría Federal de Protección al Medio Ambiente
	Federal Attorney General for Protection of Environment
PROGRESA	Programa de Educación, Salud y Alimentación (Oportunidades)
(Oportunidades)	*Programme of Education, Health and Food, (today Oportunidades)*
PRONASOL	Programa Nacional de Solidaridad
	Funding Programme for poor communities
PSP	Proveedores de Servicios Profesionales (del Programa de Desarrollo Rural)
	Professional Services Providers (of the Rural Development Programme)
PU	Predominantly Urban (OECD regional typology)
SAGARPA	Secretaría de Agricultura, Ganadería, Desarrollo Rural, Pesca y Alimentación
	Ministry of Agriculture, Livestock, Rural Development, Fisheries and Food
SCT	Secretaría de Comunicaciones y Transportes
	Ministry of Communications and Transportation
SE/SECON	Secretaría de Economía
	Ministry of Economy
SEDESOL	Secretaría de Desarrollo Social
	Ministry of Social Development
SEMARNAT	Secretaría de Medio Ambiente y Recursos Naturales
	Ministry of the Environment and Natural Resources
SENACATRI	Servicio Nacional de Capacitación y Asistencia Técnica Rural
	National Service of Rural Training and Technical Assistance
SENER	Secretaría de Energía
	Ministry of Energy
SEP	Secretaría de Educación Pública
	Ministry of Public Education
SFP	Secretaría de la Función Pública
	Ministry of Public Function
SHCP	Secretaría de Hacienda y Crédito Público
	Ministry of Finance and Public Credit
SINACATRI	Sistema Nacional de Capacitación y Asistencia Técnica Rural
	National System of Rural Training and Technical Assistance
SRA	Secretaría de la Reforma Agraria
	Ministry of Agrarian Reform
SSA	Secretaría de Salud
	Ministry of Health
STPS	Secretaría del Trabajo y Previsión Social
	Ministry of Labor and Social Prevision
UNDP	Programa para el Desarrollo de las Naciones Unidas
	United Nation's Programme for Development

ISBN 978-92-64-01152-6
OECD Rural Policy Reviews: Mexico
© OECD 2007

Assessment and Recommendations

NOTE

Please note that this publication contains a Spanish and French version of the assessment and recommendations of the review at the end of the book.

Favor de tomar en cuenta que esta publicación cuenta con la versión en español de las conclusiones y recomendaciones al final de la misma.

Veuillez noter que cette publication contient une version française de l'évaluation et des recommandations de la revue à la fin du livre.

Profile of rural Mexico: challenges and opportunities

Mexico's large rural territory and population
contrast with the low "rural" contribution to GDP.

Rural regions account for more than 80% of the land in Mexico and are home to up to 37 million people (36% of the Mexican population). That makes Mexico the country with the largest population living in predominantly rural areas in the OECD. Despite their importance in terms of territory and population, rural regions constitute a small share of the economy. The contrast is particularly visible when considering the official Mexican definition of rural (localities with less than 2 500 inhabitants) which comprises nearly a quarter of the country's population but only 2% of national GDP (see Figure 0.1).

Rural regions face challenges linked with
settlements' dispersion...

Mexico's rural population is highly dispersed: 24 million people live in more than 196 000 remote localities and an additional 13 million live in about 3 000 rural, *semi-urban* localities. Causes of this dispersion are the mountainous character of a large part of the Mexican territory and to some extent the atomisation of land and the unclear definition of property rights associated with the regime of communal property. As a result, since the land redistribution that followed the Mexican Revolution, many land owners and their descendants had strong incentives to stay close to their land but far from markets and public services and thus constrained within subsistence or low productivity agriculture.

... a declining population,...

The demographic development of rural regions has been significantly different compared to the rest of the country. In comparison to the rapid growth and concentration of the national and urban population, rural population remained relatively stable and dispersed during the second half of the 20th century, declining in relative terms. Since 2000, the population in *dispersed rural* localities declined also in absolute terms. This reduction is the

Figure 0.1. **Rural Mexico defined**

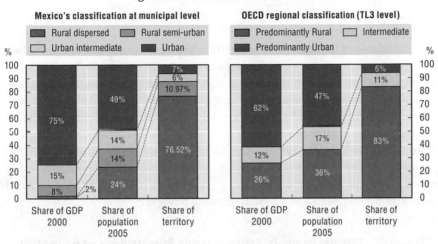

Source: OECD Regions at a Glance forthcoming and calculations with data form INAFED (2000) and INEGI (2006).

result of two combined effects: the lower fertility rates in the last decade, which have significantly reduced the dependency ratio of children and elder people; and migration of youth people to middle-sized cities and abroad, which in turn has multiple economic and social effects, including the feminisation of rural population, increases in elder people dependency ratio, and the growth of remittances as a source of income.

Figure 0.2. **Population in urban and rural areas**
1910-2005

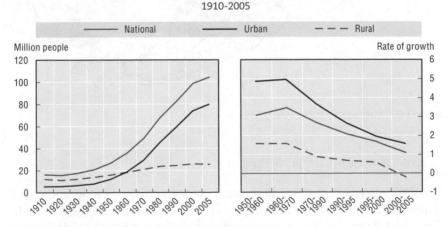

Rural refers to localities of less than 2 500 inhabitants.
Source: INEGI (2006).

The standards of living of rural population are significantly lower than urban ones and the difference is much larger than OECD standards. Whereas the average GDP per capita in urban municipalities was 141% of national average in 2000, in *dispersed rural* and *rural semi-urban* municipalities it was respectively only 27% and 43%. In fact, with the exception of certain areas in the north, almost all predominantly rural regions have a GDP per capita lower than 50% of the national average (the average among OECD countries for rural regions is 82% of national GDP). Despite the recent reductions in poverty levels since the peak reached during the 1995-96 crisis, 56% of people in rural localities live in poverty and 28% in extreme poverty.

Figure 0.3. **GDP per capita in Predominantly Rural regions as percentage of national**

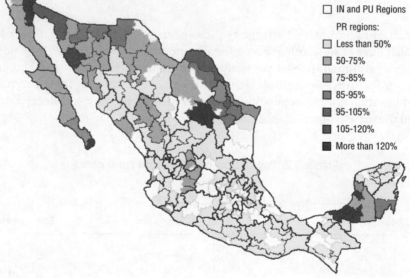

Source: OECD based on data from INAFED (2000).

The difficulty and cost of providing public services to dispersed localities has implications in the standards of living of the rural population. Less accessible localities face low levels of infrastructure, education and health services. Only 68% of the houses in *dispersed rural* areas had solid floor, only 52% had drainage, 87% had electricity and 16% had telephone service in 2000. Average schooling is less than 5 years in *dispersed rural* areas, which contrast with 7.8 in urban areas and 9.7 years in Mexico City. Only about 80% of households living in *dispersed rural* localities have access to health services at a distance of 5 km or less, and they have only 22 hospital beds and 96 physicians for every 100 000 inhabitants, in contrast with the 109 beds and 179 physicians in urban areas. This affects life expectancy rates which in certain rural municipalities are about 10 years less than in Mexico City and infant mortality rates which can be three times higher than in the capital.

There are however significant opportunities linked to the rural "demographic bonus"…

The overwhelming dimension of these challenges often blurs the perception of the heterogeneity of rural areas and the opportunities linked with abundant unexploited resources. Taking advantage of these opportunities could contribute to strengthening the country's rural economy and sustain national growth. First of all, rural population is predominantly young; the median age is 20 years. This generation, which will become part of the labour force in the next decade, is part of the "demographic bonus" that Mexico is experiencing as result of its demographic transition. It could contribute to an increase in production and economic growth as it has been the case in other OECD countries. Moreover, although the average schooling indicators of rural areas remain significantly low (because they include the adult population as well), the access and completion rates of secondary school show that the current young generation is better prepared than its previous generations. Numerous studies also highlight that Mexico's rural youth is often highly entrepreneurial and more familiar with markets opportunities and technological advances.

… a wide room for economic diversification…

Second, challenges but also opportunities are linked with the current transformation of Mexico's rural economy. The contribution of agriculture, forestry and fisheries activities to GDP declined from 8% in 1990 to 5% in 2004. In terms of employment, however, agriculture is still the most predominant activity in dispersed rural municipalities (with 44% of their population occupied in the primary sector). The share of this sector in Mexico is still higher than OECD average both for predominantly rural regions (30% vs. 10%) and for the national economy (16% vs. the 6% OECD average). Whereas large agricultural producers have been able to integrate to international markets and have considerably increased agricultural exports, the large majority of small producers are still poorly diversified, concentrated in low value-added crops and highly vulnerable to price shocks. The transition from agriculture to other activities is happening at a fast pace in rural areas. Two facts are evidence of this phenomenon. First, the share of income of non agricultural activities has grown substantially (to the point of representing more than 50% of income even in dispersed rural areas). Second, non-agricultural employment, grew more in rural regions (5.2%) than in urban regions (3.5%) between 1999 and 2004.

Figure 0.4. **Diversification of the rural economy: rural and urban employment growth rates in non-agricultural sectors**

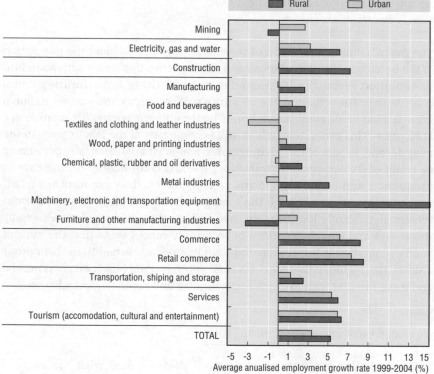

Rural includes dispersed rural localities (less than 2 500 inhabitants) and rural semi-urban (less than 15 000 inhabitants).
Source: INEGI Economic Census 1999, 2004.

The first refuge out of agriculture is retail commerce. Despite being a large sector, it had an important growth in the 1999-2004 period (8.5%). Manufacturing activities grew less, yet more than in urban areas, indicating a shift of certain industries to less urbanised contexts. It is worth highlighting

OECD RURAL POLICY REVIEWS: MEXICO – ISBN 978-92-64-01152-6 – © OECD 2007

that the manufacturing sectors that grew more in rural areas were advanced manufacturing sectors such as machinery, electronic and transportation equipment (15%, see Figure 0.4). The increasing diversification of the rural economy varies by region. Although the contribution of diversification to the improvement of standards of living is not easily quantifiable, evidence shows that GDP per capita in the most diversified predominantly rural regions (northern states such as Nuevo León, Baja California, Baja California Sur, and Coahuila) is higher than not only the rural but also the national average.

... and the presence of untapped natural, cultural and energy resources.

Third, the growth in sectors such as tourism as an alternative source of income in rural areas is worth highlighting. From 1999 to 2004 tourism was one of the sectors experiencing highest growth, again slightly higher in rural areas (6.3%) than in urban areas. By 2004, 9% of tourism employment was concentrated in rural areas. The South-eastern region and the Peninsula of Baja California contain rural areas where tourism represents a particularly significant share of the employment and GVA (more than 25%). In particular, in the South-southeast region, which is the poorest region in the country, rich natural resources, cultural heritage and archaeological and historical sites, could become key drivers of economic development. In addition, there is unused potential in terms of the renewable energy sources present in rural areas, including solar, wind, hydraulic and bio-energy. The experience of many OECD and non-OECD countries indicates that rural areas could significantly contribute to the energy provision of the country and to their own, while providing alternative income and employment opportunities for the local population.

In sum, there are different "rural Mexicos", with distinct challenges and potential.

Rural regions present a high heterogeneity: there is definitely a "rural poor", but it cannot be generalised that "rural" is "poor". There is a part of the rural economy that is strongly linked to agriculture, forestry and fisheries sector, and there are rural areas which have been able to diversify into manufacturing industries and services. There are rural regions already developed into tourist destinations and others that contain untapped natural and cultural resources. There are thus very diverse challenges for Mexico's rural policy. These include: 1) poverty alleviation, 2) provision of basic public services; 3) strengthening and diversification of the rural economy; and finally, 4) better exploiting and preserving untapped cultural, natural and energetic resources.

How is Mexico coping with rural challenges and opportunities?

*Mexico has taken innovative steps towards
a cross-sectoral, multi-tier framework
for rural policy.*

The Mexican approach to rural policy has been shifting in the past decades from a one sector policy (agriculture) in the direction of a policy that aims at integrating the actions of the different sectoral ministries and of the different tiers of government (federal, state and municipal) in rural areas. The new institutional framework for these changes is based in the Law for Sustainable Rural Development (LDRS), approved in 2001, which mandates the establishment of a federal horizontal co-ordination body specific for rural policy (the Inter-Ministerial Commission for Sustainable Rural Development, CIDRS), the constitution of participatory bodies for civil society (Councils for Sustainable Rural Development), and the elaboration a Special Concerted Programme for Rural Development (PEC). The latter has evolved into the integration of a "rural budget" appended every year to the federal budget. An analysis of this budget demonstrates that, within the federal programmes impacting rural areas, two types of policies stand out in terms of resources: social policy (which involves poverty alleviation, education and health policies) and "productive support" policies, which have mainly an agricultural focus. Other federal policies significantly impacting rural areas are the provision of basic and productive infrastructure, environmental, land and labour policies.

*The two most relevant actors of rural policy operate
programmes explicitly targeted to rural
development...*

The two ministries with most significant impact in rural areas, the Ministry of Agriculture, Livestock, Rural Development, Fisheries and Alimentation (SAGARPA) and the Ministry of Social Development (SEDESOL), within their own areas of competence, count with policies specifically oriented to rural development. On the one hand, SAGARPA's Programme of Rural Development (PDR) is one of the most decentralised federal programmes in Mexico. It supports productive investments for agriculture, livestock and non-farm activities with a demand- and project-driven approach. Two other complementary components are technical support and organisational support. This latter component has been instrumental in the construction of the institutional architecture mandated by the LDRS. On the other hand, SEDESOL leads Micro-Regions Strategy as an inter-ministerial programme,

OECD RURAL POLICY REVIEWS: MEXICO – ISBN 978-92-64-01152-6 – © OECD 2007

which specifically targets the most marginalised rural regions and is oriented to provide basic infrastructure and framework conditions for the development around selected "micro-poles of development", the so-called *Strategic Community Centres* (CECs). The specificity of its scope allows it to monitor the advances and deficits in each of the areas of support through objective and socially shared validation mechanisms called *"banderas blancas"* (white flags).

... which pursue different objectives through an integrated approach.

Both the PDR and the Micro-Regions Strategy include several aspects that are in line with OECD best practices: 1) they adopt a territorial and integrated perspective on rural development that extends outside sectors; 2) they do not focus on subsidies but rather on investments and, 3) they co-ordinate efforts of multiple actors, the PDR with a stronger vertical orientation (due to its decentralised character) and the Micro-Regions Strategy with a more horizontal perspective (due to its inter-ministerial character). However, the two programmes differ significantly in their objectives and methodology: 1) the PDR is oriented to rural areas in general, while the MR Strategy is concentrated in a subset of rural areas, those with higher marginalisation and poverty conditions; 2) the PDR is more oriented support the rural population as economic agents or producers, while the MR Strategy focuses on their rights and living conditions; 3) while the PDR is more demand driven (beneficiaries submit projects in order to obtain support), MR Strategy co-ordinates the policy supply of different ministries in specific territories.

Critical issues and priorities of action

The governance framework for rural development could be improved through enhanced leadership...

There are two sets of critical issues with regard to *horizontal co-ordination* at the federal level: The first regards the co-ordination of the 14 ministries that are included in the CIDRS. There is evidence that SAGARPA (which chairs the commission), has had difficulties in engaging and obtaining commitment from the other ministries involved. Experience from OECD countries indicates that a horizontal commission which is chaired by one sector (in this case, agriculture) may be limited in pursuing multi-sectoral objectives and hinder the full involvement of other ministries in a national rural strategy. The governance of rural policy and the engagement of the different participants could be significantly enhanced by providing the CIDRS with a stronger "meta-ministerial" leadership. This could be done for instance by assigning its Presidency to the Chief of the Executive, or via the creation of an *ad hoc* institution or the rotation of different ministries at the lead of the commission.

... better horizontal co-ordination between key federal level ministries...

A second issue is related to the co-ordination between SAGARPA and SEDESOL, which are the two ministries with higher involvement in rural affairs. On the one hand, the co-operation between them is limited by the fact that they are guided by different logics and are accountable to different laws. Each of these laws, confers upon them "authority" in inter-ministerial commissions (one about social policy and the other about rural policy) involving usually the same ministries. In addition, SEDESOL co-ordinates the Micro-Regions Strategy which counts again with an inter-ministerial body. This institutional problem is then translated to sub-national levels, where both ministries have parallel administrative structures often acting in the same territories: SAGARPA has relied fundamentally on (and constructed) the councils for rural development delineated by the LDRS, while SEDESOL relies more on the pre-existing local planning bodies (COPLADEs and COPLADEMUNs). Besides their own *delegaciones* in each of the 31 states, the two ministries have decentralised structures to operate their programmes at the local level, such as the so-called "residents" for the Micro-Regions Strategy of SEDESOL and the "promotores" of SAGARPA. There is room for finding better institutional arrangements that enable rural policy and social policy to exploit synergies and build a common network of institutions that allows both ministries to pursue effectively their policies at local level. Such changes would help to identify complementarities in their policy approaches: SEDESOL's policies are oriented to provide a basic platform for development to rural dwellers while SAGARPA's rural policy, universal in coverage and oriented to economic development, can step in effectively once that basic platform is in place.

... and a clearer definition of responsibilities among different tiers of government.

The LDRS states that federalism and decentralisation are core criteria for the implementation of the rural development agenda. However, each ministry has set different criteria and strategies for the decentralisation of the respective public policies. Thus, certain decentralised programmes at the local level are ineffective because complementary policies were not decentralised. Strengthening the process of decentralisation of rural development policy requires 1) an agreement on the policy areas to be decentralised by each ministry, with focus on the complementarities between them, 2) a definition of the responsibilities (in terms of budget and accountability) and functions (standard setting, design, implementation and evaluation) of the different tiers of government, and 3) enhancing local capacity, particularly at the municipal level and ensuring the continuity of existing capacity, which is a challenge in the context of the short terms of municipal authorities.

A more coherent, and transparent Special Concerted Programme (PEC) could enhance efficiency of rural spending…

From a policy standpoint, priorities for Mexico's rural policy include: 1) poverty alleviation; 2) provision of basic public services; 3) strengthening and diversifying the rural economy; and finally, 4) better exploiting and preserving untapped cultural, natural and energy resources. Since these policy priorities extend the scope of any individual ministry the co-ordination of actions is necessary to pursue them efficiently. Although the Special Concerted Programme (PEC) constitutes an important effort towards the design of an integrated federal policy for rural development, it still exercised more as an inventory of programmes rather than a tool to exploit synergies between programmes impacting on rural areas. The result is the inclusion of programmes and institutions that are not necessarily oriented to rural development. This produces an inaccurate picture of the federal rural policy strategy and data on rural spending that do not fully correspond to the reality. In order to take full advantage of the purpose of this innovation, efforts should be devoted to 1) improve transparency regarding the criteria for programme inclusion into the PEC and the portion of such programmes which can be considered as being directed to rural areas, 2) engage in a dialogue that could result in the merging, transferring and elimination of certain programmes with the objective of achieving a more coherent and effective set of policy tools for rural areas. There have been efforts in this direction, but the process requires stronger political will from the different ministries and significant leadership form the CIDRS. 3) Introduce monitoring and evaluation mechanisms of the outputs and outcomes of rural policies according to agreed targets.

… and orient public resources towards the policy priorities for rural development,…

At present, the federal resources invested in rural areas do not fully correspond with the priorities identified: one sector-based (agriculture) and one horizontal policy objective (poverty alleviation) dominate rural policy. Although significant investments in these two areas contribute to the priorities of poverty alleviation and strengthening of the rural economy, significant synergies could be obtained from investing greater resources in public service delivery, business development in non-agricultural activities and the sustainable exploitation of natural, cultural and energetic resources. While ministries in charge of education, health and environment have significant impact on rural development, other ministries, related to economic policy, such as Economy (SECON), Transportation and Communications (SCT), Finance (SHCP), Tourism, Labour (STPS) and Energy have very low rural focus (see Figure 0.5). The involvement of these ministries in rural areas, could significantly contribute to the strengthening of the rural economy through SME support, financial sector development and better economic infrastructure. It would also contribute to the economic diversification of rural areas by facilitating the expansion of specific sectors such as tourism and energy.

Figure 0.5. **Ministries and budget involved in rural policy**

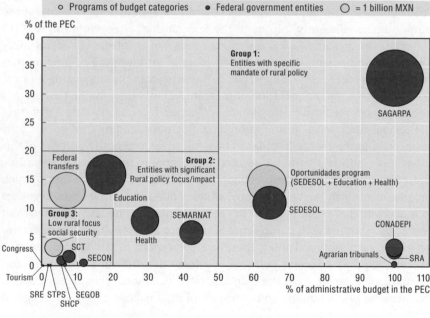

Source: PEC, 2006.

---

*... complemented by private investment
and a better use of remittances.*

The mobilisation of private resources is needed in addition to public investment in order to trigger development in rural areas. This should involve both attracting new resources and promoting a better use of the resources

OECD RURAL POLICY REVIEWS: MEXICO – ISBN 978-92-64-01152-6 – © OECD 2007

owned by rural dwellers. For new resources to come, greater flexibility in markets is needed, particularly in that of land, as well as greater personal and property rights security. In order to better exploit the resources that already reside in rural areas, mainly in the form of land and remittances, rural dwellers should be able to easily convert their property rights into economic assets, and have better access to credit, saving and investment alternatives. Remittances, which are currently biased towards consumption, could also be invested in productive ways if an investment portfolio is proposed to the senders. For instance, the 3x1 programme could be better linked with the PDR and Micro-Regions Strategy so that remittances are used in a strategic way.

RD programmes can improve their effectiveness:
in the case of the PDR, through specialisation
and a better focalisation of resources…

Both the Programme of Rural Development of SAGARPA and the Micro-Regions Strategy lead by SEDESOL could be strengthened and improved in their effectiveness and efficiency. Several evaluations of the PDR show difficulties in focusing resources on the most marginalised localities and states. On the other hand, despite receiving fewer resources, the most marginalised areas together with poorest producers and non-agricultural activities are the categories where the programme shows better results in terms of employment and income generated. Orienting efforts to these comparative advantages, particularly towards the support of non-agricultural activities, for which there is a strong demand, could result in a better use of resources. In addition, the programme should exploit complementarities between training and investment support. Evidence shows that whenever these two components are provided together the impact is higher. Advancing in these aspects will strengthen the PDR, and better link it to the multi-sectoral structure defined by the LDRS.

… and in the case of the Micro-Regions Strategy,
via the institutionalisation and better integration
with other social and economic programmes.

The strength of the Micro-Regions Strategy is the platform it offers for co-ordinated sectoral policy interventions in the most marginalised rural areas. A significant achievement of the strategy has been the completion of close to 60% of the *"banderas blancas"* that are required to fully equip each of the targeted communities with the basic infrastructure and services. However, advancements are considerably slower in some areas of support than in others, and the recent addition of new "*banderas blancas*" has further increased the scope of the programme's goals and challenges. This implies the need for greater resources and better co-ordination with the relevant sectoral ministries, in particular in the areas of road construction, sanitary services, promotion of productive activities, electricity and water provision. In this context, it is important to further "institutionalise" the strategy through formal agreements that would foster co-ordination, make explicit the responsibilities and budget commitments of the ministries involved, and guarantee the continuity of a strategy. The potential impact of the strategy could also be enhanced through greater integration with other social and economic development programmes which already channel significant resources to the most marginalised areas, with particular attention to the *Oportunidades* programme, and other resource transfers to states and municipalities.

Summing up.

The challenges faced by Mexico's rural areas are significant. Mexico's countryside is home to a large population (more than the overall population of many OECD countries) that is highly dispersed and largely living in poverty. The potential of these areas is however significant, as their vast (and young) human resources, their natural, cultural and physical assets could provide, in a more diversified economy, a greater contribution to national development. The Mexican government has had significant success in framing a multi-sector rural policy. Some of these accomplishments can provide examples of best practice for other OECD countries. The continuity and institutionalisation of these advances are a priority. In addition, efforts should be devoted to improving the efficiency and effectiveness of rural development programmes and to guaranteeing coherence with other major sectoral policies. This will contribute to addressing the country's major territorial and individual inequalities and will transform rural regions into sources of national development.

OECD RURAL POLICY REVIEWS: MEXICO – ISBN 978-92-64-01152-6 – © OECD 2007

ISBN 978-92-64-01152-6
OECD Rural Policy Reviews: Mexico
© OECD 2007

Chapter 1

Profile of Rural Mexico

The aim of this chapter is to provide a comprehensive overview of the socio-economic dynamics characterizing rural areas in Mexico and to identify the resulting policy challenges. This will lay the foundation for the discussions on current policies influencing rural development and its governance framework to be treated in the subsequent chapter. It begins by defining rural territories as the basic unit of analysis of the review. It then analyses rural regions through different lens in order to have a comprehensive understanding of the demographic, social, economic and environmental dynamics within. Finally it concludes enumerating the most significant policy challenges of rural Mexico from a territorial perspective, recognizing the heterogeneity present within rural areas.

Key points

- "Rural" comprises more than 80% of the Mexican territory and is home to an important share of the population (between 23% and 37% according to various definitions), but contributes a small share of the economy (between 10% and 26%). The contrast is particularly high for the dispersed rural localities (of less than 2 500 inhabitants) where close to 24 million people live which have an estimated contribution of only about 2% of national GDP.

- Rural population is large, dispersed and young. Historically the net growth rate (natural rate less out-migration) of rural areas has been lower than urban and national ones. From 2000 to 2005 the net growth rate became negative for the first time. Migration of young people to middle-sized cities and abroad is the main cause of this population decline, which in turn has multiple economic and social effects, including an early increase in the dependency ratio of some states, the division of families and the growth of remittances as a source of income.

- The rural-urban divide is significant in terms of standards of living: nominal GDP per capita is less than half in rural areas than in urban areas. Extreme poverty is mainly a rural phenomenon: 61% of the population in extreme poverty lived in rural areas. However, there has been a significant reduction (44%) in extreme poverty levels from the peak, during the 1995 crisis, to 2004. Several factors have contributed to closing the gap between urban and rural income. Unfortunately, only part of such improvements could be attributed to income increases, a significant portion is given by migration towards cities which has increased poverty levels in urban areas.

- The transition from agriculture to other activities is happening at a fast pace in rural areas. Two facts are evidence of this phenomenon. First, the growth in the share of income of non-agricultural activities (to the point of representing more than half of income). Second, the growth of non-agricultural employment, which grew more in rural regions (5.2%) than in urban regions (3.5%) during the period 1999-2004. The diversification into different manufacturing activities and services, such as tourism, contributes to the improvement of social conditions in rural areas. However, there are still scarce opportunities for well remunerated and formal jobs.

- Rural poverty contrasts with the richness of the natural resource endowments present in rural areas. For a long period, incentives of a growing rural population were not aligned with conservation of these resources contributing to the extension of area used for agricultural and livestock activities in detriment of forest and jungles land. Despite improvements in the control of environmental degradation, erosion of soil, pollution of soil and water, illegal fallings, forest fires, and depletion of water reserves are important threats to the environment in rural areas.

● There is not one but many rural Mexicos. There is the "rural poor", but it cannot be generalised that "rural" is poor. There is a part of the rural economy that is strongly linked to the agriculture, forestry and fisheries sector, and there is a rural diversified into manufacturing industries and services. There are rural areas where tourism is already arising as a viable alternative, and others that contain untapped natural, cultural and energy resources that could contribute to their own development, and the development of the country as a whole.

Introduction

Mexico stands out for its concentration (26% of its population is gathered in 3 metropolitan cities) and on other extreme, it also compares high on its dispersion (23% lives in localities of less than 2 500 inhabitants, and almost 40% in localities of less than 15 000 inhabitants).

This unusual concentrated-dispersed dichotomy of the country is an underlying determinant of many of the performance indicators of the country. It explains to some extent how Mexico can be among the largest 10 economies in the world in terms of GDP (75% produced in urban areas) and at the same time score low in most average indicators, from GDP per capita to PISA educational performance tests. When decomposed into their rural and urban components, these indicators depict differences closer in magnitude of the comparisons between OECD countries and poorly developed countries than the comparisons between Mexico and other OECD countries. These differences characterise in Mexico a true rural-urban divide.

Policies have not been tangential to these phenomena. Many studies have highlighted the import-substitution industrialisation (ISI) regime followed between the 1950s and 1970s as an instrumental factor of the concentration of population and income in three metropolitan poles, Mexico City, Guadalajara and Monterrey (Diaz Cayeros, 1995; Sojo, 2004). On the other hand, the regime of land property since the agrarian reform following the Mexican Revolution, tied many people (and their descendants) to atomised plots of land. The weak definition of property rights in rural areas obliged owners of communal property to remain close to their land, being an indirect cause of the attachment of population to live in isolated rural areas.[1] The demographic growth in rural and urban populations produced on the one hand, immense agglomerations as in the case of Mexico City, and on the other, a rural population for which the land availability did not grow at the same pace. In the latter case, an important part of the population is isolated from markets and public services and structurally attached to low productivity or even subsistence agriculture and lives in poverty conditions.

This quick – and possibly oversimplified – overview underlines the fact that even though rural areas in Mexico confront similar issues that other OECD countries, namely lower productivity and income, out-migration, deficient public service delivery, etc., the issue of rural development is a major priority and challenge for Mexico. Tackling effectively the problem through the appropriate policies is a matter not only of economic transcendence but mainly of equity, having substantial implications in terms of social cohesion.

The aim of this chapter is to provide a comprehensive overview of the socio-economic dynamics characterising rural areas in Mexico and to identify the resulting policy challenges. This will lay the foundation for the discussions on current policies influencing rural development and its governance framework to be treated in the subsequent chapters. The chapter is structured as follows. Section 1.1 defines rural territories as the basic unit of analysis of the review. Section 1.2 analyses rural regions through different lens in order to have a comprehensive understanding of the demographic, social, economic and environmental dynamics within. Section concludes enumerating the most significant policy challenges of rural Mexico from a territorial perspective, recognising the heterogeneity present within rural areas.

1.1. What is "rural" in Mexico?

"Rural" as a unit of analysis, is not precisely defined as a concept and even less so as a specific territory because the frontier between rural and urban in most countries is not easily identifiable. Rather, there is a continuum of population settlements which, in the case of Mexico, has at one extreme thousands of small localities (some as small as three houses) and on the other, large urban centres as Mexico City, Guadalajara or Monterrey.

Throughout this report, two different but complementary definitions of rural will be used (Figure 1.1). The first one, based on size of population, closely matches – or proxies[2] – the most frequently used categories among policymakers and academics in Mexico: *dispersed rural* (less than 2 500 inhabitants), *rural semi-urban* (between 2 500 and 15 000), *urban intermediate* (between 15 000 and 100 000) and *urban* or *urban metropolitan* (more than 100 000). The second one is a standardised category set for OECD countries, which classifies regions according to population density into three types: *Predominantly Rural (PR)*, *Intermediate (IN)*, and *Predominantly Urban (PU)*.

OECD RURAL POLICY REVIEWS: MEXICO – ISBN 978-92-64-01152-6 – © OECD 2007

Figure 1.1. **Rural defined**

Definition of rural territories according to Mexico and OECD Territorial Levels

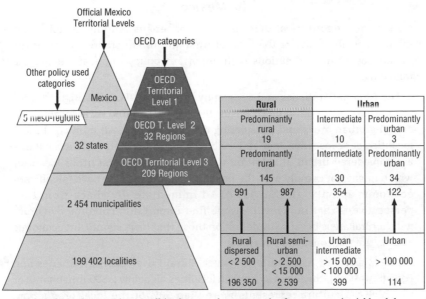

Note: Although rural categories are all in the same box, categories from one territorial level does not necessarily match the respective category under other territorial level.

Source: OECD with information from INEGI (2005).

A large share of Mexican population lives in rural areas...

Part of the difficulty of defining rural lies in the fact that the definition depends upon the territorial level of analysis. The definition provided at the lowest territorial level is the one reported by National Institute of Statistics Geography and Informatics (INEGI), which distinguishes between rural and urban localities using a population level threshold of 2 500 inhabitants. Of the *circa* 199 thousand localities, 196 thousand have less than 2 500 inhabitants, comprising close to 90% of the national territory.[3] According to this definition, in 2005, about 24.3 million people, representing 23.5% of the Mexican population, lived in rural areas (INEGI, 2005). Some studies however, refer to those communities as *"dispersed rural"* and use a higher threshold of 15 000[4] for referring to *"rural"* areas, comprising both the *"dispersed rural"* and *"rural semi-urban"* areas. Grouping these two categories is common since the living conditions of population in settlements of less than 15 000 inhabitants has characteristics closer to the "rural" environment than to an "urban" one. Using that threshold, *rural* population ascends to 38.4 million people or 37% of total population. Localities of more than 15 000 inhabitants are considered urban, however, for clearer comparison purposes; two subcategories are used in this report: *urban intermediate*, for settlements between 15 000 and

> ## Box 1.1. **Rural definitions by different government agencies in Mexico**
>
> As in many countries, there is not a consensus among agencies and institutions about where the limit of rural and urban stands. Some of the most relevant interpretations with important policy implications are the following:
>
> The National Statistics and Geography Institute (INEGI), distinguishes for the purpose of the Economic Census, between urban and rural localities by defining urban areas and considering the rest as rural. All municipal main localities or "cabeceras" and all localities with more than 2 500 inhabitants are considered urban, in addition to industrial parks and other localities which might not comply with the previous criteria but that have "significant economic activity" (INEGI, 1999). An immediate drawback from this perspective is that rarely will anyone find important economic dynamics within rural areas because by definition those that have significant economic activity are not considered as rural.
>
> The Ministry of Agriculture, Livestock, Rural Development, Fisheries and Food (SAGARPA), considers as rural all localities all below 2 500 inhabitants or in which agriculture represents more than 50% of the local production. However in a study asked by this ministry with the purpose of measuring the impact of the Rural Development Law in local communities, which will be cited frequently in this review, they use the threshold of 20 000 inhabitants.
>
> The Ministry of Social Development considers a "rural locality" any human settlement with at least three houses and a maximum of 2 500 inhabitants.

100 000 inhabitants and *urban* or *urban metropolitan* for cities of more than 100 000 inhabitants. The map in Figure 1.2 shows the territorial distribution of each of the localities of less than 2 500 inhabitants as well as of urban areas.

Any territorial level above localities constitutes an aggregation, and therefore, the boundary between rural and urban becomes less clear. Nevertheless, most information is provided either at municipal, state or national level, which makes aggregation almost unavoidable for comparison purposes at the national level and even more so at the international level. In addition, aggregation usually tells us more about the context of a specific rural region. Since there are no official classifications of municipalities into rural-urban categories, a municipal classification can be derived[5] from the classification of localities. Of the 2 454 municipalities,[6] 991 could be considered rural in a fairly strict sense due to the fact that more than 80% their population live in dispersed localities of less than 2 500 inhabitants. Using the broader definition of less than 15 000 inhabitants, and applying the same 80% criterion,

OECD RURAL POLICY REVIEWS: MEXICO – ISBN 978-92-64-01152-6 – © OECD 2007

Figure 1.2. **Map of municipalities according to the rural-urban classification**

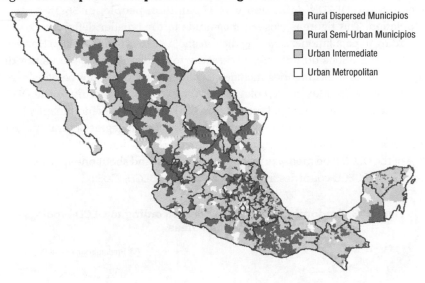

■ Rural Dispersed Municipios

▨ Rural Semi-Urban Municipios

☐ Urban Intermediate

☐ Urban Metropolitan

Source: OECD with information from (INEGI 2005).

987 municipalities should be added, thus providing 1 978 "rural" municipalities. Of the remaining 481 municipalities, 354 could be considered urban intermediate since 80% of their population lives in localities of less than 100 000 inhabitants, and only 122 could be considered urban in a more strict sense since most of their population lives in cities of more than 100 000 inhabitants. This last number increased by 24 from 2000 to 2005 indeed, which reflects, beyond normal population growth, an important urbanisation trend in the last few years (see Table 1.A1.1 in Annex 1.A1).

The OECD uses a territorial scheme to better understand and compare member countries at two sub-national territorial units: one which corresponds to the Mexican state level, Territorial Level 2 (TL2); and one which groups the 2 456 municipalities into 209 regions, Territorial Level 3 (TL3). The OECD definition of rural is based on the assessment that rural regions have low population densities *and* do not contain a major urban centre. Regions are not classified as being rural or urban pre se, but depending on the share of population living in rural communities, they are classified as Predominantly Rural (PR), Intermediate (IN) or Predominantly Urban (PU). Therefore, each of the three types of regions contains some rural and some urban communities but to a different degree. For Mexico, the OECD classifies its 32 states (TL2 regions) as follows: 19 PR, 10 IN and 3 PU. For the purpose of the current analysis, however, the most referred territorial level will be TL3, whose 209 units are subdivided as follows: 145 PR, 30 IN, and 34 PU. (A detail comparison between the Mexican and OECD typology is provided in Annex 1.A1.)

The Mexican population that lived in 2005 in predominantly rural territories, according to OECD's definition was 37.3 million people, or 36.2% of total population. This figure is close in magnitude to the broader definition of rural according to population size (using the threshold of 15 000 inhabitants) However, the two definitions do not refer necessarily to the same population since the aggregation of the categories includes localities that would not be considered "rural" under the Mexican typology (see Annex 1.A1). According to the OECD definition, the vast majority of the Mexican territory (83%) is Predominantly Rural (see Figure 1.3).OECD Countries vary significantly in their degree of rurality and in the amount of population living in predominantly rural areas. In 2001, more than 75% of the OECD land area was predominantly rural, and about one-quarter of the residents of OECD countries lived in these regions (OECD, 2005a).

Figure 1.3. **Predominantly rural regions according to OECD typology and urban areas**

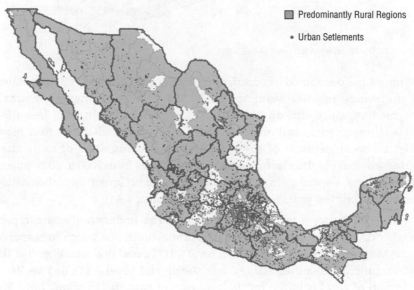

☐ Predominantly Rural Regions

• Urban Setlements

Source: OECD (2005a) and INEGI (2005).

... however, they contribute with a relatively small share of the country's GDP

An important indicator of the magnitude of "rural", in addition to population and territory is the contribution of such population and territory to the national economy, measured by GDP. Using OECD regional typology, the differences depicted between Predominantly Rural, Intermediate and Predominantly Urban regions seem not very large and relatively close to the OECD average: 26% for PR, 12% for IN and 62% for PU regions, while OECD

OECD RURAL POLICY REVIEWS: MEXICO – ISBN 978-92-64-01152-6 – © OECD 2007

Box 1.2. **OECD Regional typology**

The OECD has classified regions within each member country. To take account of the differences and establish meaningful comparisons between regions belonging to the same type and level, the OECD has established a regional typology according to which regions have been classified as Predominantly Urban, Predominantly Rural and Intermediate using three criteria:

1. **Population density.** A community is defined as rural if its population density is below 150 inhabitants per km^2 (500 inhabitants for Japan to account for the fact that its national population density exceeds 300 inhabitants per km^2).

2. **Regions by % population in rural communities.** A region is classified as predominantly rural if more than 50% of its population lives in rural communities, predominantly urban if less than 15% of the population lives in rural communities and intermediate if the share of the population living in rural communities is between 15% and 50%.

---

averages are 24% for PR, 44% for IN and 43% for PU. However, using Mexico's typology, estimates from INEGI[7] and OECD calculations[8] show a striking fact: at municipal level, the contribution of dispersed rural areas to GDP is as low as 2%. Even when considering the rural-semi urban municipalities, the contribution of rural areas to the national economy adds up to only 10%. These figures do indicate a disproportion between the population living in those localities, and the territory with their contribution to GDP.

The disproportion between GDP, population and territory[9] depicted in Figure 1.4 evidences the fact that structural obstacles impede population in dispersed rural areas (recall that they are 23 million people, more than the whole population of many countries) to be fully integrated and contribute to the national economy. If only each of these people, without much more preparation but with access and tools to exchange in the economy, contributed with the average value added of a worker in Mexico, Mexican GDP could be significantly enlarged. This comparison sets the basis for the following section where the causes and circumstances of this phenomena will be addressed with greater detail. It also invites one to look at poor rural areas from a different perspective: not as an irreversibly ill part of the country, in need of intensive care but as untapped human and land resources, that could potentially contribute much more to Mexico. A new vision might imply a substantial shift or broadening in the portfolio of policies to develop these regions.

One of the most fundamental conclusions of the most recent OECD research on rural areas, is that, although they might be in general lagging in comparison with urban areas, they are far from being synonymous with decline (OECD, 2006). On the contrary, some of them have taken a proactive

Figure 1.4. **Rural proportions and disproportions**

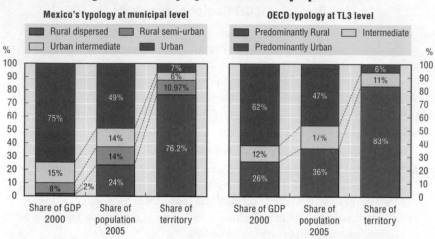

Source: OECD with data from INAFED (2000).

role in the context of globalisation. Although rural areas in Mexico face greater challenges, they certainly should not be set aside of the process of development and economic integration that the country is experiencing in other grounds.

1.2. What is happening in rural areas?

Rural development is a complex, multi-sectoral issue, which can only be assessed by looking at rural territories from different lenses. Since the launching of the Rural Development Programme in 1991, the OECD has developed a framework to analyse rural territories that addresses four main development concerns: demographic, social, economic and environmental (OECD, 1994). This section will analyse the main issues facing the rural areas in Mexico in these four areas.

Figure 1.5. **Looking at rural areas through four main development concerns**

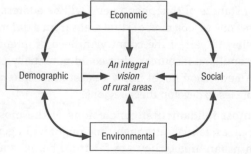

Source: OECD (1994).

OECD RURAL POLICY REVIEWS: MEXICO – ISBN 978-92-64-01152-6 – © OECD 2007

1.2.1. Population and migration

Rural population is large,...

Mexico is the 11th most populated country in the world, with 103.1 million inhabitants. As it has been already mentioned, up to 38 million people live in rural areas. This figure is larger than the population of many individual countries and it makes of Mexico the country with the largest population living in predominantly rural areas within OECD countries (Figure 1.6).

Figure 1.6. **Population living in Predominantly Rural regions**
2001

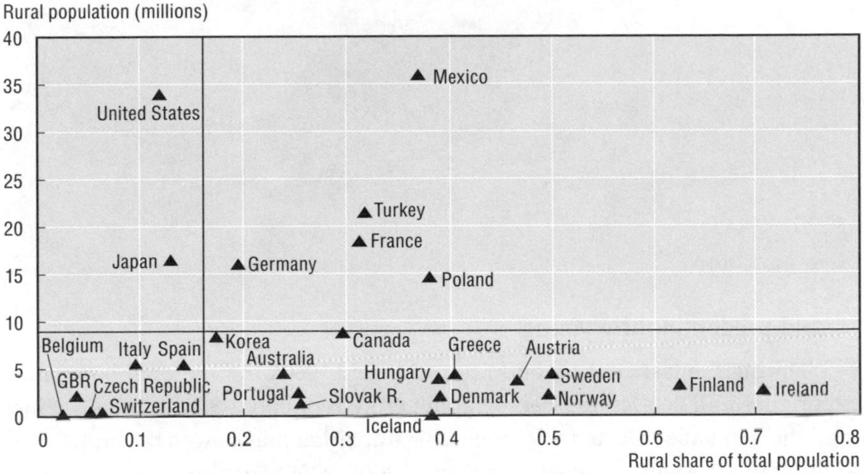

Rural population (millions)

Source: OECD Regional Database.

... dispersed,...

Dispersion is one of the main characteristics of the rural population: 24 million people live in more than 196 000 remote localities and an additional 13 million live in about 3 000 rural, *semi-urban* localities. Even though significant rural-to-urban migration occurred during the 20th century, the relatively large size of rural population is also due to some extent, to a "willingness" to stay close to the small plots of land that a significant portion of the rural population received with the land reforms that followed the Mexican Revolution. The weak definition of property rights, obliged owners of those plots and their descendants to stay close to their land but far from markets and public services and thus constrained within subsistence or low productivity agriculture.

Figure 1.7. **Map of urban and rural localities**
2000

● Localities of less than 2,500 inhabitants
■ Urban Areas

Source: INEGI (2004).

... and predominantly young

During the last century and up to the mid 1960s the national population experienced an accelerated demographic growth of about 3.3% annually. Since then the population started a demographic transition that slowed the growth rate to an average of 1% between the period 2000-2005. Fertility rates, although declining, have been persistently higher in rural areas. The average number of members of rural households was 4.4 in 2005 compared with the urban figure, which is closer to 3 persons per household. The smaller proportion of children (less than 12 years) and elder people (more than 65) has contributed to a decline in the dependency ratio[10] from 62% in 1999 to 56.4% in 2004 for dispersed rural localities and from 52.2 in 1999 to 49.4 in 2004 for rural semi-urban localities. The result is a vastly young population, with a median age of 20 years (Figure 1.8).

Currently, Mexico is about to enjoy a period of what some academics call a *demographic bonus* where the population in working age will increase up to 40% in absolute numbers by 2020 (PEC, 2002), and the dependency ratio will be considerably low for a considerable period. This is true also for rural areas. However, the lack of opportunities of youth population in the rural economy has steepened the out-migration trends in the past decades. The concentration of land ownership in elder population, among proprietors of communal land[11] (*ejidatarios*), is a clear evidence of the lack of opportunities that instigate migration (Figure 1.9).

OECD RURAL POLICY REVIEWS: MEXICO – ISBN 978-92-64-01152-6 – © OECD 2007

Figure 1.8. **Age structure of population in Mexico and in rural areas**

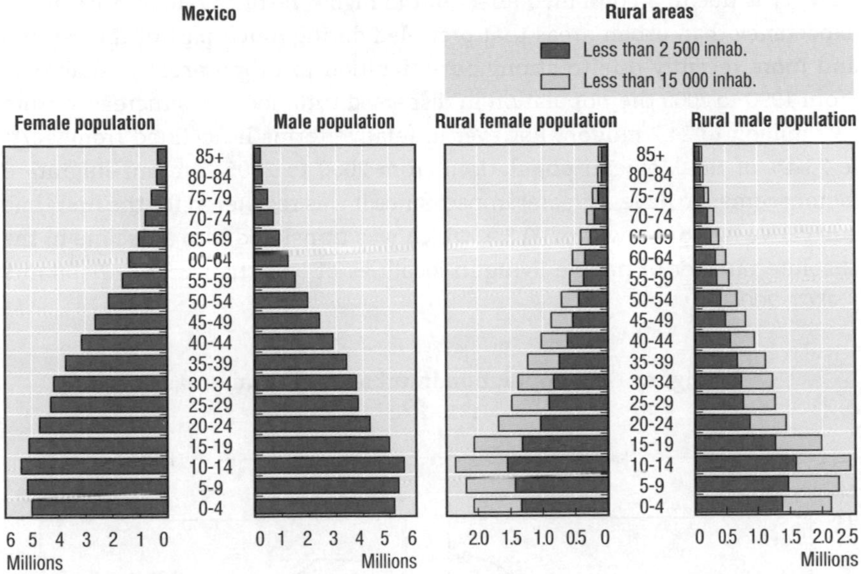

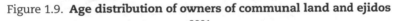

Mexico   Rural areas

■ Less than 2 500 inhab.
□ Less than 15 000 inhab.

| Female population | Male population | Rural female population | Rural male population |

85+
80-84
75-79
70-74
65-69
60-64
55-59
50-54
45-49
40-44
35-39
30-34
25-29
20-24
15-19
10-14
5-9
0-4

6 5 4 3 2 1 0   0 1 2 3 4 5 6   2.0 1.5 1.0 0.5 0   0 0.5 1.0 1.5 2.0 2.5
Millions   Millions   Millions

Source: INEGI (2005).

Figure 1.9. **Age distribution of owners of communal land and ejidos**
2001

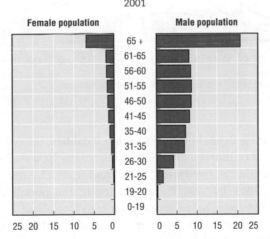

Female population   Male population

65 +
61-65
56-60
51-55
46-50
41-45
35-40
31-35
26-30
21-25
19-20
0-19

25 20 15 10 5 0   0 5 10 15 20 25

Source: Rios Piter (2006).

Rural population is declining…

The demographic perspective of rural regions is significantly different to the rest of the country. In comparison to the exponential growth of national and urban population, *dispersed rural* localities of less than 2 500 inhabitants remained considerably stable during the 20th century (Figure 1.10). Such stability is due to a combined effect of the higher fertility rate and lower life expectancy than urban areas that prevailed during much part of the century and more recently due to strong out-migration to urban areas and abroad. From 1990 to 2000 the population in dispersed rural localities increased from 23.2 million to 24.7 million, however in relative terms it declined from 28.7% to 25.4% of the Mexican population. From 2000 to 2005, the out-migration factor seemed to have a greater impact since it was registered for the first time a negative rate of growth of –0.3%, which was translated into a decline in the absolute number of people living in localities of less than 2 500 inhabitants (INEGI, 2006).

Figure 1.10. **Population in urban and rural areas**
1910-2005

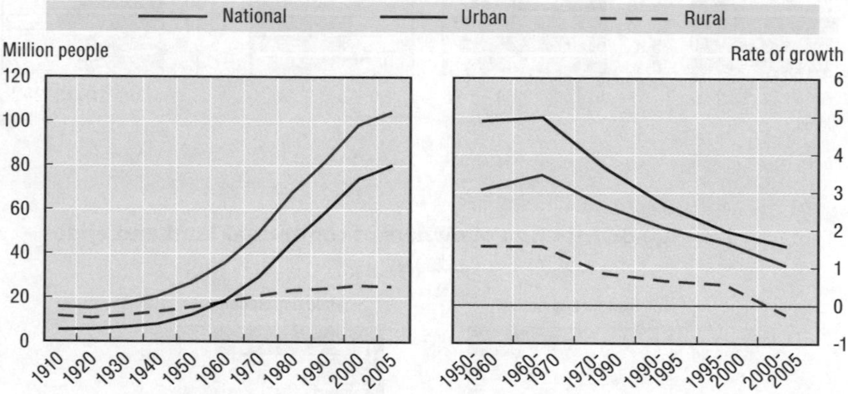

Rural refers to dispersed rural localities (less than 2 500 inhabitants).
Source: INEGI (2006).

The population living in *rural semi-urban* localities, in contrast, increased; it went from 11.2 million in 1990 to 13.3 million in 2000 and to 14.3 million in 2005. However, in relative terms, it declined from 13.9 per cent in 1990 to 13.6 per cent in 2005. By 2030, the estimation is that population in *dispersed rural* areas and *rural semi-urban* areas will increase to about 27 and 17 million respectively, but the share of total population will continue falling to 21 and 13.2 per cent of total population.

... largely due to migration of young people to larger cities and to the United States

An increasing number of youth are migrating in search of opportunities in larger cities or abroad. Migrants are in a vast majority male youth (in a proportion of 71%) of which from 1994 to 1997, 67% went to other localities of Mexico, mainly middle-size cities and 33% to the United States (see Box 1.3). (World Bank 2005) The decline in the number of youth in rural areas starts to have a significant impact in the life of rural communities. Besides the social implications of divided families, an early aging phenomenon is reflected in a higher dependency ratio of elder people, which, although still low, ascends to 16% and 15% in dispersed rural and rural semi-urban areas compared to 11% per cent in urban areas. For some states, this ratio reaches much higher levels in dispersed rural localities close to major urban centres or with strong emigration to the United States: 23.6% for Nuevo León, 20.6% for Zacatecas, 19.7% for Tamaulipas, 19.4% for Jalisco, 18.7 for Durango, 18.6% for San Luis Potosí, and 18.5% for Oaxaca (CONAPO 2004).

On the other hand, migration has provided rural areas with remittances, a new source of income that has become increasingly important as percentage of household income (see Figure 1.17., included as private transfers). In 2004, internal remittances were close to 2% of rural household net income on average and remittances from the United States ascended to up to 11% of household net income (Ceron Monroy, 2004). Foreign remittances, which totalled 20 034.8 million dollars in 2005, have surpassed foreign direct investment as a source of foreign exchange in Mexico. The principal recipient states are Michoacán, Guerrero and the State of Mexico. Close to 4.4% of homes receive remittances, but in the case of Michoacán, Durango and Nayarit, it is around 10%.

Migration of youth male has also conduced to a feminisation of the rural population both on dispersed rural and rural semi-urban localities, particularly for ages between 15 and 49 years (see Figure 1.10, above). The proportion of women for each 100 male which was 108 among youth and 110 among adults in 1999, increased to 114 among youth and 113 among adults in 2003 for dispersed rural localities. In rural semi-urban localities, this phenomenon is even stronger, with higher impact on the adult population. The growth for the referred period for adults was from 115 to 120 and for youth was from 113 to 117 (Presidencia de la República, 2004).

Another important demographic characteristic of rural Mexico is the presence of indigenous population. In 2005, 82% of the population speaking indigenous languages (6 million) lived in rural localities (62% in dispersed rural and 20% in rural semi-urban localities) and were concentrated in 12 states particularly in the South South-East region (INEGI, 2006). Despite the cultural richness of this population, they are the group in the poorest condition, with the lowest education and health levels. Of the localities that concentrate 70% and more indigenous population, 95.4% are classified as localities of high or very high marginalisation.

Box 1.3. **The issue of migration is in essence an issue of disparities in regional development**

Migration flows, mainly out-migration, have long been an issue impacting Mexico's rural landscape. While out-migration from rural Mexico continues at a high rate, there have been changing trends in the destination choices (internal or international) and the employment sector (farm or non-farm) the migrants are joining at their destination.

In terms of internal migration, the rural-urban migration stream has begun to experience changes as the attractiveness of the largest metropolitan areas has begun to diminish in comparison to the small and medium-sized cities, which are now attracting not only rural migrants, but also inhabitants from other cities of varying sizes. For example, CONAPO indicates that from 1995-2000, 1.2 million people emigrated internally from rural localities (< 2 500 persons), and of those, roughly 127 000 moved to small cities (15 000-99 999), 400 000 moved to medium cities (100 000-999 999) and 339 000 moved to big cities (> 1 000 000). The shift in attractiveness of migrant destinations is also demonstrated by the decline of Mexico City (the Federal District and State of Mexico) as the main internal migrant destinations (in relative terms) and the growing importance of states such as Baja California, Chihuahua and Tamaulipas (see below figures). The case of Baja California and Chihuahua exemplifies the important role of "bridge states" that receive large numbers of internal immigrants and later witness large outflows of international emigrants headed to the USA.

Migration flows in Mexico, 1955-60 and 1995-2000

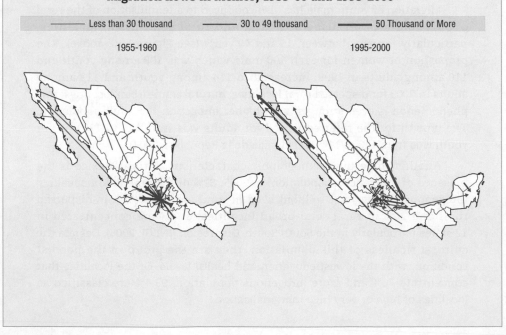

——— Less than 30 thousand   ——— 30 to 49 thousand   ——— 50 Thousand or More

1955-1960   1995-2000

Box 1.3. **The issue of migration is in essence an issue of disparities in regional development** (cont.)

Apart from the net emigration from rural Mexico on a permanent basis, Mexico also displays high rates of temporary internal migration. In particular, this refers to agricultural migrants (jornaleros agrícolas) who migrate to search for agricultural employment during the planting and harvesting seasons. According to SEDESOL, in 2000 there were between 2.7 and 3.7 million jornaleros in Mexico, a large majority of which permanently reside in the southern states, such as Oaxaca and Guerrero which have the highest number of jornaleros. There are three types of jornaleros: jornaleros pendulares who leave their place of origin for 4-6 month periods, but return to their place of residency when the job is finished; jornaleros golondrinos who move constantly, all year long, from one place to the next working on different crops; and jornaleros locales who are employed in areas relatively close to their place of origin enabling them to go to work and return home the same day. Of particular concern are the large numbers of children that work as jornaleros, as SEDESOL estimates that it could be as high as 40%.

A 2005 study by Mora and Taylor, using the findings from the 2003 Mexico National Rural Household Survey (Encuesta Nacional a Hogares Rurales de México, or ENHRUM),* indicates that the percentage of Mexico's rural populations working at internal and international migrant destinations rose significantly from 1980-2002 (see figure below). Over 50% of all rural Mexican migrants end up in Mexican destinations, yet the propensity to migrate to jobs in the USA more than doubled from 1990 to 2002. There are also interesting trends in the employment sector choices made by the migrants which mirror the decline in overall agricultural employment as well as the share of agricultural production in the Mexican economy dating back to the 1990s. The ENHRUM data highlights a growing percentage of rural inhabitants employed as non-farm migrant labourers both internally and internationally, as well as a much less pronounced upward trend in the percentage in US farm jobs. Internally, there has been a decrease in migrants working in agriculture. In 2002, an average of 14% of the rural Mexican population was working in the USA, a figure which is higher than the percentage for the total Mexican population, which in 2002 was 9% (in 2002, 9.82 of the estimated 103 million Mexicans resided in the USA). The majority of rural Mexico's international migrants, 82%, were employed in US non-farm jobs. On average 15% of rural Mexican populations were observed as internal migrants, of which, 90% were non-farm labourers.

* ENHRUM provides detailed data on assets, socio-demographic characteristics, production, income sources, and migration from a nationally representative sample of rural households surveyed in January and February 2003. The sample includes 7 298 individuals from 1 782 households in 14 states. INEGI designed the sampling frame to reliably characterise Mexico's rural population (living in localities with under 2 500 inhabitants), but for cost reasons excluded disperse populations in localities with under 500 inhabitants. Thus, the sample is representative of more than 80% of the population INEGI defines as rural.

Box 1.3. **The issue of migration is in essence an issue of disparities in regional development** (cont.)

Labour migrants as percentage of rural Mexican population, by migrant destination and sector of employment, 1980-2002

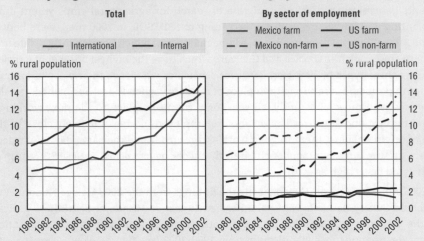

Migration decisions in rural Mexico, as everywhere in the world, are in essence based in regional development disparities. Individuals and households compare the utility associated with migrating to different locations and labour markets with the utility associated with not migrating. Mora and Taylor's empirical study models the selectivity of internal and international migration to farm and non-farm jobs, combining individual, household and community variables to provide a picture of the determinants of migration from rural Mexico. Other things being equal, the following can be said for total migration from rural Mexico:

● Household heads are significantly less likely to migrate than non-heads-of-household;

● Males are significantly more likely to migrate than females;

● Probability of migration increases with age, but at a decreasing rate;

● Probability of migration increases significantly with years of completed schooling of the individual;

● As the value of family landholdings increases, the probability of migration decreases;

● Migration networks have a positive and highly significant effect on migration;

● Migration increases with rural localities' transportation access to commercial centres;

● Individuals in rural localities with insecure access to outside markets are more likely to migrate than those in localities where market access is secure; and

● Migration decreases when non-farm enterprises are present in the localities.

OECD RURAL POLICY REVIEWS: MEXICO – ISBN 978-92-64-01152-6 – © OECD 2007

Box 1.3. **The issue of migration is in essence an issue of disparities in regional development** (*cont.*)

While the above are general results for the determinants of migration as a whole, the significance of different variables actually varies according to the destination and employment sector. For example, individuals' schooling has a significant positive effect on internal migration to non-farm – but not farm – jobs. Yet schooling has no significant effect on international migration, since rural Mexican international immigration heavily entails unauthorised entry and employment in low-skill jobs where the returns to schooling obtained in Mexico are likely to be small (as is the case with Mexican agricultural jobs). Migration networks in the USA significantly affect international migration to both farm and non-farm jobs, reflecting the greater costs and risks associated with international migration and thereby the greater value of family contacts, and networks in Mexico significantly affect internal migration, but much less for farm than non-farm jobs. Overall, there is no evidence at the local level that integration with outside markets discourages migration. The level of transportation infrastructure is positively linked to migration, especially internally. And when access to markets outside the rural localities is insecure, probabilities of migration increase. Finally it should be said that the current US immigration debate over legalisation policies and guest worker programmes will likely play a role in the future strength of migration networks and thus impact rural migrants' location decisions.

Source: Mora, J. and J.E. Taylor (2006), Wodon, Q. *et al.* (2002) and McKenzie, D.J. (2006).

1.2.2. Social well-being and equity

The rural-urban divide is significant in terms of standards of living

The contrast between rural and urban population in terms of standards of living can be assessed by almost any indicator. Rural and urban levels of GDP per capita are shown in Figure 1.11. Whereas the average GDP per capita in urban municipalities was 141% of national average in 2000, in dispersed rural and semi-urban municipalities it was only 27% and 43%. Even urban intermediate municipalities show a strong discrepancy with respect to urban ones. The average GDP per capita in urban intermediate municipalities was 70% of the national average.

A similar contrast exists within OECD categories. Whereas Predominantly Rural and Intermediate regions had in 2000 a GDP per capita of 71% and 70% of national average, Predominantly Urban were 34% higher than the national average.[12] The mapping of these regions in Figure 1.12. shows an important fact: with exception of certain PR regions close to the US frontier and the ones that have a high GDP due to mineral resources, almost all PR regions have a GDP per capita lower than 50% of the national average.

Figure 1.11. **Estimated GDP per capita by type of municipality and region**
2000

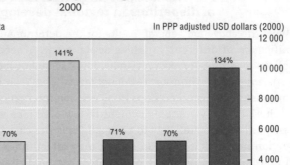

As percentage of national GDP per capita

In PPP adjusted USD dollars (2000)

Note: OECD typology refers to TL3 level.

Source: OECD calculations based on GDP per capita and population figures by municipality from INAFED (2000).

Figure 1.12. **GDP per capita in PR regions as percentage of national**

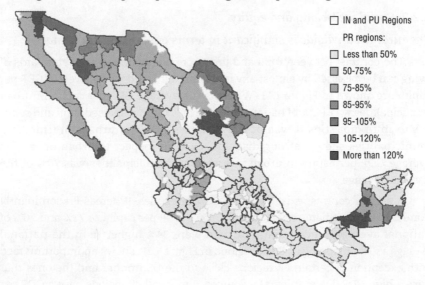

Source: OECD based on data from INAFED (2000).

OECD RURAL POLICY REVIEWS: MEXICO – ISBN 978-92-64-01152-6 – © OECD 2007

Although inhabitants of urban regions frequently enjoy the highest level of GDP per capita, not only in Mexico but in most countries, differences between regions are much higher in Mexico. Figure 1.13 shows the differences in GDP per capita between PR, IN and PU regions for OECD countries. In 2001, GDP per capita in predominantly urban regions in OECD countries was on average 36% higher than the national, but intermediate and predominantly rural regions had a GDP per capita that was 93% and 82%, respectively, of the national average. Mexico shares with the Czech Republic, Hungary, Poland, the Slovak Republic and Turkey, large differences between urban and rural GDP per capita.

Doing the same exercise for states within Mexico gives important information about the level of development of rural areas in the different states and the degrees of inequality within states. Some states, such as Nuevo León, Baja California, Baja California Sur, Campeche and Coahuila have GDP per capita in predominantly rural areas higher than the national GDP per capita average. For some states the distance between urban and rural income is considerably high, such as Aguascalientes, Guerrero, Nuevo León and Quintana Roo.

Despite recent reductions, poverty is prevalent in rural areas

Although urban poverty has recently become a more significant phenomenon, rural residence (together with educational attainment) has been the leading characteristic defining the profile of the poor in Mexico. According to the referred poverty classification (Box 1.4), 60.6% of the population in extreme poverty lived in rural areas in 2004. Besides this, several studies indicate that the number of dispersed rural localities in each municipality has a strong negative correlation with the level of GDP per capita (FAO 2005) and a positive correlation with extreme poverty rates (OECD, 2003a). Isolation of dispersed rural localities constitutes not only a challenge for the provision of public and private services like education and health, instrumental in the process of leaving the situation of poverty, but also a barrier that prevents the exploitation of new opportunities. This fact has contributed to the further marginalisation of the rural population since the drive towards economic liberalisation, which for other sectors of population has opened economic opportunities (OECD, 2003a).

Efforts to have standard, independent measurements of poverty have paid off not only for the value of possessing information but also for the favourable results that they have provided with regards to poverty fighting programmes. These measurements indicate that rural poverty has reduced substantially since 1996, when the financial crisis increased the absolute and relative number of people in poor conditions both in rural and urban areas. In fact, the reduction of rural poverty has been more significant than the reduction within urban poverty. From 1996 to 2004 the number of people

Figure 1.13. **GDP per capita by type of region in OECD countries and in Mexican states**

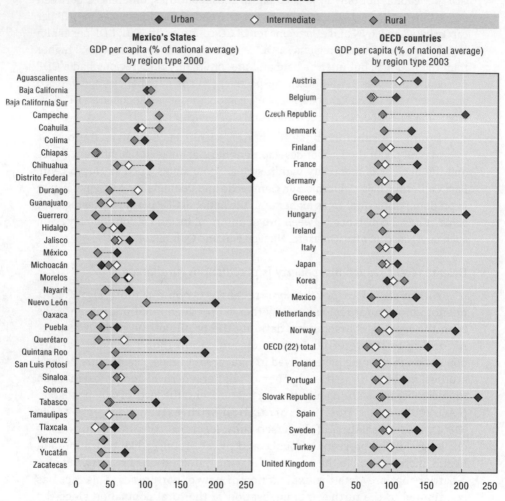

Note: Countries for which no data on GDP per capita at TL3 level is available are excluded.
Source: OECD regional database and INAFED (2000).

in rural areas under the category of food poverty (extreme poverty) decreased by 44% from 19.8 to 10.9 million. However, they still represent 28% of rural population. The population under poverty of capacity and poverty of assets have also declined by 37% and 26% in rural areas. Despite this improvements, in total 56.9% of people in rural localities live under some kind of poverty condition. (Figure 1.14).

OECD RURAL POLICY REVIEWS: MEXICO – ISBN 978-92-64-01152-6 – © OECD 2007

Box 1.4. **Alternative measures of standards of living used in Mexico**

Since GDP per capita sometimes fails in capturing a complete picture of the differences in standards of living, several alternative measures have been developed or adopted by Mexican policymakers. Among these are the Index of Marginalisation, UNDP's Index of Human Development and the three poverty lines defined and measured by an independent Technical Committee for Measurement of Poverty. These measures are described here.

The Marginalisation Index developed by the Consejo Nacional de Población (CONAPO) since 1996, combines 9 variables: the percentage of illiterate individuals over 15 years of age, the percentage of individuals without completed primary school, the percentage of individuals living in their private house with no drainage service, the percentage of individuals living in private houses with no electricity, the percentage of individuals living in their private house with no drinking water system, the percentage of private houses characterised by overcrowding, the percentage of individuals living in private houses with soil floors, the percentage of population living in localities of less than 5 000 inhabitants, and the percentage of working population earning less than two minimum wages.

Municipalities and states are classified according to five categories: very high marginalisation, high, medium, low and very low. This index has been extensively used in policymaking for example for defining the initial focalisation of the Progresa (today Oportunidades) programme and to define the target zones of the Micro-Regions Strategy.

Municipalities according to the degree of marginalisation

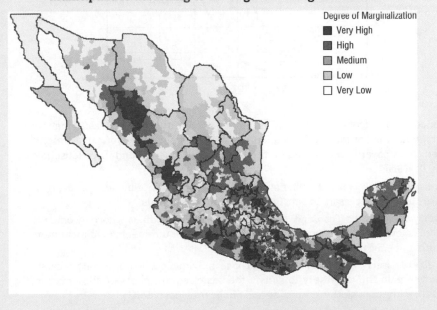

Degree of Marginalization
- ■ Very High
- ■ High
- ▨ Medium
- ◻ Low
- ☐ Very Low

Box 1.4. **Alternative measures of standards of living used in Mexico** *(cont.)*

Human Development Index developed by the United Nations Programme for Development (UNDP) which is published yearly at country level in the Human Development Report since 1990, has been proxied at state and local level in Mexico in co-ordination with CONAPO. The index includes four measures of development: adjusted GDP per capita, an index of adult literacy, an index of schooling and infant mortality rates. The IIDI is at municipal level is strongly co-related with the Marginalisation Index. The following graph shows the contrast between all the municipalities in various states ordered according to the HDI.

Human Development Index by municipalities for selected states

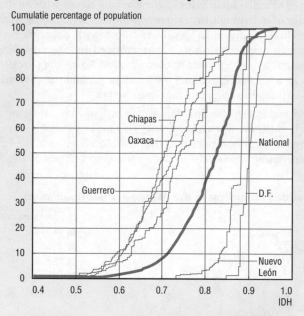

Mexico's Classification of Poverty. The Technical Committee for Measurement of Poverty, which is conformed by academics of different independent institutions, defined three poverty lines based on the National Income-Expenditure Household Survey (ENIGH):

1. Poverty of food (*Pobreza Alimentaria*): Those individuals whose income per capita is lower than the necessary to satisfy basic alimentation needs.

2. Poverty of capacities (*Pobreza de Capacidades*): Those individuals whose income per capita is lower than the necessary to fulfil the basic requirements of alimentation, health and education.

3. Poverty of assets (*Pobreza de Patrimonio*): Those individuals whose income per capita is lower than the necessary to satisfy the basic requirements of alimentation, health, education, clothing, housing and public transportation.

Box 1.4. **Alternative measures of standards of living used in Mexico** (cont.)

Poverty lines in current MXN

	Poverty lines		
	2000	2002	2004
Urban			
Food	626.00	672.27	739.60
Capacities	769.98	826.90	909.71
Assets	1 258.89	1 351.94	1 487.34
Rural			
Food	492.90	494.77	548.17
Capacities	586.06	588.29	651.77
Assets	899.54	902.96	1 000.41

Source: CONAPO (2001a, 2001b) and SEDESOL (2006).

Figure 1.14. **Incidence of rural poverty**

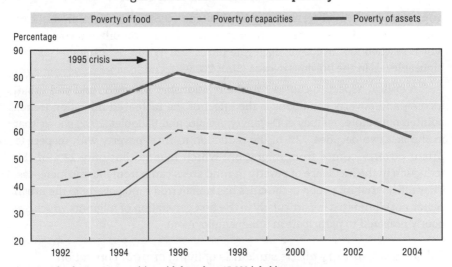

Note: Rural refers to communities with less than 15 000 inhabitants.
Source: SEDESOL (Comité Técnico para la Medición de la Pobreza 2005).

On the other hand, according to the Income-Expenditure Surveys, rural income has increased at a greater pace than urban income in the past few years. From 2000 to 2004 aggregate household income per capita in rural areas increased from $3 442 MXN to $3 543 MXN (at 2000 prices), which means a 2.93%

Figure 1.15. **Rural-urban per household income ratio**
1992-2004

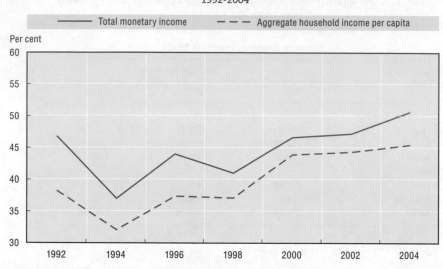

Source: OECD calculations based on SIAP (2006) and Ruiz Castillo (2005).

improvement in real terms compared to the –0.63% in urban areas (Ruiz Castillo, 2005). The result has been an increase in the rural-urban income ratio, which reached 51% in 2004 in aggregate terms and 45% in per capita terms, the highest levels in the previous decade (SIAP, 2006).

A critical aspect to consider in the relationship between rural and urban income and poverty conditions is the effect of the increased migration trends pointed out before. A study of De Janvry, Araujo, and Sadoulet (2002) shows that in the last two decades, 77% of the reduction in rural poverty with respect to urban poverty comes from migration, which means that only 23% of the reduction in the incidence of poverty in rural areas came from income increases. They affirm that migration to the cities has transferred rural poverty to the urban sector not eliminated it, particularly in the first generation of migrants which are poorly prepared to participate in urban employment.

Public service delivery affects standards of living of rural population

Many indicators of social well-being are closely linked to the provision of public services. This is why, increasingly, public service delivery to rural areas in OECD countries is being considered as providing "basic rights" to all population regardless of their location. The dispersed character of rural population in Mexico increases the difficulty to establish a critical mass of infrastructure, public and private services.

OECD RURAL POLICY REVIEWS: MEXICO – ISBN 978-92-64-01152-6 – © OECD 2007

Of the 196 000 rural localities, about 15% live close to an urban centre, however, 44.3% is far from cities but close to a road functional all year and 32%, where about 4.6 million people live, are isolated. Accessibility therefore is a major priority. The current network of rural roads extends to 172 000 paved kilometres and 78 000 unpaved roads (Presidencia de la República 2005). These roads are in general of poor quality and often not functional during the whole year. Nevertheless they are a crucial communication asset for the 19 000 localities that they access, where about 60% of rural population lives (PEC, 2002).

Despite significant improvements in the figures from 2000 to 2005 (Table 1.1), a large number of houses or shelters in dispersed rural municipalities still do not count with appropriate conditions. Houses with solid floor increased from 68% in 2000 to 83% in 2005; houses with their own sanitary from 73% to 89%, houses with drainage had a significant increase from 52% to 80%; electricity coverage increased from 87% to 93%. Still, these figures contrast with the urban metropolitan figures which are in most of these indicators higher to 90% coverage. Interestingly however, several indicators show a decrease for urban intermediate and urban metropolitan categories. These shifts are related to the migration patterns.

Although Mexico has one of the highest levels of coverage of electric power in Latin America, reaching 94.7% of total population, about 5 million people in rural areas does not have access to electricity, most of them in indigenous communities in the states of Veracruz, Chiapas, Guerrero, Oaxaca, San Luis Potosí and Chihuahua. This also constitutes an obstacle to the provision of other public services, such as drinking water, telecommunications, remote education and health services.

In terms of telecommunications, technological advances have really facilitated access to remote localities in the past decade. For example, the challenge of fixed telephone coverage has been reduced with mobile and satellite telephone infrastructure, which allowed to increase the provision of this service, from 1995 to 2005, from 18 600 to 50 500 rural localities, mainly the South-South-eastern region (Presidencia de la República, 2005). In a similar way, through the E-Mexico network, the Mexican government has installed 3200 Digital Community Centres to provide at least one point of high-speed connectivity at each and every municipality in the country, where educational, health, business and government services are provided.

Education, as previously mentioned, has been regarded as the most important factor explaining rural poverty in Mexico, in as much as 47% compared to 29% in Latin America (Attanasio and Szekely, 1999). Several studies coincide also in the fact that years of schooling have proved to have significant returns for the rural population and influence their choice of economic activity (Yunez and Taylor, 1999). In the context of high migration to urban areas, investment in

Table 1.1. **Social and public service delivery indicators**

Municipalities columns: Rural dispersed, Rural semi-urban, Urban intermediate, Urban metropolitan. Regions (TL3) columns: Predominantly Rural, Intermediate, Predominantly Urban.

2000-2005	Rural dispersed		Rural semi-urban		Urban intermediate		Urban metropolitan		Predominantly Rural		Intermediate		Predominantly Urban	
	2000	2005	2000	2005	2000	2005	2000	2005	2000	2005	2000	2005	2000	2005
Living conditions														
Houses with solid floor (%)	68	**83**	80	**86**	88	**88**	94	**91**	78	**81**	80	**84**	95	**91**
Houses with sanitary (%)	73	**89**	80	**90**	87	**90**	92	**92**	81	**88**	84	**91**	90	**92**
Houses with water (%)	68	**83**	80	**84**	83	**86**	92	**90**	76	**80**	80	**83**	92	**90**
Houses with drainage (%)	52	**80**	64	**84**	79	**86**	90	**90**	65	**76**	72	**82**	91	**91**
Houses with electricity (%)	87	**93**	94	**94**	96	95	98	**94**	91	**93**	94	**95**	99	**94**
Skills														
Population (15 >) literate (%)	81	**90**	85	**91**	90	**92**	95	**96**	86	**88**	87	**89**	95	**96**
Population (15 >) with basic school (12 yrs) (%)	14	**21**	17	**21**	18	**22**	20	**22**	16	**19**	16	**19**	21	**23**
Population (15 >) higher than basic ed. (%)	15	**28**	16	**31**	23	**30**	36	**42**	20	**25**	23	**28**	35	**39**
Average schooling years	4.7	**5.7**	5.8	**6.1**	6.8	6.4	7.8	7.3	5.1	**5.7**	5.3	**6.0**	6.9	**7.7**
Performance in Reading (points/600)	340		383		406		435							
Performance in Math	335		368		389		417							
Performance in Sciences	362		388		407		434							
Performance in Problem Solving	327		362		391		421							
Health														
Infant mortality rate (per 1000 births)	34		30		25		21		31		31		25	
Life expectancy at birth (years)	71		75		79		85		74		73		81	
Hospital beds per 100 000 inhabitants	23		36		54		110		54		69		101	
Physicians per 100 000 inhabitants	97		97		104		180		117		131		167	
Population with Social Security (%)	20	**43**	25	**45**	38	**49**	52	**54**	33	**43**	33	**43**	48	**51**
Accessibility														
Distance in minutes to closest city	51		31		29		7		43		21		11	
Aggregate Measures														
Index of Human Development	0.65		0.70		0.76		0.82		0.68		0.69		0.76	
Index of Marginalisation[1]	**0.57**	0.59	-0.08	**-0.10**	-0.79	**-0.79**	**-1.64**	-1.61	**0.15**	0.16	0.11	**0.08**	**-0.91**	-0.89

1. For the Index of Marginalisation, negative values are better (less marginalisation) than positive values (more marginalisation).

Source: INAFED with data from INEGI (2005) and CONAPO (2000), OECD PISA (2003).

OECD RURAL POLICY REVIEWS: MEXICO – ISBN 978-92-64-01152-6 – © OECD 2007

education is of the highest return. The previously referenced study from De Janvry, Araujo, and Sadoulet (2002) highlights the fact that while migration provides rural population with higher wages, the critical factor that increases income is education and particularly secondary education (after the 6 years of *educación primaria* and 3 years of *educación secundaria*).

The Mexican government has done an important effort in the improvement of the coverage of education in rural areas. From 2000 to 2005 average schooling in dispersed rural municipalities increased one year from 4.7 to 5.7, the proportion of population of more than 15 years with basic education (12 years of *primaria* and *secundaria*) increased from 14% to 21% and the percentage of such population with higher than basic education increased from 15% to 28%. Still, average schooling is 5.7 years in dispersed rural areas, which contrast with the 7.8 recorded in urban metropolitan areas in 2000 (which declined to 7.3, probably because the same migration phenomenon in 2005) and with the 9.7 years in Mexico City (INEGI, 2000).

The challenge to provide education services to disperse localities is very significant. In many of the localities of less than 100 inhabitants, where almost one million children of less than 14 years live, one teacher educates children of different grades in all the areas of knowledge. Mobility and lower education or even illiteracy of parents (which reaches close to 20% in rural areas) are factors that have important repercussions on children's education. An elevated number of children in rural areas (between 400 000 and 700 000 according to diverse estimations) have very high mobility because of the movement of their parents working as *jornaleros* in different parts of the region (see Box 1.4). These factors affect the quality of education. OECD student performance tests (PISA, 2003) evidence that students in dispersed rural localities and rural semi-urban localities have significantly lower performance than students in urban areas, which in general are already low by OECD standards.

Provision of health services is subject to similar challenges. Only about 80% of households living in rural localities have access to health services at a distance of 5 km or less, and there were only 22 hospital beds and 96 physicians for every 100 000 inhabitants in dispersed rural areas in 2000. The lower levels of infrastructure translate into lower health standards measurable by almost any indicator. For example, life expectancy in rural areas of Oaxaca, Guerrero and Chiapas is 10 years less than in urban areas of Baja California Sur, Nuevo León and the Federal District (PEC, 2002). Infant Mortality Rates were in 2000 as high as 67 deaths per 1 000 live births in some dispersed rural municipalities in contrast with 17 in metropolitan municipalities.

The access to health services and ability to face financial contingencies due to illness, accidents, maternity or death are important factors of well-being. The disparities in coverage of social security in rural areas (20% in dispersed rural compared to 52% in urban areas in 2000), were to some extent reduced in the past few years through several mechanisms have been implemented to insure the rural population such as the Seguro Popular. The population in dispersed rural areas and rural semi-urban areas rose to 43% and 45% respectively by 2005.

1.2.3. Economic structure and performance

Agriculture has reduced its role in the overall economy...

Rural economy has undergone an important transformation since the beginning of the 1990s characterised by a reduction in the role of agriculture and a consequent increase of non-agricultural activities. The contribution of Agriculture, Forestry and Fishing (AFF) activities to GDP declined from 8% in 1990 to 5% in 2004. There are of course substantial regional differences in the way this shift has taken place, between 1993 and 2003, farming activities accounted on average for 5% of GDP in northern states and up to 15% for southern state[13] (FAO, 2005).

In terms of employment however, agriculture is still the predominant activity in dispersed rural municipalities, where in 2000, the share of occupied population in the primary sector reached 43.7%. This figure declines to 32% for rural semi-urban municipalities and to 30% when referring to predominantly rural regions, which is still three times higher than the 10% average or PR regions among OECD countries. The relative importance of agriculture as a source of employment in Mexico is also evident by the fact that at the national level, the share of employment in agriculture (14.3%) is more than double of the average among OECD (6%).

Agriculture itself has had an important transition in the past 15 years. Production of basic grains remained stalled due to a reduction in the harvested area affected by adverse climate, a decline in the producer prices, increasing costs of supplies and inefficient scale of production. In contrast, production and harvested area of fruits and vegetables linked to more profitable national and international markets has grown substantially (PEC, 2002). However, increases in agricultural productivity and exports have done little to improve the living conditions of population in rural dispersed localities since most of them dedicates to agriculture for self-consumption of basic grains such as beans, maize and coffee. This is true even in regions where there is a clear vocation for high value added crops such as fruits and vegetables, which give good profits to larger producers. In exceptional cases, public and private institutions have successfully aided the transition of small producers to exportable crops, and innovative collaboration systems have allowed them to profit from higher export prices, such as in the case of avocado production in Michoacán (OECD, 2005b).

The limits of agriculture are also set by the fact that of the 198 million hectares of the Mexican territory, only 11% are arable territory and most of it is

OECD RURAL POLICY REVIEWS: MEXICO – ISBN 978-92-64-01152-6 – © OECD 2007

Figure 1.16. **Sectoral composition of occupied population according to different territorial levels and definitions of rural areas**

2000

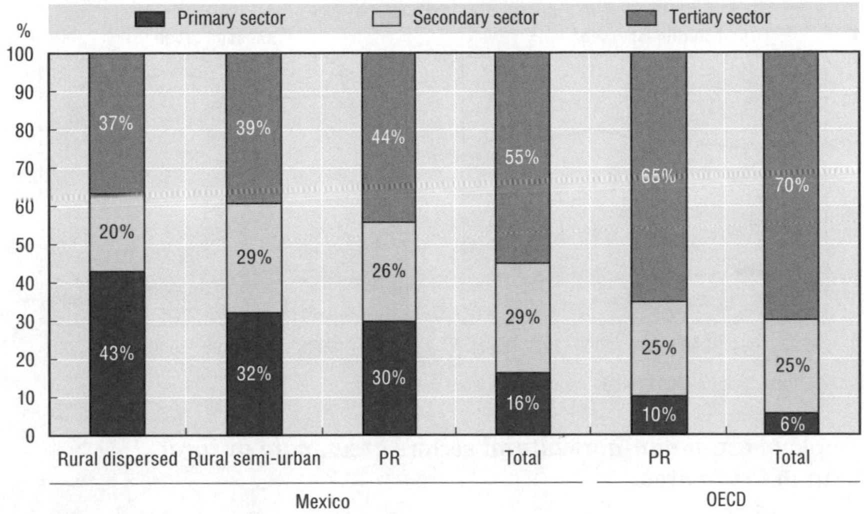

Source: INAFED (2000) and OECD Regional Database.

already with that use. Where agriculture has room for improvement is in terms of productivity. Unfortunately only large producers, in general, have scale and access to financing and technology which are the major drivers of productivity increases.

Therefore, most opportunities for economic development are thus more and more linked to non-farm activities. This transformation of the rural economy is noticeable increasingly in the change in the composition of rural families' income and in the employment and output shares of non-farm sectors in rural areas.

... as well as in the income of rural families

Non-agricultural activities accounted for 51% and 62% of family income in dispersed localities and in rural semi-urban localities in 2004. In contrast, income derived from agriculture (both independent farming and wage labour) has declined from 41% and 23% in 1992 to 19% and 11% for dispersed and semi-urban localities respectively (Ruiz Castillo, 2005). The other sources of income that have increased significantly are public and private transfers, the former as a result of an substantial increase in the coverage of the two main programmes of direct transfers to rural areas, *Oportunidades* and Procampo, the latter is related to the remittances from family members living in the United States.

Figure 1.17. **Distribution of income by source in rural localities**
1992-2004

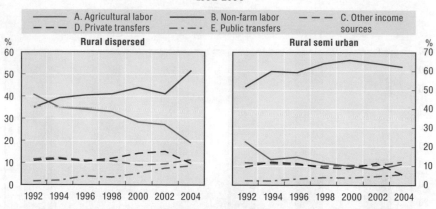

Source: Ruiz Castillo (2005) with information from SIAP (2004).

Employment in non-agricultural sectors grew more in rural than in urban areas

According to the Economic Census of 2004, rural municipalities contributed with only 8.2% of total non-agricultural employment[14] (1.1% by dispersed rural and 7.1% by rural semi-urban). Using the OECD typology, PR regions have 26% of employment. The most important industries in rural areas are mining, retail commerce, manufacturing and certain services such as tourism. For all these sectors, the share of employment in rural areas of the sector is higher than the share of total employment in rural areas. These shares are 21.5, 11.3, 9.8 and 9.1 per cent respectively.

Figure 1.18 shows the dynamics of non-agricultural employment in rural areas. From 1999 to 2004, non-agricultural employment increased at an average annual growth rate of 5.2% in rural municipalities (both in rural dispersed and in rural semi-urban), which contrasts with the 3.5% growth in urban municipalities. The contrast between predominantly rural and predominantly urban growth rates is similar (4% to 3.17%), which implies that the contribution to employment growth during that period was larger from rural areas than from urban areas (see Table A2 in Annex 1.A1 for details).

... markedly in manufacturing activities

This fact is particularly true for Manufacturing employment which grew 2.6% annually in rural municipalities (1.25% for PR regions) and declined in absolute terms 0.13% annually in urban municipalities (–0.1% for PU regions). Among manufacturing activities the most prevalent industries in rural areas are food and beverages on the one hand and textiles, clothing and leather industries on the other. In 2004 these industries employed approximately 113 000 and

Figure 1.18. **The rural economy: employment growth by non-agricultural sector**

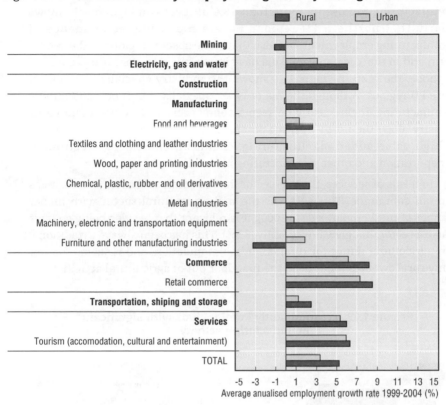

Source: INEGI 2006.

115 000 people in rural municipalities, which accounts for 13.4% and 15.6% of total employment in those industries, respectively. Although most of the employment in these activities takes place in rural semi-urban municipalities, both activities have more than 12 000 employees in municipalities with all their population living in dispersed rural localities. Despite the fact that these two manufacturing sectors grew more in rural than in urban areas, their growth was not very significant (2.6% and 0.2% respectively).

In contrast, other manufacturing sectors showed more dynamism in rural areas. It is worth highlighting that advanced manufacturing sectors such as machinery, electronic and transportation equipment manufacturing were the ones that showed greater growth in rural municipalities. This group of sectors grew 15.1% (44.3% in dispersed rural municipalities and 14% in rural semi-urban municipalities) in contrast with the 1.9% growth in urban areas. Other manufacturing sector that grew more than average was the metal manufacturing industry.

The map in Figure 1.19 depicts the Predominantly Rural regions for which manufacturing represents more than 15% of local employment. It shows clearly that northern PU regions have a much higher incidence of manufacturing employment, but also that some specific regions in the centre, south and in the Yucatan Peninsula have important manufacturing activities. Of those, the map in Figure 1.20 shows the industry specialisation within these PU regions. Although the majority are specialised in Food and Clothing manufacturing, it can clearly be seen a zone specialised in wood and paper industry along the north-west region and a clear concentration in the north of high value added manufacturing (chemical, machinery, electronics, transportation and other manufacturing industries).

In terms of services, the sub-sector that has more relevance in rural areas is retail commerce. This sector is the non-agricultural sector with higher number of rural employees (454 000). It is relevant that besides being so large is also a sector that grew importantly (8.5%). This has been always a traditional non-agricultural refuge for rural (an urban) population, and it seems that for many rural dwellers it has been the first door out of agricultural activities.

Figure 1.19. **Predominantly Rural regions with significant manufacturing activity**
2004

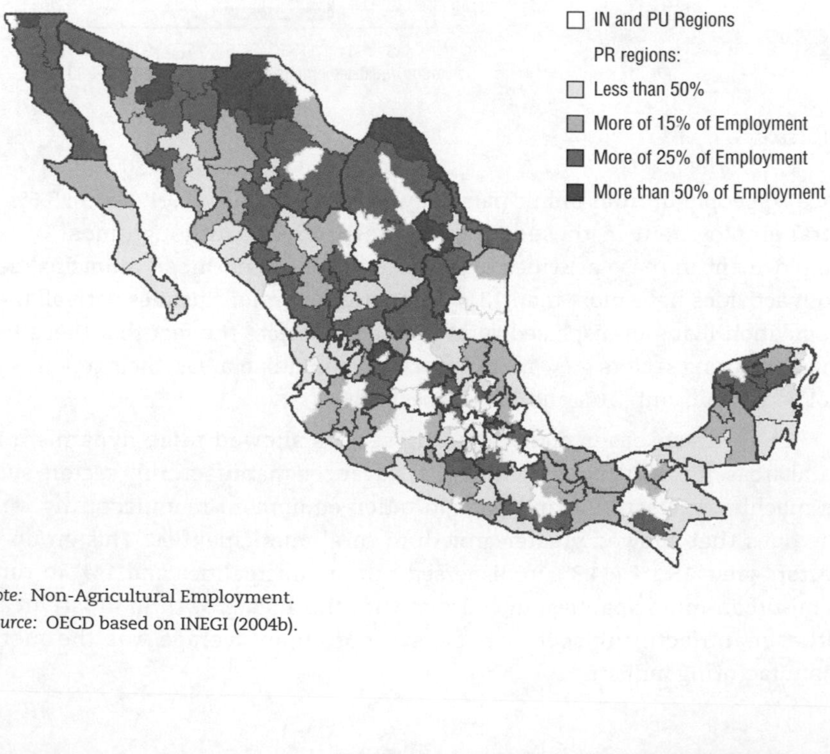

☐ IN and PU Regions
PR regions:
☐ Less than 50%
▨ More of 15% of Employment
▨ More of 25% of Employment
▉ More than 50% of Employment

Note: Non-Agricultural Employment.
Source: OECD based on INEGI (2004b).

Figure 1.20. **Industry specialisation of PR with more than 15%
of employment in manufacturing**

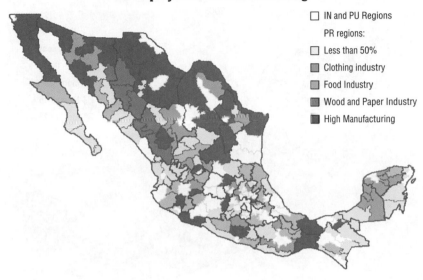

☐ IN and PU Regions

PR regions:

☐ Less than 50%

▨ Clothing industry

▨ Food Industry

▨ Wood and Paper Industry

▨ High Manufacturing

Source: OECD based on INEGI (2004b).

... and in services such as tourism

The growth of tourism as an alternative way of income in rural areas is worth highlighting. This sector employed 123 876 people in rural municipalities in 2004, 9.1% of all tourism employment (27% for PR regions). This activity is one of the sub-sectors with the largest growth in terms of employment from 1999 to 2004, which was also – slightly – higher in rural areas than in urban areas (6.3 *vs.* 5.9%) The regional perspective indicates that the South-southeast and the Peninsula of Baja California contain the rural areas where tourism already represent a significant share of occupied population and certainly where tourism has increasing potential as an alternative to agricultural activities (Figure 1.21). The substantial water resources, forest cover, bio-diversity, and archaeological sites constitute important assets that are unused or underused with respect to the economic potential that they could represent for the local population. The OECD has already highlighted that is room for policy intervention to find ways to attract tourist resources from mass resort destinations to surrounding areas (see OECD, 2003). Mexico ranks eighth in the world regarding tourist inflows and has approximately 2 million jobs in the sector.

The higher growth of non-farm employment in rural than in urban areas during the period 1999-2004, is an important indication of the potential of rural areas as alternative engine of employment growth for Mexico. This is not an isolated phenomenon in Mexico. For several OECD countries, the region with highest employment growth was a rural region (OECD, 2005a).

Figure 1.21. **Predominantly Rural regions where tourism has
a relevant importance**
2005

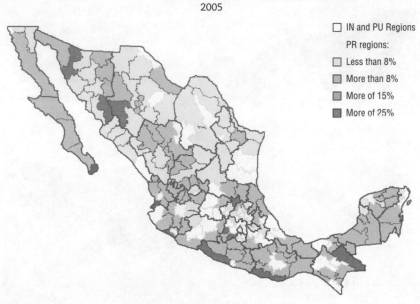

- ☐ IN and PU Regions
- PR regions:
- ☐ Less than 8%
- ▨ More than 8%
- ▨ More of 15%
- ▨ More of 25%

Note: Employment refers to Non-Agricultural Employment.
Source: OECD based on INEGI (2004b).

Figure 1.22 shows the average yearly employment growth of OECD countries during the period 1998-2003. For a growing number of OECD countries (they were 3 in the 1996-2001 period and 8 in the 1999-2003) the rate of employment growth is higher in predominantly rural areas (PR) than in predominantly urban (PU) or intermediate (IN) areas.

During the period 1995-2000, Mexico depicted higher growth rates of employment in urban than in rural areas, this situation was reverted in the period 1999-2004. The states that drove this higher rural employment growth can be identified in Figure 1.22: Baja California, Chihuahua, Guanajuato, the State of Mexico, Nayarit, Nuevo León, Puebla, San Luis Potosí, Tabasco and Yucatan show higher employment growth in their Predominantly Rural regions that in the urban regions, which is usually the capital of the state. Campeche should be considered an exception because all its regions are considered PR and it obtained a very high growth, but it might be related to the importance of the oil industry in the state. This result is very relevant since most of these states have been building industrial parks outside of the main cities.

Still, there are scarce opportunities for well remunerated, formal jobs

While the opportunities for economic development are increasing in non-farm activities, rural population face important obstacles to access other

Figure 1.22. **Employment growth by type of region**

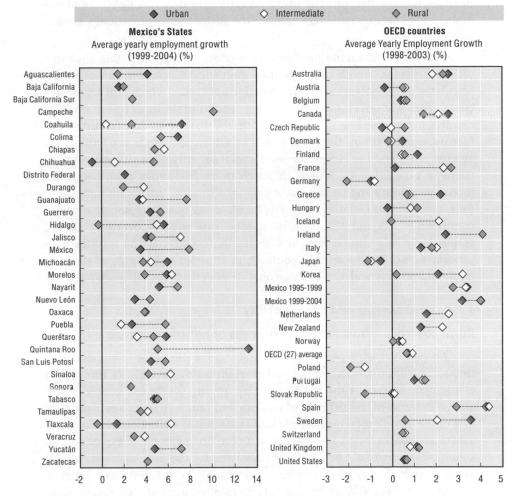

Note: For Mexico, employment refers to Non-Agricultural Employment.
Source: OECD Regional Database and INEGI (2004b).

activities than agriculture. The structural adjustment of the rural economy has increased significantly the number of unemployed people both in rural dispersed and rural semi-urban localities. In both cases the number of unemployed ascended in 2004 to close to 110 000 people (from 77 000 in rural dispersed and 83 000 in rural semi-urban in 2000), which added make about 220 000 unemployed people in rural areas (Presidencia de la República, 2004). The sharp difference in the average earnings of workers across sectors exemplifies the difficulties facing the rural population that cannot manage to access activities other than agriculture. Average earnings in other sectors were nearly ten times that of agriculture, forestry and fisheries by 2000 and the highest paid sectors generally enjoyed the fastest rates of earnings growth (OECD, 2003).

In addition, when the rural population does manage to obtain a job in a different sector, which often implies migrating to semi-urban or urban populations, this job is usually in the informal sector, which still segregates them from higher standards of living. Individuals in extreme poverty condition face the low quality of informal jobs due to certain structural factors, among them: their low levels of education, their low protection against risks, and the lack of access to social security. This situation obliges them to take informal jobs with much more frequency than people in moderate poverty and people out of poverty situation. Within households in extreme and intermediate poverty, 80.6% does not have social security compared to 56% and 32% of people in moderate and no-poverty condition, respectively. In a similar way, 47% of people in extreme and intermediate poverty do not have a written contract, in contrast with 39.6% of those in moderate poverty and 22% of those outside poverty (Sojo-Villareal, 2005).

1.2.4. Environment and sustainability

Rural poverty contrasts with the richness of natural resources

An environmental perspective of rural regions allows the identification of important opportunities for rural development as well as important challenges. Mexico is the fourth country among the 12 considered *mega-diverse* in terms of the richness of its flora and fauna. It hosts approximately 12% of the world's total biodiversity (OECD, 2003c). By definition most of these assets are concentrated in rural areas. These endowments if exploited in a sustainable way, could be a valuable resource for the development of rural areas. Unfortunately destruction and degradation of forests and jungles, extinction of flora and fauna, unlimited exploitation of certain fish species, degradation and desertification of soil, the loss and contamination of subsoil water inventories and the inadequate disposition of toxic and dangerous residuals, are important threats to rural environmental assets that call for further policy intervention.

Forests and Jungles. One of the most important characterisations of the environmental diversity of Mexico are its forest and jungles. Mexico's territory is covered in 33% by these types of vegetation (17% forest and 16% tropical forest or jungles). The distribution of the 39.3 million hectares of these endowments, including primary and secondary vegetation, are concentrated particularly in the South-Southeast region, which has close to 4 million hectares of forest and 15 million of jungle. To a lesser degree the centre-west

OECD RURAL POLICY REVIEWS: MEXICO – ISBN 978-92-64-01152-6 – © OECD 2007

and north-west regions are also rich, especially in forests (see Map in Figure 1.23 and Figure 1.24). For the South-East region the value of this endowment is particularly noteworthy. This region has 44% of the national area covered by primary and secondary forests and 71% of the national area covered by jungle. The environmental richness of the region contrasts with the poverty of its population.

It has been difficult for poor population in rural areas to obtain economic value of the natural richness. During the past four decades, the growth of population and internal migration within rural areas propitiated land use changes and expanded the agrarian frontier at the costs of forests, without significantly improving the poverty condition of its inhabitants. It is estimated that since 1960, Mexico has lost 30% of the forests and jungle present at that time (see Maps in Figure 1.23). The weak definition of property rights has been an important related factor: 51% of the Mexican territory is social land (*ejidos* and communal land, see Box 1.5). The property regime of 85% of the forest land falls within this type of property, which makes control difficult since sometimes there is no clear responsibility of the good or bad use of these assets.

Figure 1.23. **Change in vegetation coverage, 1976-2002**

- ☒ Humid Jungle
- ☐ Sub-humid Jungle
- ☒ Mountain Forest
- ☒ Forest
- ☐ Natural Grass

- ☒ Gipsophylic and Halophytic Vegetation
- ☐ Xerophylic Grass
- ☒ Mangle
- ☐ Other hydropholic
- ☐ Other types of vegetation

- ☐ Induced and cultivated grass
- ☒ Forest plantation
- ☐ Agriculture

Source: SEMARNAT.

Nevertheless, in the past few years there have been important efforts to promote sustainable forestry practices. In 2004, 12 million hectares were already classified as being under "responsible forestry management" which include multiple cases of *ejidos* which have succeeded in attaining good forestry practices and profiting from activities such as eco-tourism. The

Figure 1.24. **Forest and jungle vegetation area by region and state**

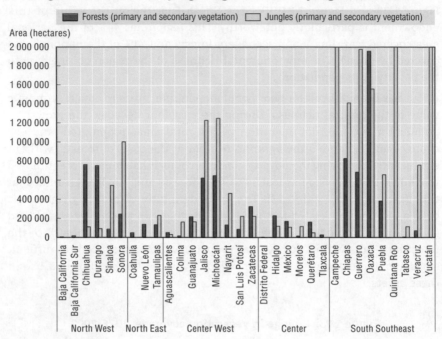

Source: SEMARNAT (2002).

extension of Natural Protected Areas (ANP) is close to 19 million hectares, which represent approximately 9.5% of the Mexican territory. 90% of these areas are comprised in 15 states: Baja California, Baja California Sur, Campeche, Sonora, Quintana Roo, Chihuahua, Chiapas, Colima, Nayarit, Tamaulipas, Yucatán, Coahuila, Querétaro, Puebla and Tabasco.

Still, about 12 million people lived in 2000 in forest zones and it remains an important challenge the consolidation of sustainable practices in the totality of these zones as well as the prevention of inadequate exploitation of them since an important part of this population still has incentives for transforming forest land into arable or cattle land or affecting them through parcel burning and illegal exploitation.

Water. As in many other countries the sources and uses of water are significantly "rural". Mexico consumes about 80 km^3 of water annually, which represent about 17% of the natural availability and comes in 68% from superficial water and 32% underground. Although that level of use puts the resource in a "moderate pressure" category, for the centre, north and north-west regions, the level of use is 47% of the natural availability, which is considered of "high pressure". The most predominant use is agriculture, which takes a share of 76%, followed by public use 12% and industrial 5%.

OECD RURAL POLICY REVIEWS: MEXICO – ISBN 978-92-64-01152-6 – © OECD 2007

Box 1.5. **Land property regime in Mexico**

In Mexico, in addition to public property, Article 27 of the Constitution recognises two forms of land property

1. Small Property (Private Property) – Regulated in general by the civil right and controlled by the public registry of the property, which according to the Agrarian Law cannot exceed 100 hectares (Has) of irrigation, 200 Has of rain fed land, 300 Has for fruit trees, 800 Has of forest or the necessary to maintain up to 500 heads of cattle (although there are certain exceptions, this is the general application). It is estimated that this type of property reaches an area of 75 million hectares.

2. Social Property – Regulated in general by the agrarian right and controlled by National Agrarian Registry (RAN), structured in two modalities:

   ● Ejidos, characterised by the fact that their origin is derived from the agrarian distribution of land or extension of land for (agrarian groups), whose proprietors can dispose of the land as urban estate, parcels or land for common use. The certification rights for the first two cases is individually, for the latter, it is proportional according to the number of ejidatarios that integrate the agrarian group. In this modality, it is allowed to sell rights of land among the recognised ejidatarios in the agrarian group, being able to accumulate up to 5% of the total surface of the ejido or the limits of the small property, whichever is reached first. It is also allowed to reach (full rights) with the agreement of the two thirds of the general assembly of the ejido, in order to sell the land to any third person.

   ● Communal land, which is characterised by the fact that its origin derives from the confirmation or restitution of land to indigenous communities that originally were established there and made use of them. In this single case the rights can be sold only among relatives or people in the vicinity, and it is prohibited the accumulation of rights by on single commoner. La agrarian distribution in the case of the agrarian property, is synthesised in the following picture:

Property regime	Agrarian groups	Land (Has.)	% of national land	Beneficiaries
Small (Private) Property		75 000 000	38.2	
Social land	30 939	101 06 921	51.7	4 236 900
Ejidos	28 721	84 352 527	43.0	3 517 965
Communal land	2 218	17 054 394	8.7	718 935

Source: SRA, Información Agraria Básica Nacional, December 2005.

The intensive use of water in agriculture is related to the dependency of this sector on irrigated water, which has increased irrigated land from 750 thousand hectares 1926 to 9 million hectares in 2002, being more than half in arid and semi-arid zones of the northern and centre regions (see Figure 1.25). It is however, that land, which represents only 29% of agricultural land, where 55% of agricultural output is produced and the origin of 77% of agricultural exports (Alvarado and Kemper, 2001). There is room for improvement in the use of water for agricultural purposes, since it is estimated that the average efficiency of the use of irrigated water is 46% (PEC, 2002).

Figure 1.25. **Rain fed and irrigated agricultural land by region and state**

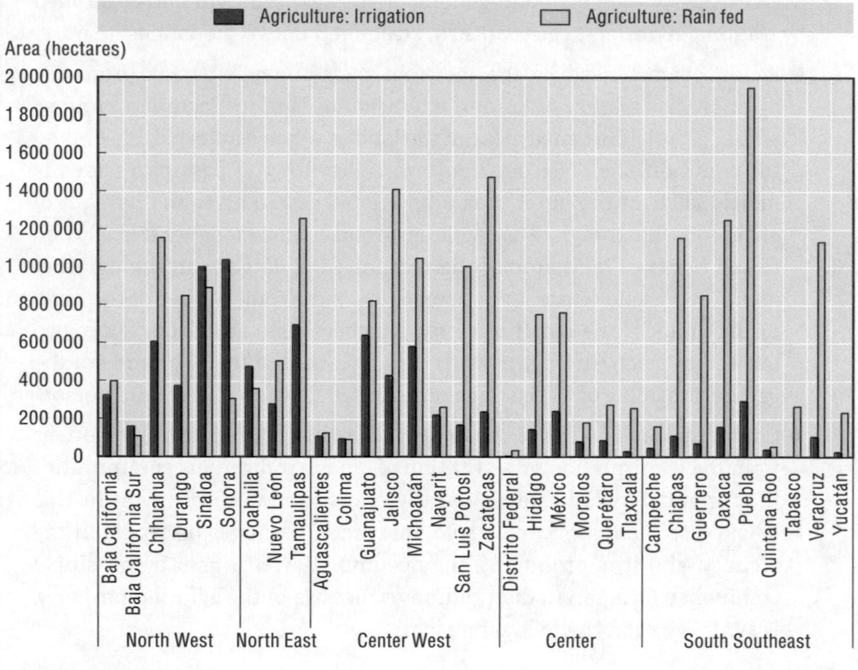

Source: SEMARNAT (2002).

Coasts and marine habitats. Having 11 122 km of coast and more than 2.9 million hectares of internal water bodies, Mexico has enormous potential for generating economic benefits for rural areas from better organised fishing and aquaculture activities. Of the more than 2 million hectares of salt water, 450 000 are good for shrimp harvesting and 1.6 for other species, however only 16 000 are used for shrimp and 30 000 on other species. In sweet water the potential is of 900 000 hectares and are used 754 000 in a very limited way. Water pollution is a direct threat to this potential both in internal and coastal ecosystems. The deficiency of port infrastructure for fish capturing is also an important concern.[15]

There is also large potential in terms of cultural and energy resources

Culture. The heterogeneity of Mexico in its culture is a valuable asset in its local expressions such as language, ways of living, typical dressings, dances, food and culinary expressions. These assets are complemented by the rich archaeological and historical sites, many of which are considered mankind's heritage. Rural areas have many of these amenities or are close to them and could profit better from sharing its richness with the Mexican population and international visitors.

Energy. In the same sense, Mexico is the seventh country in the world with mineral resources potential, and as of today only 20% of the national territory has been explored. Again, rural areas can be an important source of energy and minerals with economic value, which could potentially serve as alternative sources of employment and income for their population (PEC, 2002). In particular, rural areas have strong potential as sources of renewable energy. There are plenty of experiences among OECD countries of rural areas being providers of energy for close urban areas and for self-sufficiency. Wind energy, for example is an alternative utilised in a very narrow way in Mexico that might well provide of their own energy to many rural municipalities. Bio-fuel is another alternative with great potential both from agricultural and livestock sources. Although the Congress has pushed for increasing use of ethanol as source of energy, important political obstacles are present, mainly from sugar cane producers that would eventually be the greatest beneficiaries of such a step. The case of Brazil with this respect is not longer seen as a political adventure but as a true best practice by OECD countries in a context of high oil prices that does not seem to end in a near future.

Conclusion

The previous analysis highlights the heterogeneity of rural regions in Mexico. Generalising into "rural" therefore, might be misleading, since the great challenges of certain rural regions might completely blur relevant opportunities for other rural regions.

The definition of "rural" is important to define the policy challenges. A narrow perspective of rural, limiting its definition to localities of less than 2 500 inhabitants translates into a propensity to label "rural" as synonymous of dispersion and "poverty". As it has become clear through this chapter, from a broader vision of rural areas, such relationship is not necessarily true, and constitutes a barrier to development both for poor rural regions and non-poor rural regions. The multifaceted vision approach of this chapter allows talking at least about 5 different types of "Rural Mexicos":

1. *The rural poor,* which is dispersed, inaccessible, with low levels of public services, almost isolated from markets and thus characterised by low productivity or subsistence agriculture.

2. *The rural with intensive agriculture,* which has had significant productivity gains and is increasingly oriented towards export markets. However, it depends highly on irrigation and therefore contributes to the depletion of water reserves.

3. *The rural diversified,* which is in a process of adoption of the economic vocation of the region or the nearby cities and becoming location for industrial parks and/or services taking advantage of lower costs.

4. *The rural peri-urban,* whose life is closely integrated to urban areas. There are two extremes in these areas. On the one hand the poverty belts generated by migration from rural areas which require extending poverty alleviation policies to urban contexts. On the other, there are rural areas which have also become home for accommodated people seeking a calm refuge to live out of the big cities, leading to increasing commuting flows to and from urban areas, and a growing demand for services.

5. *The rural with large natural, cultural and energetic resources potential* that could generate substantial economic value if exploited in a sustainable way. In particular there are opportunities for better organised forestry and fishing/aquiculture activities and of enlarging the tourism potential of these regions taking advantage of the richness in natural, landscape and cultural amenities.

There are thus very diverse challenges for Mexico's rural policy. These include: 1) poverty alleviation, 2) provision of basic public services; 3) strengthening and diversification of the rural economy; and finally, 4) better exploiting and preserving untapped cultural, natural and energetic resources. These challenges will be referred to in the next chapter which analyses current rural policy in Mexico.

Notes

1. In Mexico exists a model of social property of land integrated by more than 30 000 agrarian groups denominated ejidos and comunidades agrarias (see Box 1.4).

2. Since the most precise definition of rural is based on localites, but most detailed information is provided by municipio, a classification of municipios was made classifying them as dispersed rural if more than 80% their population lived in localites of less than 2 500 inhabitants and so on for 15 000, for 100 000 and more than 100 000.

3. Some sources, based on the territory covered by the 196 000 localities measure up to 95%. An approximation using municipalities in Figure 1.6 shows less due to the fact that urban municipalities are larger than the urban areas.

OECD RURAL POLICY REVIEWS: MEXICO – ISBN 978-92-64-01152-6 – © OECD 2007

4. Other sources use 20 000 as the higher threshold for rural semi-urban areas, however since the most used both by the main source, INEGI and by many analysis is 15 000 this report uses also this figure as threshold.

5. This purpose of this classification is not to approximate the classification of localities in terms of population but to show in the most clear way the specific characteristics of rural municipalities. The heterogeneity in terms of size of municipios in Mexico might lead to misleading results since, there are states with very large municipios that contain an important proportion of rural areas but contain also a city and might be classified as urban, while states as Oaxaca and Chiapas that have a disproportionaly large number of municipios, mostly rural what might overestimate rural figures.

6. The 2005 Conteo de Población y Vivienda form INEGI includes 2 454 Municipios, which adds 11 municipios to the 2 443 that appear in various sources related to the 2000 Censo General de Población y Vivienda, which is used in several of the analysis referred in this Review. For details on these additions see *www.inegi.gob.mx/est/contenidos/espanol/sistemas/conteo2005/municipios.asp*

7. Although INEGI does not publish an official figure, within the methodology of the Economic Census it clarifies that the contribution of localities of less that 2 500 inhabitants to the economy is about 1% and therefore the measurement of the Census in these localities, having in consideration its small share, for budget reasons is made by a sample instead of censing them all. The background report provided by SAGARPA for this report as well as interviews with relevant policy makers agreed on the figure of around 1.8% of GDP.

8. Calculated based on the GDP per capita figures at municipal level obtained in the Sistema Nacional de Información Municipal (SNIM) of INAFED multiplied by population figures of 2000. The original source of those GDP per capita figures are estimates of CONAPO used in the Human Development Index at municipal level, which is done based on State GDP proxied at municipal level with income levels from the Income-Expenditure Surveys. The categorisation of municipalities done for this calculation is the same used throughout the document: dispersed rural, those municipalities with 80% or more of its population living in localities of less than 2 500 inhabitants, rural semi urban, those municipalities with 80% or more of its population living in localities of less than 15 000 inhabitants, and so on. It is important to clarify that this categorisation is intended to capture the living conditions of the population in dispersed rural regions, however since many of dispersed rural localities are located in municipalities which also have larger settlements, this categorisation underestimates the population and territory of dispersed rural localities. Therefore the population shares in Figure 1.4 are at locality level, and the territory calculations are explained in the note 9. Strictly, using the 80% categorisation the values for population and territory are the following:

Municipalities	Share of GDP	Share of population	Share of territory
Rural dispersed	2.0%	7.5%	25.8%
Rural semi-urban	8.0%	17.6%	38.1%
Urban intermediate	15.4%	21.9%	21.9%
Urban metropolitan	74.6%	53.0%	14.2%

9. Territory calculations in Figure 1.6 differ form calculations at locality level (close to 95%) because the calculation is based on *municipios* in the figure. The purpose of this approximation is not to come with an actual value but to have a better idea of

the magnitude. For this calculus was not used the same categorisation of municipalities used throughout this report but one that instead of classifying rural first, classified urban first. This is, the municipalities of which more than 80% of their population was in localities of more than 100 000 were classified as urban metropolitan, those that 80% was in localities of more than 15 000 as urban intermediate, and so on. This slight difference in measurement allows a larger residual of dispersed rural that better approximated the territory covered by these localities.

10. The dependency ratio is the proportion of people of less than 12 years and more than 65 years as percentage of the total population.

11. The different types of land property are explained in detail in Box 1.4.

12. Interestingly at OECD territorial level 3, GDP per capita of PR and IN is almost the same, at TL2 (states) level, the proportion of average GDP per capita in PR regions is 80% and for IN is 96%.

13. 13. Northern states refer to Baja California, Coahuila, Chihuahua, Nuevo León, Sonora and Tamaulipas. Southern status refers to Chiapas, Guerrero, Michoacán and Oaxaca.

14. The Economic Census, performed by INEGI with a periodicity of 5 years contains information on employment, firms and production of all economic activities in Mexico to an X digit level of detail with exception of agriculture. For this sector it only includes the fishing and aquaculture subsector.

15. For a more detailed examination of the fisheries sector in Mexico please refer to OECD (2006)

OECD RURAL POLICY REVIEWS: MEXICO – ISBN 978-92-64-01152-6 – © OECD 2007

ANNEX 1.A1

Exended Tables and Methodological Notes

Table 1.A1.1. Detail of localities, municipalities and OECD TL3 regions by state

	LOCALITIES					MUNICIPALITIES					REGIONS			
	Dispersed rural <2 500	Rural semi-urban >2 500 <15 000	Urban intermediate >15 000, <100 000	Urban >100 000	Total	Dispersed rural <2 500	Rural semi-urban >2 500, <15 000	Urban intermediate >15 000, <100 000	Urban >100 000	Total	Predominantly Rural PR	Intermediate IN	Predominantly Urban PU	Total
AGUASCALIENTES	1 835	16	4	1	1 856		6	4	1	11		1	1	2
BAJA CALIFORNIA	4 041	37	6	3	4 087			2	3	5		3	1	4
BAJA CALIFORNIA SUR	2 728	13	3	1	2 745		2	2	1	5		4		4
CAMPECHE	3 073	24	2	2	3 101	1	6	2	2	11		4		4
COAHUILA	4 166	26	14	5	4 211	10	10	13	5	38	1	4	1	6
COLIMA	1 254	14	4	1	1 273	1	5	2	2	10		2	1	3
CHIAPAS	19 311	131	14	3	19 459	38	59	18	3	118	3	6		9
CHIHUAHUA	12 814	37	9	2	12 862	38	17	8	4	67	1	11	1	13
DISTRITO FEDERAL	449	10	6	15	480			1	15	16			2	2
DURANGO	6 218	35	3	2	6 258	16	17	4	2	39	1	8		9
GUANAJUATO	8 821	81	26	4	8 932	6	11	25	4	46	2	1	1	4
GUERRERO	7 594	109	13	3	7 719	25	40	13	3	81		6	1	7
HIDALGO	4 497	83	15	1	4 596	38	31	14	1	84	6	6	1	13
JALISCO	11 081	139	34	5	11 259	24	65	30	5	124	1	8	1	10
MEXICO	4 442	338	42	19	4 841	20	58	28	19	125		4	4	8
MICHOACAN	9 505	158	20	3	9 686	20	71	19	3	113	1	4	1	6
MORELOS	1 256	70	12	3	1 341	1	18	11	3	33	2	2	3	7
NAYARIT	2 567	38	6	1	2 612	3	11	5	1	20		4	1	5
NUEVO LEON	5 683	28	8	7	5 726	17	17	10	7	51		6	1	7
OAXACA	10 360	145	13	1	10 519	435	119	15	1	570	1	7		8
PUEBLA	6 296	234	24	2	6 556	94	97	24	2	217	2	3	2	7
QUERETARO	2 424	53	4	1	2 482	7	7	2	2	18	1	3	1	5

OECD RURAL POLICY REVIEWS: MEXICO – ISBN 978-92-64-01152-6 – © OECD 2007

Table 1.A1.1. **Detail of localities, municipalities and OECD TL3 regions by state** (cont.)

	LOCALITIES					MUNICIPALITIES					REGIONS			
	Dispersed rural <2 500	Rural semi-urban >2 500, <15 000	Urban intermediate >15 000, <100 000	Urban >100 000	Total	Dispersed rural <2 500	Rural semi-urban >2 500, <15 000	Urban intermediate >15 000, <100 000	Urban >100 000	Total	Predominantly Rural PR	Intermediate IN	Predominantly Urban PU	Total
QUINTANA ROO	2 147	15	3	2	2 167		3	2	3	8		3	1	4
SAN LUIS POTOSI	7 251	46	5	3	7 305	22	28	5	3	58		3	1	4
SINALOA	6 177	76	8	3	6 264	2	8	5	3	18	1	4		5
SONORA	8 049	46	11	4	8 110	37	22	7	6	72		12		12
TABASCO	2 513	80	11	1	2 605	1	7	8	1	17	1	2	1	4
TAMAULIPAS	8 780	34	7	6	8 827	14	17	6	6	43	2	2		4
TLAXCALA	1 164	71	10		1 245	8	42	10		60	1	2	6	9
VERACRUZ	21 757	226	42	8	22 033	64	101	39	8	212	3	4		7
YUCATAN	3 276	75	11	1	3 363	29	64	12	1	106		7	1	8
ZACATECAS	4 821	51	9	1	4 882	20	28	8	2	58		9		9
Total	196 350	2 539	399	114	199 402	991	987	354	122	2 454	30	145	34	209

Note: Localities information is for 2005, Municipalities are classified as dispersed rural if more than 80% of their population in 2005 lived in localities of less than 2 500 inhabitants, rural intermediate if 80% lives in localities of less than 15 000 inhabitants and is not considered dispersed rural, and so on.

Source: OECD based on SNIM (2003) and INEGI (2006).

Table 1.A1.2. **Non-agricultural employment by territorial level (2004)**

	LOCALITIES	MUNICIPALITIES							REGIONS		Grand total
	Rural localities	Rural dispersed	Rural semi-urban	Total rural	% of sector	Total urban	PR	% of sector	IN	PU	
Mining		6 448	19 882	26 330	21.5	96 310	79 249	64.6	16 799	26 592	122 640
Electricity, gas and water		5 370	10 245	15 615	7.1	205 689	56 844	25.7	38 581	125 879	221 304
Construction		1 938	6 900	8 838	1.4	643 549	151 609	23.2	95 366	405 412	652 387
Manufacturing	250 440	45 509	367 992	413 501	9.8	3 784 793	1 186 290	28.3	501 439	2 510 565	4 198 294
Food and beverages		12 474	101 156	113 630	13.4	731 216	261 949	31.0	149 825	433 072	844 846
Textiles and clothing and leather industries		15 834	99 258	115 092	15.6	620 981	173 581	23.6	156 758	405 734	736 073
Wood, paper and printing industries		4 475	18 202	22 677	8.4	246 349	59 539	22.1	29 825	179 662	269,026
Chemical, plastic, rubber and oil derivatives		4 487	51 184	55 671	8.6	592 193	140 054	21.6	58 809	449 001	647 864
Metal industries		2 326	25 349	27 675	7.9	322 291	81 893	23.4	41 944	226 129	349 966
Machinery, electronic and transportation equipment		3 389	51 833	55 222	5.4	976 216	385 565	37.4	39 716	606 157	1 031 438
Furniture and other manufacturing industries		2 524	21 010	23 534	7.4	295 547	83 709	26.2	24 562	210 810	319 081
Commerce	510 998	74 606	435 946	510 552	10.2	4 485 280	1 421 889	28.5	778 185	2 795 758	4 995 832
Retail commerce		68 629	386 003	454 632	11.3	3 579 215	1 194 221	29.6	645 392	2 194 234	4 033 847
Transportation, shiping and storage		3 864	28 753	32 617	5.1	602 318	150 492	23.7	90 898	393 545	634 935
Services	181 866	50 460	378 958	429 418	6.5	6 147 364	1 496 780	22.8	855 981	4 224 021	6 576 782
Tourism (accomodation, cultural and entertainment)		16 802	107 074	123 876	9.1	1 237 717	374 753	27.5	205 156	781 684	1 361 593
TOTAL		171 393	1 141 602	1 312 995	8.2	14 727 586	4 168 400	26.0	2 172 093	9 700 088	16 040 581
Percentage of national employment		1.1	7.1	8.2		91.81	26.0		8 537 725.94	536.53	100.0

Source: INEGI (1999 and 2004).

OECD RURAL POLICY REVIEWS: MEXICO – ISBN 978-92-64-01152-6 – © OECD 2007

Table 1.A1.3. **Growth in non-agricultural employment by territorial level 1999-2004**

Average yearly percentage change 1999-2004

| | LOCALITIES | MUNICIPALITIES | | | | | REGIONS | | | | Grand total |
	Rural localities	Rural dispersed	Rural semi-urban	Total rural	% of sector	Total urban	PR	% of sector	IN	PU	
Mining		−0.2	−1.4	−1.1	−2.6	2.6	1.6	0.0	−2.2	5.2	1.7
Electricity, gas and water		8.3	5.0	6.1	2.4	3.1	4.2	0.7	5.5	2.3	3.3
Construction		125.2	2.1	7.1	7.1	0.0	4.1	4.1	1.1	−1.4	0.0
Manufacturing	3.4	2.5	2.6	2.5	−0.1	1.2	1.1	0.7	−0.5	0.1	1.5
Food and beverages		−1.4	3.2	2.6	1.1	1.3	1.4	−0.1	2.5	1.2	1.5
Textiles and clothing and leather industries		7.9	−0.7	0.2	3.1	−3.0	−2.0	0.7	−0.8	−3.4	−2.6
Wood, paper and printing industries		4.9	2.2	2.7	1.7	0.8	−1.9	−2.7	1.6	1.9	0.9
Chemical, plastic, rubber and oil derivatives		−1.1	2.7	2.3	2.5	−0.3	0.2	0.3	0.4	−0.3	−0.1
Metal industries		5.5	5.0	5.0	6.1	−1.2	1.4	2.3	−0.7	−1.5	−0.8
Machinery, electronic and transportation equipment		44.3	14.0	15.1	13.0	0.8	4.1	2.6	3.7	−0.3	1.3
Furniture and other manufacturing industries		−2.9	−3.3	−3.3	−4.3	1.9	1.8	0.4	−0.7	1.5	1.4
Commerce		8.1	8.2	8.2	1.4	6.2	6.9	0.4	7.1	5.9	6.3
Retail commerce		8.4	8.5	8.5	0.8	7.3	7.6	0.1	7.9	7.2	7.4
Transportation, shiping and storage		2.0	2.6	2.5	1.1	1.2	2.3	0.9	1.1	1.0	1.3
Services		3.4	6.4	6.0	0.5	5.3	4.5	−0.7	4.9	5.8	5.4
Tourism (accomodation, cultural and entertainment)		5.2	6.5	6.3	0.3	5.9	4.7	−1.0	5.4	6.9	6.0
TOTAL		5.2	5.2	5.2	1.5	3.4	4.0	0.4	4.0	3.2	3.5

Source: INEGI (1999 and 2004).

Relationship between OECD and Mexico's typology of rural urban areas

Although the population figure derived from OECD aggregation of *predominantly rural regions* (37.3 million) is similar to the one obtained according to the previously defined *rural* category of localities of less than 20 000 inhabitants (40.2 million) and higher than the *dispersed rural* category of localities of less than 2 500 inhabitants (24.3 million), it is important to be aware that since OECD aggregates have a territorial perspective, they do not refer necessarily to the same population. Table 1.A1.4 below provides a measurement of the degree to which these categories coincide, where it can be seen that 61.3 per cent of the *dispersed rural* population and 55.2 per cent of the *rural* is comprised in the PR category, but this category as a whole contains up to 40.6%, population that lives in localities of more than 20 000 inhabitants.

The advantage of the territorial perspective, however is that it places rural regions in their regional context, and regional differences are sometimes more pronounced than differences in population level. Throughout this review, depending on the type and source of the information utilised, four territorial levels are used as reference: state level, regional level (OECD TL3 regions), municipal level and to a lesser degree locality level. Therefore, the definitions of *dispersed rural, rural* (for municipalities and localities) *and predominantly rural* (for regions) are used, seeking to obtain the most clarifying picture from them and providing comparisons between them when possible.

Table 1.A1.4. **Degree of urban and rural population contained in OECD typologies for Mexico**

OECD typology	Mexico classification	RURAL			URBAN		TOTAL
		Dispersed rural (less than 2 500)	Rural total (less than 20 000)	% of row	Urban total (more than 20 000)	% of row	% of row
PR	Population	14.9	22.2	59.4	15.2	40.6	**37.4** **100**
	% of column	61.3	55.2		24.1		**36.2**
IN	Population	5.8	10	53.6	8.2	46.4	18 100
	% of column	23.9	23.6		13.1		17.2
PU	Population	3.6	8.5	17.7	39.6	82.3	48.1 100
	% of column	14.8	21.2		62.8		46.6
TOTAL	Population	**24.3**	**40.2**	**39.0**	63.0	61.0	103.3
	% of column	**100**	**100**		100		100

OECD RURAL POLICY REVIEWS: MEXICO – ISBN 978-92-64-01152-6 – © OECD 2007

ISBN 978-92-64-01152-6
OECD Rural Policy Reviews: Mexico
© OECD 2007

Chapter 2

Rural Policy in Mexico

This chapter describes the evolution of Mexico's approach to rural policy and the new institutional framework for rural policy defined by law since 2001. It analyses in general, the existing sectoral policies, budget and programs influencing rural development and in particular, two integrated policies for rural development: the Program of Rural Development of the Ministry of Agriculture, Livestock, Rural Development, Fisheries and Food (SAGARPA); and the Micro-Regions Strategy lead by the Ministry of Social Development (SEDESOL).

Key points

- The Mexican approach to rural policy has been shifting in the past decade from an interventionist agricultural policy towards a multi-sector, bottom-up policy with an increasingly territorial perspective.

- In this process, Mexico has taken innovative steps such as the creation of co-ordination mechanisms between the different ministries involved in rural policy at the federal, state and municipal levels, and the inclusion of civil society in the discussion and planning of their respective rural policy. These aspects have been institutionalised in a specific Law for Sustainable Rural Development (LDRS).

- Another significant innovation is the legal requirement of having a concerted rural development plan and the identification of a "rural budget", integrating the programmes of the different ministries oriented to rural areas.

- Social policy, which involves poverty alleviation, education and health policies, has acquired an increasingly relevant role in rural policy, to the point of becoming its largest component. Basic and productive infrastructure policies, which rely heavily on decentralised resources, are closely linked to social policy.

- Productive support policies, the second most important group of policies, have mainly an agricultural focus and are undertaken by the Ministry of Agriculture (SAGARPA). This ministry also has a significant role in the rural policy of the Mexican government through a programme oriented specifically to rural development.

- SAGARPA's Programme of Rural Development (PDR) is one of the most decentralised programmes of the federal administration. It supports productive investments for agriculture, livestock and non-farm activities with a demand- and project-driven approach. Two other complementary components are technical support and organisational support. This latter component has been instrumental in the construction of the institutional architecture of defined in the LDRS.

- The Micro-Regions Strategy is a multi-sectoral effort, led by the Ministry of Social Development (SEDESOL), which specifically targets the most marginalised rural regions and is oriented to generate "micro-poles of development". The specificity of its scope allows it to monitor the advances and deficiencies in each of the areas of support through objective and socially shared validation mechanisms called "*banderas blancas*" (white flags).

Introduction

Rural Mexico was analysed through different lenses in Chapter 1. From this diagnosis it is evident that rural areas stand out by themselves as a specific territory with challenges and opportunities clearly differentiated from the urban context. In addition, the dynamics of globalisation which has differentiated impact in rural areas has in many countries highlighted the importance of counting with a specific rural policy. However "rural policy" can mean different things. In most OECD countries rural policy used to be equivalent to agricultural policy for a long time, and it is not until recently, in a new context in which agriculture is no longer the backbone of the rural economy, that the portfolio of policies oriented to rural areas, independently of their sectoral approach is being labelled as "rural policy".

The question to be addressed by this chapter is whether Mexico deals with the rural challenges and opportunities with a consistent "rural policy". From the analysis performed in Chapter 1, a set of policy objectives can be derived. These objectives should in principle, although not necessarily explicitly, be an integral part of the institutional framework and programmes that integrate the policy approach to rural Mexico. They could be summarised as follows:

Rural Policy should have a territorial perspective. The fact that rural areas comprise close to 90% of Mexican territory, and in consequence also most of the territories of each of the states and regions individually, calls for the specific questioning of what is the actual value that states, regions and Mexico as a whole accrue from its vast territory. In addition, a significant heterogeneity was evidenced within rural territories, which means that there is no one size fits all policy for every rural region.

Rural Policy should have a multi-sector perspective. The diversification of the rural economy is a reality that requires policy to perform accordingly. Several of the opportunities and challenges of the rural territories implicate the involvement of different government entities that might not have had a rural perspective in the past. Strong leadership is important for the co-ordination of efforts of multiple agencies.

Rural Policy should be part of the country's competitiveness strategy; that is, it should actively contribute to the improvement of income *but also* the sources of income, i.e. economic growth, jobs and assets. There is evidence that there has been a significant increase in the level of income of rural households, even at a greater rate than urban income. The diversification of household income, public transfers and remittances, have contributed to this improvement. However it is important to keep in mind that in the long term, the significant sources of improvement of income are economic growth, more and better paid jobs and accumulation of assets. Rural areas cannot be exempt from the economic dynamics occurring in the country.

Rural Policy should be effectively targeted and progressive. The poverty conditions of rural areas call for a special attention to the most needed. Some studies argue that poverty reduction has occurred mainly at levels of income close to the poverty line. Policy should be carefully targeted to reach and empower those in the lowest deciles of the population and provide them with opportunities to reach higher levels. This has implications both for the agricultural policies and as for the social policies. Both policies can contribute substantially to the reduction of poverty if they are adequately focused on the right beneficiaries.

This chapter is divided as follows: Section 2.1 describes the evolution of Mexico's approach to rural policy. Section 2.2 describes the institutional framework for rural policy defined by law. Section 2.3 describes the existing policies influencing rural development by analysing the budget and programmes associated with the entities involved in rural affairs. Finally, Section 2.4 analyses in detail two integrated policies for rural development.

2.1. The evolution of Mexican rural policy

Rural policy has shifted from an interventionist agricultural policy…

The Mexican approach to rural policy has significantly changed in the past decade. The logic of rural policy during most part of the 20th century was based on three main pillars: the agrarian reform and the communal property of land, the prevalence of an agricultural focus, and the vision that rural economy was in a pre-market condition.

The agrarian reform was one of the institutions resulting from the Mexican Revolution, which had a major impact in shaping the structure of rural policy. Land ownership, which was concentrated in hands of 0.2% of the population in 1905, changed dramatically by 1940 due to the policy of redistribution of land, which abolished the *latifundios* (large amounts of land owned by a wealthy minority) and created social land structures: the *ejido* and *agrarian communities*. The extension of social land is until today around half of Mexico's territory (101 million hectares, see Box 1.5). The pre-market condition of rural areas was firstly determined by the limited individual property rights of the *ejido* system, but also by the agricultural support commitments of the post-revolutionary governments with their new agrarian constituency, which included government intervention at all stages of commodity distribution channels, generous price supports, barriers to imports, and subsidies in inputs such as credit, irrigation, energy, fertilisers, technical assistance (OECD, 2006c).

Three events in the past three decades unchained a series of policy actions that reconfigured rural policy: First, the entering of Mexico to the GATT, which started the dismantling of the pre-market logic by introducing prices to the rural environment. Second, the financial crisis of 1982 forced the government to cut significantly the expenditures to the sector and to reform agricultural policy mechanisms. Third, the introduction of NAFTA in 1994 started the phasing out of agricultural import restrictions to be finished in 2008, and has evidenced the differences between the internationally competitive agriculture, done by private producers and focused on certain niche products, and the low productivity and subsistence agriculture, still significantly tied to the *ejido* structure.

... towards a multi-sector policy

The redesign of the Mexican approach to rural policy has come gradually. The importance of having a specific strategy for poverty alleviation has increased in relevance since the 1950-1960s and attention to rural areas has therefore stopped being exclusive responsibility of the Secretary of Agriculture (and the Secretary of the Agrarian Reform). Generally speaking there have been three generations of these types of policies: The "first generation" was mainly characterised by subsidies to goods and services. The second generation, of which PRONASOL was a major component[1] was launched at the end of the 1980s and was designed to provide safety nets consistent of income compensation for the most poor. The current third generation, which began in the mid-1990s represented a significant policy shift. The core of the strategy was the introduction of an integrated programme: the Programme of Education, Health and Food (PROGRESA), after 2002 renamed *Oportunidades*.

This process was conducive to an important reallocation of public expenditure to rural areas from agricultural support, or the so called "productive" rural expenditure, to human development and anti-poverty programmes or "social" rural expenditure. In addition, agricultural policies themselves have changed substantially. Four major changes can be identified: 1) steps towards commodity market liberalisation, 2) introduction of a new system of support based on direct payments tied to historical use of land 3) steps toward deregulation of inputs markets, with greater support for introducing technical improvements, and 4) the reform to the land tenure system (OECD, 2006c).

An important recent cornerstone in the evolution of rural policy is marked by the introduction of a new piece of legislation, the *Ley de Desarrollo Rural Sustentable* (LDRS). By the time President Fox started his mandate in 2000, which marked the end of an era of one ruling party in Mexico, there was already an ongoing debate about the institutionalisation of rural policy. Many of the agrarian corporative structures affected by the international openness and new policy context, pushed for a legislation which sought to reverse the reforms and return to the previous status quo. Such legislation was approved after 28 days of the beginning of the Fox administration. Fox vetoed such law, which was in fact, a difficult and controversial decision at the beginning of his mandate, since no President had vetoed a law since 1923.[2] At the end, the law was significantly changed gaining a territorial vision of rural development and provisions to strengthen the participation of civil society and was approved in 2001 by unanimity with significant political support. The law can't be regarded as the solution to rural challenges, it ended up being a complex and long law, with 18 chapters and almost 200 articles, but it certainly set up a new framework meant to initiate a process of social and economic transformation in rural areas and improve of the living conditions of its population.

2.2. The institutional framework for rural policy

The Law for Sustainable Rural Development...

The Law on Sustainable Rural Development (LDRS), enacted in 2001, is ambitious in its purpose of creating a new institutional framework for rural policy. Three characteristics of its purpose are to be highlighted. First, the *multi-sector approach*. The law dictates the creation of an Inter-Ministerial Commission for Sustainable Rural Development (CIDRS). This commission is meant as a cross-sector horizontal co-ordination organ at federal level, which unites the heads of the different Ministries having a scope of influence in the rural context. Second, its *bottom-up territorial approach* which aims to support the design, execution, and consolidation of local-based and engineered projects. The law initiated a process of decentralisation of the rural development efforts to state and municipal level, and most rural development measures have changed from being supply-based to having a much more demand-based focus. Third, its *participatory fashion*. The law encourages the creation of Rural Development Councils that act as the institutional organ within which the rural population and their organisations can participate in the rural policy decision and implementation process.

The institutional framework as well as the policies themselves are not exempt from having conflicting issues. However, this chapter will have a more descriptive character, while the next chapter will address in detail the conflicting issues.

... which foresees a federal horizontal co-ordination body specific for rural policy,...

While in many OECD countries there is significant debate about how to provide a multi-sectoral perspective to rural policy, Mexico has leap-frogged many countries with the creation of the CIDRS as a horizontal co-ordination body at the federal level, specifically with the purpose of planning and implementing rural policy. The CIDRS (see Figure 2.1) is conformed by all the ministries involved to some extent in rural development and it is presided by the Ministry of Agriculture, Livestock, Rural Development, Fisheries and Alimentation (SAGARPA).

Figure 2.1. **Structure of the Inter-Secretariat Commission for Sustainable Rural Development**

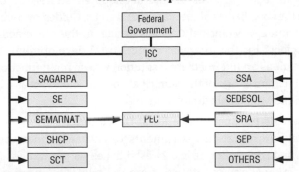

SAGARPA – Ministry for Agriculture, Rural Development, Fisheries, and Food Security.
SE – Ministry for Economy.
SEMARNAT – Ministry for Environment and Natural Resources.
SHCP – Ministry of Finance and Public Credit.
SCT – Ministry for Communications and Transport.
SSA – Ministry for Health.
SEDESOL – Ministry of Social Development.
SRA – Ministry of Agrarian Reform.
SEP – Ministry of Public Education.
OTHERS – Any other Ministries or entities that the executive powers consider necessary.
Source: SAGARPA (2006).

The law foresees also the creation of Inter-Ministerial Commissions (CIDRSs) at state level specifically set up to help co-ordinate the rural interventions of the different state ministries. The CIDRSs at state level are responsible for formulating a State Rural Development Plan. This integrated plan is meant to be the basis for the concerted efforts of all public programmes having a rural scope of influence that are designed or managed by the state administration.

... participatory bodies for civil society at different territorial levels,...

Another institution created by the LDRS as an advisory body to the Federal Government that contributes to the integration and co-ordination of rural development efforts at federal level is the Mexican Council for Sustainable Rural Development (Federal Council). The membership of the Federal Council is composed by the CIDRS along with accredited representatives from social and private national organisations having their scope of action within rural areas (LDRS art. 17). The Federal Council is meant as a forum for sharing experiences, emitting opinions, and co-ordinating activities linked with rural development. The Federal Council is also expected to form special working committees to stimulate a concerted vision of Mexico's rural development efforts.

The law prescribes the integration of Councils for Sustainable Rural Development not only at national level but also at state level, at district level (which is an intermediate level already in place for agricultural policy), and at municipal level. State Councils, in collaboration with their respective governments are meant to develop a rural development strategy at state level that is adapted to the specificities of the state's rural areas. Guided by their state's rural development strategy, Municipal Councils decide on the acceptability of locally proposed projects for the interests of local rural development. The District Council is meant as an intermediary institution whose main function is to assist the capacity building efforts of the Municipal Council and to act as a link between the State and the Municipal administrations.

The Councils for Sustainable Rural Development are meant to be the main vertical co-ordination instruments to be used under the LDRS (see Figure 2.2). The LDRS under article 24 establishes as permanent members of these Councils those representatives from the related institutions belonging to administrative levels immediately above and below that of the set council. This guarantees the vertical participation and exchange of information between the different administrative levels involved in the rural development policy-making and implementation process.

Figure 2.2. **Councils for Rural Sustainable Development**

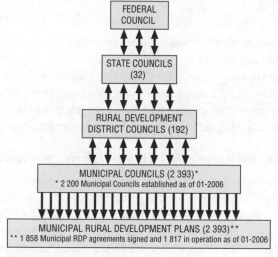

Source: OECD based on information from SAGARPA.

... and an official, integrated "rural" budget

The CIDRS, as it is the case for other similar commissions that have been created in the country, has to cope with the reality that the budget and policy responsibility remains within the scope of the different ministries. However, another significant innovation is the Special Concerted Rural Development Programme ("*Programa Especial Concurente*", PEC), which is an official

OECD RURAL POLICY REVIEWS: MEXICO – ISBN 978-92-64-01152-6 – © OECD 2007

document, issued in 2002 for the period 2002-2006, containing the main federal rural development programmes, intended to have a coherent strategy and co-ordinate the actions of the relevant ministries. This document, which according to the law must be approved by the president in the six months following the publication of the National Development Plan, contains a relevant diagnostic of rural areas and states that the new policy of rural development in Mexico is in transition, among various dimensions:

- from a primary sector approach as universe of attention to a regional approach with linkages to other economic activities;
- from a centralised approach in the definition of rural policies to the greater involvement of states and municipalities through the participatory councils;
- from programmes oriented to advanced producers to programmes which open opportunities to the most needed people;
- from primary production to the integration of productive vertical chains with industries, services and markets;
- from homogeneous sector-based policies to differentiated policies responding to the social, productive and regional heterogeneity of rural areas and its ecologic diversity.

As a result of the PEC, an accounting exercise is made every year since 2003, grouping the budget of each ministry that will be directed towards programmes and efforts that have a rural scope.[3] This document constitutes an official "rural" budget, since it is published as an annex of the Federal Budget Decree. Figure 2.3 shows the evolution of public expenditure in rural areas from 1994 to date, broken down into two main items already acknowledged: "productive" expenditure, i.e. agricultural support, and "social" expenditure, or actions to combat poverty, education and health policies. The total amount did not grow much during the 90s, but it has in recent years. It is important to see these figures only as indicative because the methodology of aggregation of rural budget has not necessarily been the same from year to year and most evidently from one administration or another, as it is the case in Figure 2.3. According to the officially provided aggregations, in the early years, productive allocation received more attention, but subsequently both productive and social received similar resources.

Compared to the total federal budget for 2006, the PEC is still modest: it only accounts to 7.1%, a substantially lower participation than the percentage of rural population at 23.5%. However, when compared to the total budget of the ministries involved in the CIDRS (Table 2.1), the figure is by no means insignificant; it represents 43% of their aggregate budget. The importance of rural spending is also evidenced by the fact that it is equivalent to one half of agricultural GDP (the highest in Latin America) and close to 2% of national GDP (World Bank 2006).

Figure 2.3. **Public expenditure for sustainable rural development**
1994-2006

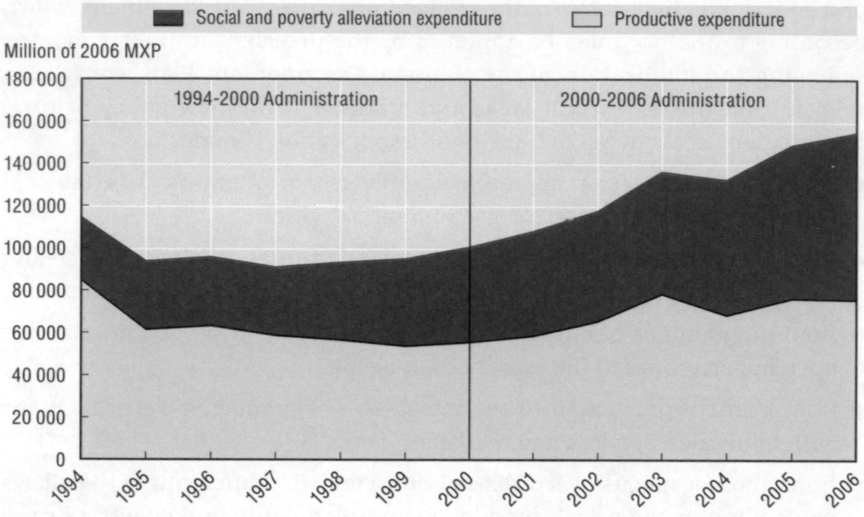

Source: SHCP (2006).

Table 2.1. **"Rural" budget by ministry**

Ministry	PEC budget								Administrative budget			
	2003		2004		2005		2006		2003	2004	2005	2006
	Million MXP	%	Million MXP	%	Million MXP	%	Million MXP	%	Million MXP			
SECON	576	0.5	965	0.8	1 016	0.7	889	0.6	5 404	5 380	7 018	7 619
SAGARPA	40 583	34.7	43 814	36.9	49 221	33.5	51 021	33.0	41 783	36 373	48 396	51 021
SALUD	6 829	5.8	6 827	5.7	14 206	9.7	12 268	7.9	20 867	20 973	34 024	42 356
SCT	1 092	0.9	2 948	2.5	2 151	1.5	2 505	1.6	23 124	22 746	36 694	33 687
SEDESOL	15 574	13.3	13 449	11.3	17 448	11.9	17 147	11.1	18 978	21 099	23 744	26 573
SEMARNAT	8 977	7.7	8 004	6.7	11 305	7.7	9 022	5.8	17 404	16 008	24 483	21 343
SEP	17 554	15.0	17 443	14.7	23 830	16.2	24 732	16.0	106 355	113 414	127 668	137 590
SHCP	10 310	8.8	4 539	3.8	6 918	4.7	6 524	4.2	21 785	23 620	26 916	27 212
SRA	3 566	3.0	3 505	2.9	4 856	3.3	4 436	2.9	2 759	2 806	4 856	4 436
STPS	866	0.7	126	0.1	75	0.1	76	0.0	3 151	3 328	3 185	3 262
TURISMO	16	0	75	0.1	4	0	2	0.0	1 459	1 230	1 147	1 227
Others	11 153	9.5	17 196	14.5	15 735	10.7	26 150	16.9				
Total	117 097	100	118 892	100	146 765	100	154 761	100	263 068	266 978	338 133	356 325
% of admin. budget	44.5		44.5		43.4		43.4		100	100	100	100

Source: SAGARPA for 2003, Federal Budget for other years.

OECD RURAL POLICY REVIEWS: MEXICO – ISBN 978-92-64-01152-6 – © OECD 2007

2.3. Federal programmes impacting rural areas

Despite their heterogeneous participation in the overall "rural budget" the policies of the federal ministries included in the CIDRS were catalogued in the original 2002-2006 *Programa Especial Concurrente* (PEC) document, into 6 categories that, it can be assumed, correspond to the objectives set for the concerted rural policy strategy. These categories are *social conditions, production support, basic and productive infrastructure, labour conditions, land conditions and environment*. Table 2.2[4] provides a breakdown of the main programmes of the ministries included in the PEC for each of the six categories. The detailed revision of all these programmes is not within the scope of this review. Several of them have been subject to thorough analyses by the OECD and other international organisations. This section will provide a brief overview of them as part of the overall rural policy.

Social development

Social policies such as education, healthcare, social security and job training represent a great share of total public expenditure: 61.9% in 2006, up from 38.2% in 1990. They also represent the largest share of the "rural budget" (PEC): close to 36% (see Table 2.2). Despite its relative importance, the fact that Mexico has one of the lowest levels of public spending among OECD member countries, makes social expenditures in Mexico also low by OECD standards. This fact was already acknowledged in the OECD Territorial Review on Mexico (OECD, 2003).

Since broad-based social policies do not necessarily reach all categories of the population, and particularly poor population in rural regions, Mexico has developed a specific strategy for poverty alleviation. The Ministry of Social Development, SEDESOL, operates this strategy. The most important component is the well known programme of *Oportunidades* (originally named PROGRESA), which is an inter-institutional programme which involves also the Health and Education Ministries oriented to fight poverty by improving income, education and health of poor population.[5] PROGRESA/Oportunidades represents a major change from previous anti-poverty programmes in Mexico in that it went beyond offering only temporary safety nets to include strong incentives to accumulate human capital. Its main innovation is the conditionality of the support, that is, "eligible" families can receive support as long as they meet certain obligations, i.e., send their children to school, and provide them with the "basic package" of illness prevention and health care.[6] It has three pillars, in each of which different ministries play an important role. In the education pillar the Ministry of Education is involved. *Oportunidades* provides student grants and school supplies to poor families to promote school attendance.[7] The health pillar involves the Ministry of Health

Table 2.2. **Budget by PEC objectives classification**

Programme	2005		2006		Responsible government unit
	MXN	% PEC	MXN	% PEC	
Social conditions					
Oportunidades	27 924	19.0	30 276	19.6	SEP, Salud, SEDESOL
Desarrollo Capacidades	9 976	6.8	4 573	3.0	SEP, Salud
SPSS	5 395	3.7	1 972	1.3	Salud
IMSS-Oportunidades			4 689	3.0	Social Security
CONADEPI	4 213	2.9	5 076	3.3	SHCP
Alimentation programmes	4 514	3.1	1 466	0.9	SEDESOL
Rural housing programme	887	0.6	1 538	1.0	SEDESOL
Other SEDESOL programmes	1 424	1.0	911	0.6	SEDESOL
Other SEP programmes	3 957	2.7	5 913	3.8	SEP
Production support					
Procampo	14 885	10.1	15 272	9.9	SAGARPA
Alianza (rural development)	2 959	2.0	2 062	1.3	SAGARPA
Alianza (livestock and agriculture)	5 205	3.5	4 166	2.7	SAGARPA
Support to commercialisation	6 755	4.6	9 134	5.9	SAGARPA
Progan	1 708	1.2	1 920	1.2	SAGARPA
Support funds: FACRP, FIRCO, FOMAGRO,FCCEA	5 005	3.4	7 284	4.7	SAGARPA
Institutions: INIFAP, UAC	2 209	1.5	2 312	1.5	SAGARPA
FONAES	669	0.5	558	0.4	SECON
Other SECON programmes	948	0.6	277	0.2	SECON
Rural financial institutions (Financiera Rural, FIRA, etc.)	1 660	1.1	1 346	0.9	SHCP
Basic and productive infrastructure					
FISM productive infrastructure	4 234	2.9	4 460	2.9	Federal Transfers
FISM social infrastructure	7 811	5.3	8 218	5.3	Federal Transfers
Hidroagrarian infrastructure	5 105	3.5	2 673	1.7	SEMARNAT (CAN)
Hidraulic programmes	2 732	1.9	2 924	1.9	SEMARNAT (CAN)
Micro-Regions	530	0.4	464	0.3	SEDESOL (+SECON)
Rural roads	962	0.7	1 250	0.8	SCT
Environment					
Forestal	1 875	1.3	1 972	1.3	SEMARNAT
Other SEMARNAT programmes/institutions	1 593	1.1	1 453	0.9	SEMARNAT
Land policies					
SRA programmes and admin. budget	3 911	2.7	3 450	2.2	SRA
Agrarian registry, general attorney and tribunals	1 519	1.0	1 560	1.0	SRA, Agrarian Tribunals
Labour conditions					
Temporary employment programme	1 420	1.0	1 488	1.0	SCT, SEMARNAT, SEDESOL, STPS
STPS programmes	75	0.1	76	0.0	
Total	132 058	90.0	130 733	84.5	

Source: SAGARPA for 2003, Federal Budget for other years.

OECD RURAL POLICY REVIEWS: MEXICO – ISBN 978-92-64-01152-6 – © OECD 2007

and provides basic health services for all members of the beneficiary families with particular emphasis on preventive care. The third component is nutrition, which includes a fixed monetary transfer to improve food consumption, as well as nutritional supplements to pregnant and breast-feeding mothers. In 2006, the programme was extended to provide elder people in beneficiaries' families with a pension (*IMSS-Oportunidades* programme). Including this extension, *Oportunidades* accounts to 22.6% of the PEC, which makes it the largest individual programme in it.

The conditionality of the grants has been a crucial success factor of the PROGRESA/Oportunidades programme, which has been labelled internationally as a "best practice" and has gained importance and budget in the Mexican administration.[8] The programme has been expanded significantly during the Fox administration along three axes: territory, beneficiaries and scope. Territorially, the programme was gradually extended from rural localities (of less than 2 500 inhabitants) to semi-urban, urban intermediate and finally urban areas. Today, the programme has presence in all municipalities of the country. In terms of beneficiaries, during its first year, PROGRESA benefited around 300 000 families; in 2005, it covered almost five million beneficiary families, which represent close to 25 million people, that is close to one quarter of the Mexican population is recipient of the programme, 69.1% were living in rural dispersed zones, 17.4% in semi-urban zones and the rest in urban concentrations. Finally, the programme has grown in scope: in its education pillar, it was extended to cover secondary education (until 12th grade) and saving and pension provisions have been incorporated into the programme. Another important characteristic of the programme is that it includes an elaborated monitoring and evaluation system.[9]

Other poverty alleviation programmes of SEDESOL include rural housing, food provision and programmes oriented to the attention of specific groups such as the migrant peasants (*jornaleros agrícolas*), elder population, women, etc. Within this array of programmes, two highlight for their amount of budget: the rural housing programme and the food programmes. The first is oriented to support the construction, expansion and improvement of houses in rural areas. The second refers to food subsidy programmes and the supply of basic and complementary products to rural areas, which is done mainly through two institutions, LICONSA and DICONSA. A programme that seeks to take advantage of the incoming remittances to rural areas is the 3x1. The programme promotes investment in community projects matching with public funds (1 from the federal government, 1 from the state government and 1 from the municipal government) the resources that migrants to the US send for projects in their localities of origin.

Educational and health policies are important components of the policy strategy to alleviate poverty and develop rural areas. The most important programme of the SSA in rural areas is the System of social protection in health (SPSS).[10] This system seeks to respond to the obligation of the State to guarantee access to health to its inhabitants through the combination of interventions in the promotion of health, prevention, diagnosis, treatment and rehabilitation. It is co-ordinated by the Health Ministry and provided at state level.

The Ministry of Education (SEP), on its part, provides education services through a large network of rural schools and teachers. Despite the challenge that dispersion of localities represents in rural Mexico, educational policies have achieved significant improvements. Primary school enrolment in Mexico reaches rates close to 97%. In many small, dispersed settlements, however, there is nearly no opportunity for education beyond the primary level. This brings down enrolment rates in secondary education to 81.9% for women and 75.8% for men in 2003 (WDI, 2006). CONAFE, which is an agency in the structure of SEP, has developed programmes for children who live in remote rural areas, in partnership with local communities that are involved in the day-to-day running of the schools. Technology advances have been instrumental in reaching remote communities. A first step in this direction was the creation of a satellite network of educational television (Edusat) that transmits, among other channels, the *Telesecundaria* programme, which delivers broadcast lessons for all three levels of lower secondary school. During the Administration of President Fox (2000-2006), SEP has innovated in bringing technology to the school class. This has been done through the *Enciclomedia* programme, which is a technological tool created to support teaching in the classroom with a new pedagogic concept based on the digitalisation of free text books. The programme is national and has evidently advanced much faster in urban contexts; however, its incipient integration to rural contexts is already contributing to the reduction of the technological divide. In addition, SEP counts with some specific programmes such as the farm education programme[11] provided through the Directorate General of Agricultural and Livestock Technological Education (DGETA), whose object is to provide agricultural and livestock technological education at the level of bivalent baccalaureate in 332 educational units.[12]

Many poverty alleviation programmes and social policies implicitly target the indigenous population. However, in 2003 the Mexican government created the National Commission of Indigenous People and Communities (CONADEPI),[13] in substitution of the National Indigenous Institute (INI). CONADEPI is a decentralised, non-sector entity of the federal public administration to promote the integral development of the indigenous people. Its most important programmes include schools, basic infrastructure, promotion and development of indigenous cultures, regional funds, productive organisation for indigenous women and promotion of agreements in matters of justice, among others. It operates in 24 states through 110 indigenous development co-ordinating centres. Although for budgetary issues CONADEPI is circumscribed to the Ministry of Finance (SHCP), it is an independent institution, which in 2006 received a budget of 5 076 million MXP, or 3.3% of the PEC.

Productive (agricultural) support

Most productive support programmes fall within the scope of the Ministry of Agriculture, Livestock, Rural Development, Fisheries and Alimentation (SAGARPA). The ministry has three *pillar* programmes: The first is PROCAMPO (*Programa de Apoyos Directos al Campo*), which is also the most important in terms of budget: 15 272 million MXP, almost 10% of the PEC. The programme started in 1994 in substitution of direct price support programmes and as an explicit strategy of support to farmers in the context of the introduction of NAFTA, and therefore, was intended to be phased out by 2009, when the open trade in terms of agricultural products is expected to enter into force between Mexico, the US and Canada. PROCAMPO consists of direct payments linked to historical use of land, rather than current production. This provision was intended to help farmers switch to more profitable crops in the context of a more competitive economy. In benefit of poor farmers, the programme introduced a minimum payment size of 1 hectare that applies even for those who own less land. Initially, the programme was oriented to the support of only nine crops,[14] however it has gradually expanded its scope. Today the benefit applies for the eligible surface that is planted, that is kept under livestock or forest activities, or that is under an eligible ecologic project.

A second pillar is *Alianza contigo* (formerly *Alianza para el campo*), which started in 1996 as an umbrella of more than 100 programmes, oriented to increase agricultural productivity and the capitalisation of farmers. Today it has three main components, one of them being the Rural Development Programme (PDR) which will be analysed with further detail in the next section, explicitly oriented to poor farmers and which extends supports beyond the primary sector. The other two are the agricultural and livestock development programmes. The most important characteristic of *Alianza* is its decentralised character since several of their programmes have been part of a process of federalisation, oriented to transfer not only funds but also the responsibility of implementation and even federal staff to states. In addition, *Alianza* is the only production support programme that has been decentralised to the municipal level (World Bank, 2005). The third pillar of SAGARPA's productive support programmes are the programmes of support to commercialisation. These programmes are oriented to help producers and traders to adjust to the transition from the previous direct purchase, distribution and commercialisation system of the Mexican Government through CONASUPO,[15] to a more market driven framework. Nevertheless, the Target Income programme, which is the larger in terms of budget, is intended to guarantee an income for the producers in the context of lower prices.[16]

SAGARPA counts as well with a wide variety of funds for specific types of support. The *Fondo de Apoyo a la Competitividad de las Ramas Productivas* (FACRP) seeks to strengthen the productive systems and the more sensitive production-consumption chains against international market conditions. FIRCO[17] is an agency of SAGARPA operating since 2002 promoting instruments of public and private promotion of the development of new agro-business or those already organised. FIRCO operates with the Shared Risk Fund for the Development of Agro-Business (FOMAGRO). Finally, SAGARPA introduced recently an energy cost compensation fund (*Fondo de Compensación a Costos Energéticos Agrícolas*, FCCEA) which is a mechanism that guarantees a fixed preferential price for the diesel fuel used by peasants, fishermen and aquaculture. In addition, two academic and research institutions are funded by SAGARPA's budget.[18]

According to the PEC, little productive support is done in rural areas in a sector other than agriculture. Forestry programmes, although might be considered productive support are in this report included in the environmental category, below. About the productive support to sectors other than AFF it might be highlighted the role of the *Fondo Nacional de Apoyo a Empresas Sociales*, (FONAES), which used to be part of SEDESOL but was transferred to the Ministry of Economy (SECON) during Fox's administration. About half of the budget of this fund (558 million MXP) is considered "rural" and therefore incorporated in the PEC. However it only represented 0.4% of the PEC in 2006. Its total budget is neither very large (1 187 million MXP); however, it seems to be the most important support for micro and small enterprises in rural contexts. In 2006, it had close to 25 000 projects and its support reached about half million people. It comprises four strategies: capital formation, business development, commercial promotion and financial intermediaries' formation and the main sectors that it supports are manufacturing of regional craftsmanship, furniture and jewellery. Other SECON funds and programmes included in the PEC include support for rural women (FOMMUR) a business incubator for youth entrepreneurs and a small share of the Fondo PYME (A fund for SME support), however, in total they add only 0.2% of the PEC.

Infrastructure

The provision of basic and productive infrastructure represents together with the social policy and productive support policies an important part of the broad rural policy and in particular of the poverty alleviation strategy. Federal transfers play an important role in the provision of basic and productive infrastructure. Within the federal transfers allocation in the budget, the *Fondo para Infraestructura Social Municipal* (FISM) is divided into two parts which are earmarked, one for basic infrastructure and the other for productive infrastructure. These funds together accounted 8.2% of the PEC in 2006. The transfers are regulated in the Fiscal co-ordination Law (LCF).[19] Other federal transfers, (representing 4.6% of the PEC), were not included in Table 2.2, since they don't have a specific label, but some of them are likely to be used also in infrastructure.

A major challenge in terms for the provision of basic and productive infrastructure is the dispersed character of rural settlements, which seriously hinders development opportunities and raises costs of public service delivery. Furthermore, some social and productive programmes *de facto* exclude small communities. In this context, a relevant programme in the provision of basic and productive infrastructure to the most marginalised regions is the Micro-Regions Strategy,[20] which is a co-ordinated strategy, lead by SEDESOL, in which many other ministries are involved. Its objective is to co-ordinate public policy for the least developed rural areas (263 areas of application spread across 1 334 municipalities in 31 different states) and to promote bottom-up participation from targeted communities. The OECD has followed closely the development of this strategy since it broke previous centralist schemes in exchange of a territorial perspective. The strategy will be described in detail in the next section.

The Ministry of Environment (SEMARNAT) and the Ministry of Communications and Transportation (SCT) play an important role in the provision of rural infrastructure. The former, through the National Commission of Water (CNA), takes care of an important part of the water related infrastructure in rural areas, both for human consumption and irrigation. The *Hydro-agricultural infrastructure programme*[21] is intended to increase the efficiency and productivity in irrigation and temporal zones. The *Hydraulic programme*, on the other hand, is oriented to the development and construction of basic hydraulic infrastructure to provide potable water and sewerage services to rural population. These programmes together received resources equivalent to 7% of the PEC in 2006. The SCT on its part has a specific rural commitment with the rural roads programme.[22] The programme received a budget of 1 250 million MXP which was matched by almost the same quantity assigned to the programme of temporary workers, contracted to build and maintain the network of rural roads.

Environmental, land and labour

In addition to the three largest rural policy areas (social policy, productive support and basic and productive infrastructure), three other are considered explicitly in the PEC, linked to the role of specific ministries. These categories are environment, land issues and labour issues. With respect to environmental policy, besides the already acknowledged contribution of SEMARNAT to the development of rural infrastructure, since its existence in 1996, this ministry has contributed to provide greater order to the use of environmental resources in rural areas. The National Forest Commission (CONAFOR),[23] created in 2001 is responsible for public policies to revert the processes of degradation of the forestry resources and promote its sustainable use. Through the Forestry programme, CONAFOR deals with the incorporation of lands into technical management, establishment of commercial forest plantations, reforestation, plant health diagnostic actions, execution of work for the prevention, conservation and restoration of soils, and incorporation of lands into payment for environmental services through the capture of carbon. This programme receives resources for almost 2 billion MXP or 1.3% of the PEC. The budget assigned to rural areas from SEMARNAT includes also 1.4 billion MXP that correspond to the Federal Protected Areas and the Federal Attorney General for Protection of Environment (PROFEPA). Through these institutions the environmental enforcement has been broadened to address unsustainable use of natural resources (OECD, 2003c).

Land issues are specifically tied to the Ministry of Agrarian Reform (SRA). SRA is intended to provide juridical certainty in matters of landholding by the ordering of the territory and the regularisation of rural property. One of the most important programmes of SRA is the Programme for the Regularisation of Community Property Rights and Entitling of Parcels (PROCEDE). Its actions have been concentrated on the consolidation of programmes for the ordering and regularisation of rural property seeking to resolve, definitively and under the law, conflicts derived from possession of the land. Apart from the SRA, there are a number of institutions included in SRA's budget oriented to achieving the mentioned objectives: the Agrarian Registry (RAN) and the Agrarian General Attorney. In addition, there are specific tribunals, with a separate budget, which deal with conflicts of land. In total, the institutions devoted to land issues have a budget of more than 5 billion MXP, accounting for 3.2% of the PEC.

Although labour issues constitute a specific sub-category of the PEC, by the size of labour-related programmes included in the PEC, one would conclude that labour issues in rural areas receive low attention. This might not be necessarily true since many of the different programmes are oriented to generate employment and better employment conditions. However, the programmes clearly related to labour issues account to only 1% of the PEC. The temporary employment programme (PET), as mentioned before serves for creating temporary jobs related to infrastructure development. Several ministries have this programme under their budget, totalling 1.4 billion MXP. Other programmes of the Ministry of Labour (STPS) are related to migrant workers in Mexico (*jornaleros*) and abroad (SEAMLE for workers in Canada). The programmes of the Ministry of Foreign Relations (SRE) and the Ministry of Interior (Gobernación), have the same focus. They are however a very small share of the PEC, which do not reach 1%.

The wide array of policies impacting in rural areas, even if properly accounted and with the intention of constituting a comprehensive rural programme, as it is now in Mexico, does not constitute a policy for rural development. Therefore, this review will focus its attention on the two main actors of rural policy, SAGARPA and SEDESOL, and in particular on their policies specifically targeted to rural development.

2.4. Policies targeted to rural development

The two main actors of Mexican rural policy, SAGARPA and SEDESOL, within the scope of their own attributions, the former with a more productive focus, the latter with a poverty alleviation mandate, have also been "policy entrepreneurs". That is, they have innovated and designed/redesigned policies to address explicitly rural development.

Both the Rural Development Programme of SAGARPA and SEDESOL's Micro-Regions Strategy are policies specifically oriented to the development of rural areas, and therefore will be analysed with greater detail in this section. The two programmes share several aspects: 1) they have a territorial perspective, one rooted on its decentralised character, the other based on a top-down geographic identification of target areas. 2) They have an integral perspective of rural development that extends outside of the sectoral boundaries. 3) They do not focus on subsidies but rather on investments, one based on projects, the other oriented to fulfil deficits of basic services and infrastructure. 4) They co-ordinate efforts of multiple actors, one with a clearer vertical orientation and the other with a more horizontal perspective. 5) They constitute a relatively small share of the budget of their respective ministries, but 6) their net resources are larger than their budget, either because federal resources are complemented by state, municipal and participant resources, as it is the case of the PDR or because they pool resources from different ministries, as it is the case of Micro-Regions; and 7) they have grown in importance within their own ministries and therefore have received significant real increases in their budget in the past years (Figure 2.4).

Besides these common features, the two referred programmes have clearly different objectives and approaches. The first important difference is in scope, whereas the PDR is oriented to rural areas in general, the MR Strategy is concentrated in a subset of rural areas, those with higher marginalisation and poverty conditions. Secondly, the PDR is more oriented to the rural population in their role as economic agents or producers, while the MR Strategy focuses on them as "subjects of development" with an emphasis on improving their living conditions. Finally, the PDR has a demand character in the sense that beneficiaries seek the support of the programme and are encouraged to organise themselves to benefit from the programmes of

Figure 2.4. **Resources of the PDR and Micro-Regions**

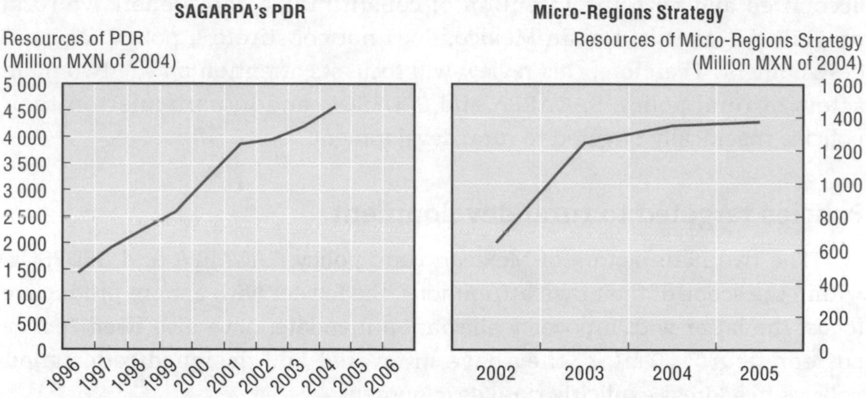

SAGARPA's PDR   Micro-Regions Strategy

Resources of PDR   Resources of Micro-Regions Strategy
(Million MXN of 2004)   (Million MXN of 2004)

These figures include Federal, State, Municipal and Beneficiaries resources in both cases.
Source: FAO 2005 for SAGARPA PDR, SEDESOL for MR Strategy.

different ministries, while the MR Strategy co-ordinates the institutional supply of different ministries for specific territories while encouraging beneficiaries to actively participate in the development of their communities.

Both the PDR and the Micro-Regions Strategy are described with greater detail in this section. Specific issues resulting from the external evaluations of the programmes and critical issues are addressed in Chapter 3 along with recommendations for each of them.

SAGARPA's *Programa de Desarrollo Rural*

The Rural Development Programme (PDR) is undertaken by the Undersecretary of Rural Development of SAGARPA, and as its name indicates is oriented to attaining rural development in a broader sense outside the boundaries of the agriculture, livestock and fisheries sectors which are also part of the mandate of the ministry. This programme is part of *Alianza Contigo (Alianza)*, one of the flagship programmes of SAGARPA, which was created in 1996 (with the name *Alianza para el Campo*) as an umbrella for different programmes that the ministry ran. *Alianza* has evolved substantially in its 10 years of existence. Originally it was conformed as a programme oriented to strengthen the agricultural sector in the context of the introduction of NAFTA. Today, the specific objectives of the *Alianza*, as defined in their Rules of Operation are: to foster the economic organisation of farmers, to foster investment in rural areas, to foster development of capacities of the rural population, to strengthen the organisation of rural units of production and to improve the levels of sanitary and safety of farm and fishery products.

The PDR has also evolved significantly since 1996, when *Alianza* was created. At that time, what today is the PDR was named *Programa de*

Equipamiento Rural (Programme of Rural Equipment). In the subsequent years other programmes oriented to support poor producers were created expanding its budget and scope (see Table 2.3). In 2000, 9 different sub-programmes existed that more or less directly embarked upon rural development support efforts, with frequent overlapping, strong dispersion of investments and contrasting development philosophies. In 2002 a redesign of *Alianza* launched what today is the Rural Development Programme merging all the programmes oriented to rural development in *Alianza* with the rationale of avoiding dispersion of supports and concentrating them in projects that would detonate processes of sustainable development, with significant multiplier effects.

Table 2.3. **Evolution of the rural development programmes in Alianza**
1996-2006

1996	1998	2000	2003-2006	
1 programme	6 programmes	9 programmes	1 programme	
Programme of rural equipment	Support for rural development	Support for rural development	PDR	PAPIR Subprogramme of support to rural investment projects
	Training and extension	Training and extension		
	Programme of support of coffee	Programme of support of coffee		
	Elementary programme of technical assistance	Integral Development of rural marginalised zones		PRODESCA Subprogramme of development of rural capacities
		Elementary programme of technical assistance		
	Programme of support of rubber	Programme of support of rubber		PROFEMOR Subprogramme of strengthening of enterprises and rural organisation
	Programme of support of cacao	Programme of support of cacao		
		Women in rural development		
		Organisation and training for commercialisation		

Source: Adapted from FAO (2005).

The stated objectives of the PDR today are: fostering of capitalisation of the units of production, the promotion of sustainable use of natural resources, development of projects for the primary sector while incorporating manufacturing and services, development of capabilities of rural areas, and fostering and consolidation of entrepreneurial organisations in rural areas. The most relevant defining characteristics of the programme are the following:

The PDR is organised based on an "integral rural development model". This model seeks to promote economic growth through the investment in three complementary types of capital: physical, human and social capital. The three main subprogrammes of the PDR respond to that logic: the Programa de *Apoyo a*

Proyectos de Inversión Rural (Programme of support to rural investment projects, PAPIR), which is oriented to support investment in physical capital. In turn, the *Programa de Desarrollo de Capacidades en el Medio Rural* (Programme of development of rural capacities, PRODESCA), is oriented to contribute to human capital development and the *Programa de Fortalecimiento de Empresas y Organización Rural* (Programme for strengthening rural enterprises and organisation, PROFEMOR) is devoted to construction of social capital.

The PDR is demand and project driven. The Rural Development Programme has changed the traditional supply-based public policy approach for one demand-based, that is, oriented to the needs of eligible beneficiaries which can openly apply for support to the programme. More recently the rules of operation of the programme introduced a further change to become project driven. While in the first years all the investment support of Papir were allocated by free demand, in 2004, 80% of the beneficiaries of this programme obtained their support through projects.

This new approach has significant benefits in terms of transparency, and has aided an explicit strategy to concentrate resources in less beneficiaries having greater impact. In addition it has introduced a new approach in the relationship of rural producers and the government, which fosters entrepreneurship and an active role of the recipient in using the resources with criteria of return and market orientation, in contrast with the paternalistic approach that prevailed before.

PDR is a targeted programme both in terms of people and in terms of regions. According to the Rules of Operation of *Alianza* the resources allocated to the PDR should be oriented to the following purposes: 20% to high-priority groups (indigenous population, women, youth, elder and handicapped people), 70% to high-priority regions (namely regions with high and very high marginality index, according to the CONAPO classification), and 35% to agro-alimentary chains subject to high social exclusion. Several evaluations of the programme (FAO [2005], World Bank [2006]) highlight the difficulty that the programme has had to achieve the targeting objective. This issue will be commented in the next chapter.

The PDR is the most decentralised programme of the federal government. The alliance concept behind *Alianza por el Campo* and afterwards *Alianza Contigo* comes precisely from the fact that is intended to be a common effort between the federation, states and municipalities. The three so-called *programas federalizados* of *Alianza*, the PDR, the Agriculture and Livestock Programmes have been involved in the process of federalisation, which started in the mid-90s intended to transfer not only programme implementation and funds but also SAGARPA's staff to state's governments. This process has encountered significant obstacles, however, as of today, most funds of these programmes have been transferred to states and in the case of PDR to municipalities, and important parts of the

OECD RURAL POLICY REVIEWS: MEXICO – ISBN 978-92-64-01152-6 – © OECD 2007

implementation process are pursued by local authorities (World Bank 2006). In 2003 the Operation Rules of Alianza established that 35% of PDR resources should be oriented to projects validated by the municipal councils (CMDRS), and in 2004 started the municipalisation process of the programme, which implied that 50% of its budget was to be administrated by the municipal authorities. The advances of this process are shown in Table 2.4. As of today, the PDR has become the main instrument of public policy of rural municipalities after the transfers of the Ramo 33 (Presidencia de la República 2005).

Table 2.4. **Advances in the process of decentralisation**

	2004	2005
Number of states	16	32
Number of municipalities	658	2 300
Number of CMDRS	2 110	2 200
Number of CDDRS	165	192
Number of municipal co-ordinators	1 420	1 665

Source: Presidencia (2005).

PDR subprogrammes

The Programme of support to rural investment projects, PAPIR

PAPIR is the core subprogramme of the PDR and the one that receives the highest share of resources (66%, see Figure 2.5). The programme seeks to revert the low capitalisation of producers in rural areas. Its stated objective is to promote capital investment of the eligible rural population through support for the start-up of productive projects that enable producers to attain better technologies; re-convert their production to more productive niches; store, prepare and transform primary products; generate of rural non-farm jobs and services, and improve the position of products in markets.

The subprogramme has three variants of execution: national, federalised and municipalised. Projects with high complexity, high level of investment or social impact are usually performed with the national variant, were the provision of resources come directly from SAGARPA or a technical agent of SAGARPA, usually the INCA Rural.[24] The federalised variant is the most frequent. Under this type of execution, State governments in co-ordination with the local delegations of SAGARPA have the responsibility of the operation of the programme, according to an agreement that SAGARPA has subscribed with each of the 32 states. The municipalised execution variant started in 2004, as a step further in the process of decentralisation. In this variant, the operation of the programme is ceded to the municipal governments with the support of the Municipal Councils of Sustainable Rural Development (CMDRS).

Figure 2.5. **Distribution of federal PDR budget**
Million MXP, 2006

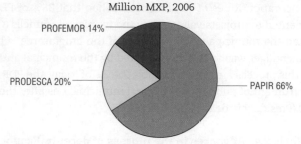

Source: PEC 2006.

Programme of development of rural capacities, PRODESCA

PRODESCA is oriented to cope with the deficit of technical assistance available in rural areas, both on the demand and supply sides, since the deficit is associated with the lack of qualified technicians but also with the lack of demand of technical assistance from producers. The objectives of the subprogramme are subsidise the cost of external professional services that groups and organisations of producers require, provide to the beneficiaries an open and competitive network of providers of professional services (PSP by its initials in Spanish) and strengthen the supply of PSP through on site or on line with the support of two institutions: INCA Rural and the *Centros de Calidad para el Desarrollo Rural* (Centres for Quality in Rural Development, CECADER).

Through PRODESCA the PDR has created a market of professional services for rural producers, which constitutes a radical change from the prevailing status quo where government employees delivered these services. The new scheme establishes the "payment for service" approach based on an explicit demand from producers instead of the salary paid with extension mechanisms (FAO 2005). To accede to the programme, producers present a support inquire and propose the accredited PSP that they want to hire for that purpose, from the network of accredited PSPs, publicly available,[25] where they can compare profiles and capacities or from other service providers, since the process is intended to be open and competitive. From the beginning of the process and until the conclusion of it, CECADER supervises the provision of services according to the programme and evaluates the performance of the PSP (SAGARPA 2006).

Programme for strengthening rural enterprises and organisation, PROFEMOR

This subprogramme is oriented to the attention of prioritary groups (women, youth, indigenous, disabled and elder population) and economic organisations of rural producers. It has two main goals. On the one hand, the promotion of organisation of rural family production units in order to obtain

OECD RURAL POLICY REVIEWS: MEXICO – ISBN 978-92-64-01152-6 – © OECD 2007

Box 2.1. **The PDR and the construction of the institutional architecture of the LDRS**

The PDR has become the vertical column of a network of programmes and institutions that make operational the Sustainable Rural Development Law (LDRS). In addition to the three main subprogrammes, the Under-secretary of Rural Development of SAGARPA counts with other programmes and instruments that support them in its overall rural development strategy. Although the scope of the law is intended to expand beyond SAGARPA, as of today, the institutional framework there established has been constructed by SAGARPA within its PDR strategy and used by SAGARPA for attaining the objectives of the PDR.

PROFEMOR has been the arm of SAGARPA to develop the institutional structure dictated by the LDRS, particularly for the constitution of more than one thousand Municipal Councils of Sustainable Rural Development. This explains the growth in its budget in the past years, since through the programme was financed the contracting of municipal co-ordinators and the formulation of diagnostics and rural development plans in each of those municipalities. The municipal co-ordinators, are in charge of elaborating the municipal diagnostics, formulate the development plan and co-ordinate its implementation in a participatory fashion at the municipality.

The construction of the institutional architecture of the LDRS at municipal level has also required an important training effort ranging in objectives from transmitting the new philosophy to learning the basics of developing a municipal rural development plan. The Sistema Nacional de Capacitación y Asistencia Técnica Rural Integral (SINACATRI), which is one of the systems established by the LDRS (arts 22, 41-52) has been an instrumental tool. SINACATRI, installed in June of 2003, is the formal instance of articulation of the training programmes of the ministries involved in the PEC. It operates through a Technical Committee co-ordinated by the training arm of SAGARPA, the INCA Rural and structure provided by the Servicio Nacional de Capacitación y Asistencia Técnica Rural Integral (SENACATRI). The SINACATRI has been able to conform a model of institutional concurrence based on the instrumentation of local training programmes for which the resources and infrastructure of different agencies are articulated to cover the demand of rural population with this respect. This has been done through a set of co-ordination agreements between the federal, state and municipal governments as well as the horizontal co-ordination at each of these levels.

The contribution of INCA Rural, to the process of municipalisation of the PDR has two variants, one related to entrepreneurship and the other to social participation. Within the entrepreneurship training programme a network of 243 accredited trainers and more than 8 000 accredited professional service providers (PSP) has been built. In terms of the social participation area, workshops

Box 2.1. **The PDR and the construction of the institutional architecture of the LDRS** (cont.)

organised by INCA Rural have been instrumental in the constitution of the 2 200 municipal councils for sustainable rural development, and the conformation of 1 858 municipal plans. It has contributed also to the training of 1 665 municipal co-ordinators. INCA Rural contributes closely to the development of the PDR also by being in charge of the operation and administration of the *Unidad Técnica Operativa Nacional* (UTON).

Important complementary programmes, but outside the budget of Alianza are PATMIR and PIASRE. PATMIR is oriented to the provision of financial services oriented to the rural population promoting savings and reducing the distance between supply and demand of financial services in rural areas. PIASRE is oriented to the conservation and appropriate use of land, water and vegetation in zones frequently affected by natural phenomena in order to diminish the vulnerability of producers, and the re-conversion of production to less vulnerable and more sustainable ones.

SAGARPA has also set up the *Sistema de Monitoreo, Seguimiento y Evaluación del Desarrollo Rural* (SIMOM) as an internal monitoring system of the process construction of the institutional architecture and the implementation of the LDRS. In order to direct the necessary information to the pertinent decision makers within the vertical planning process of its rural development programmes, the SAGARPA needed a monitoring system that could identify the main problems that surface during the implementation of its measures. To accomplish this task, SIMOM was developed. This monitoring system was designed in a way that would include the institutional evaluation elements internal to the SAGARPA together with a permanent interaction with key actors involved in the implementation of rural development programmes, and popular consultations with all those affect by these measures.

SIMOM allows for the periodic accumulation of relevant, first-hand information and evidence concerning the advances or set-backs of Mexico's rural policy achievements. The system is also meant to raise the policy-makers' awareness of the practical difficulties implied by the implementation of the development initiatives. SIMOM attempts to establish a communication flow between those formulating the rural development policy and the affected rural population. The information collected by SIMOM is made available to the public via internet.[*]

[*] *www.simom.org.mx.*

higher scale, access to programmes and value added and productivity increases. On the other hand, the increase of participation of the rural population in the decision making process of rural development.

The supports of these programme are institutional strengthening, particularly for the state, district and municipal councils of sustainable rural development; organisational consolidation, of different types of organisation (labelled of 1st, 2nd and 3rd level), and enterprise support through scholarships, exchange of experiences, publications and specialised seminars. The institutional strengthening aspect of the programme has been instrumental in the conformation of the network of institutions delineated by the Law on Sustainable Rural Development (LDRS), particularly at municipal level, which in turn is a cornerstone strategy for the successful implementation of PAPIR and PRODESCA.

SEDESOL's Micro-Regions Strategy

The National Strategy for the Micro-Regions[26] was initiated in February 2001 as an effort to break the pervading tendency of "sectorialisation" between ministries or between the state and the federal levels and to avoid the duplicity of public investments addressed to lagging rural regions.[27] The strategy partially draws from previous experience and from tools developed during past administrations. The most relevant defining characteristics of the strategy are the following:

MR is not a programme but a multi-sector and multi-tier strategy. Although SEDESOL is the entity directly responsible of the strategy and has a specific budget allowance for the "Local Development Programme" (LDP) or "Micro-Regions Programme", the strategy goes beyond SEDESOL since it consists of a set of horizontal and vertical contracts in order to co-ordinate public service delivery for the least developed rural areas. The strategy's main normative instrument is the Principles for Inter-ministerial Co-operation and Co-ordination[28] signed by 12 Ministries in May 2001, which, with only one exception, are the same ministries that conform the Inter-secretarial Commission for Sustainable Rural Development (CIDRS).[29] The funding of the strategy therefore comes on important part from the ad hoc LDP allocation administered by SEDESOL, but complemented by the budgets of the 68 programmes of the different ministries that operate under the strategy, and by municipal and state resources (see Figure 2.6).

The strategy relies on a multi-tier co-ordination mechanism. At the federal level, political co-ordination among different ministries is enforced through the Inter-sectoral Committee for Micro-Regions, chaired by the Chief of the Executive and with co-ordination mechanisms at Vice-ministers and Director General levels. At the state level, an intermediate or "approval" tier is represented by the Sub-Committee for the Attention of Regions of High Priority

Figure 2.6. **Investment of the MR Strategy by source**

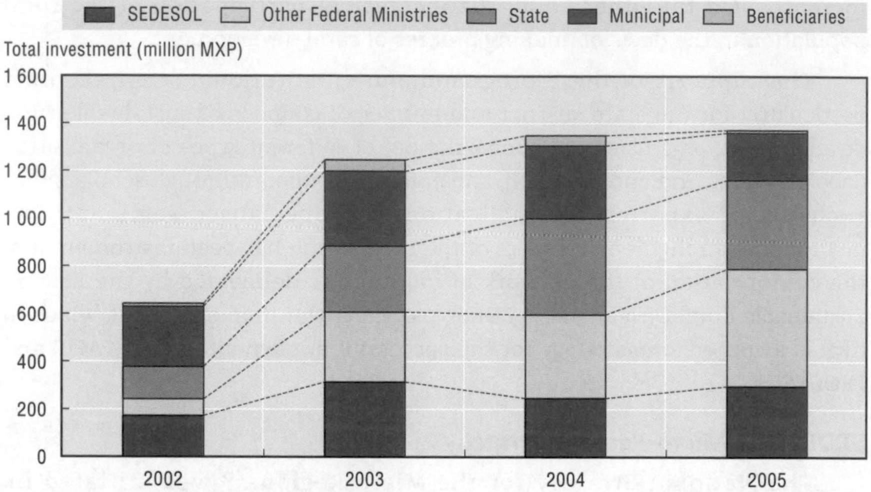

Source: SEDESOL.

(SARP), mainly known in the different states as the COPLADE,[30] which is a wide-ranging state development council chaired by the State Governor that has a special *mesa* (workgroup) for the micro-regions co-ordinated by the State Delegate of SEDESOL. At *the local level*, co-ordination takes place through the Committees for Municipal Development or COPLADEMUN. In the cases where the micro-region boundaries exceed the municipal administrative ones – which is often the case – a new figure, the "Micro-regional Committee", is formed by bringing together each municipality's COPLADEMUN.

MR is a territorial strategy. In contrast to most of the typical government programmes designed as response to specific policy issues, sectors or problems, MR is probably the most clearly territorial policy of the Mexican government in the sense that it was born from a mapping exercise. The identification of the strategy's beneficiaries was based on the Marginalisation Index developed by the National Council of Population (CONAPO).[31] The Micro-Regions Strategy focuses on the municipalities of "Very High and High Marginalisation".[32] These municipalities are depicted in Figure 2.7. The exact boundaries of the resulting 263 micro-regions (that may group from 1 to 25 municipalities) were then defined considering the territory's geographic proximity, ethnic and cultural identity and geo-economic characteristics.

Initially, the *co-operation principles* identified 250 rural micro-regions of very high and high marginalisation, as its targets. 13 more micro-regions were added to the initial 250 in order to include all the municipalities where at least 40% of the population spoke an indigenous language. Thus, the strategy targets 263 areas of application spread across 1 334 municipalities in 31 different states.

OECD RURAL POLICY REVIEWS: MEXICO – ISBN 978-92-64-01152-6 – © OECD 2007

Figure 2.7. **Municipalities with High and Very High Marginality Index**

Source: OECD Based on CONAPO classification.

These 263 micro-regions contain more than 99 000 localities, and host a population close to 20 million. The profile of these micro-regions in terms of various development indicators are depicted in Table 2.5.

Table 2.5. **Indicators of marginalisation and socio-economic profile of micro-regions**

	Micro-regions	National
Total population	19.9	97.4
Share of population over 15 years of age that is illiterate	23.2%	9.5%
Share of population over 15 years of age that did not completed primary education	51.9%	28.5%
Share of population that lives in houses without sewerage and separate sanitary room (?)	27.5%	9.9%
Share of population that lives in houses without access to electricity	15.4%	4.8%
Share of population without access to water facilities	30.3%	11.2%
Share of population that lives in a condition of crowding	62.1%	45.9%
Share of population that lives in houses with ground floor	41.5%	14.8%
Number and share of municipalities that expel population	515	765
	38.7%	31.3%
Total Employed Actively Population (EAP) (millions)	5.7	33.7
Share of Total EAP that has incomes of less than two minimum wages	76.4%	51.0%
Share of Total EAP that works in the primary sector	49.7%	15.2%
Share of Total EAP that works in the tertiary sector	29.1%	53.6%

Source: SEDESOL (2003).

MR Strategy is oriented to detonate "micro-poles of development". The objective of the strategy is to induce endogenous development through the creation of "micro-poles of development", labelled as *Strategic Community Centres*[33] (CEC by its Spanish acronym). The CEC have the function to concentrate the necessary basic infrastructure for the local population and the surrounding settlements. Authorities expect that these "centres" will be able to help overcome the difficulties linked with the provision of basic services and even foster a concentration of population around them to create larger rural hubs and contain migration towards urban areas.[34] In the process of identification of the CECs, SEDESOL has employed GIS[35] analysis to co-relate socio-economic variables of marginalisation at the level of states, municipalities and localities.[36] In addition, other elements were considered to warrant its potential to assume local leadership, among them its dynamism, potential in terms of economic activity, and the ability to influence surrounding areas from a commercial, cultural, or religious perspective. Within the 263 micro-regions, 2 966 CECs were selected, around which investment and development policies are organised. They have following characteristics: population between 500 and 5 000 inhabitants; relatively good year round road accessibility; a certain endowment of basic services; strong links with surrounding communities; and strong productive vocations.

MR is deficit oriented. The goal of counting with CECs in each micro-region with the adequate resources to generate dynamics of endogenous development has conduced to the development of objective criteria for the validation of progress in each CEC based on flag indicators. For each of the CECs, the stated objective is to reach eleven "white flags" or *banderas blancas* (a second set of three white flags is considered as eligible, see chart below). A *bandera blanca* certifies that a target area has been endowed with a certain level of infrastructure or service. In practice fulfilling the deficit of banderas blancas in the 100% of the CECs has become a quantifiable medium term goal that orients the direction of the strategy. Of the close to 33 000 *Banderas Blancas* required in the almost 3 000 localities to fully work as CECs, almost one third (9 650) were already established in 2000 and the "presidential goal" of the Fox administration was to complete another third (10 400) by the end of the sexenio.

MR promotes bottom-up participation of communities. Although in its design the MR Strategy is essentially a top-down policy, its objective of endogenous growth relies strongly in the participation of local actors in the definition of their own projects, in the establishment of targets and evaluation of results. In a context of high marginalisation of target areas and little experience at any level of government in territorial development policies, an initial top-down approach to the strategy was certainly adequate, but the programme has been developing structure and capacity at the local levels. SEDESOL's officials have worked in framing a central-local systematic dialogue with local leaders and

Table 2.6. **Evaluating progress, the Banderas Blancas (white flags)**

White Flag	Criteria for evaluation	Institution which validates
1) Basic service of electricity	When the construction of the electricity plant with the capacity to supply the 100% of demand of work-shops and houses of the locality is completed	Federal Electricity Commission/Municipal Government
2) Road connected to the state or federal road network	When there is a road for motor vehicles operative during all the year conducing to the state or federal road net-work	Ministry of Communications and Transportation/ Municipal Government
3) Basic educative service	When there is full coverage of the service of basic education for the CEC and its area of influence with qualified infrastructure and personnel	Municipal Government
4) Public telephone service	When the service is operative in the locality	Municipal Government
5) Basic health-service coverage	When the service is delivered in a permanent basis and with up-dated equipment according to the definition of official health-care procedures and standards	Ministry of Health
6) Public service of computers and internet access	When the connectivity service reaches a minimum of six computers in a Learning Community Centre (CCAs for its Spanish acronym) open to the population in general and the agreements of operation and maintenance have been signed with the municipal mayor office; otherwise, when the service is provided by an institution or a third party	Micro-Regions Unit (SEDESOL)
7) Water provision	When the construction of the hydraulic plant with the capacity to supply the eventual of 100% of the locality is completed	Municipal Government
8) Basic food-stuffs provision	When service is delivered in a permanent basis in the Diconsa Service Centre, or in at least three private shops or a public market	Municipal Government/ Diconsa
9) Sanitary services	When at least 80% of all households dispose of a "dry" type latrine and/or the construction of the sewerage and water treatment system is completed	National Water Commission
10) Promotion of productive activity	When the CEC locality and/or in the influence area exists an formal and acting association where: exist a *caja de ahorro* (community savings cooperative) that finances productive projects, and/or exist a viable productive project technically approved in terms of eco-efficiency, self-sustainability, return, scope and projections, or exists a planning committee that evidences its functionality	Micro-Regions Unit (SEDESOL)
11) "Solid floor"	When the number of households with concrete floor in the CEC locality reaches the average at the state level according to the data in the federal census of 2002	Municipal Government
12) Local urban planning (eligible)	When the Local Development Plan of the population centre is approved by the municipal Council and registered with the participation of the community	Municipal Government
13) Legalisation of rural patrimony (eligible)	When in the municipalities where a CEC is established, the 100% of the land property is certified and registered, and the cases documented where land property in under dispute	National Agrarian Registry
14) Juridical identity (eligible)	When the CEC and its area of influence reach 80% of its population its registered and receives its identity code (CURP)	Civil Registry/Municipal Government

Source: SEDESOL.

information databases that should allow a better understanding of local needs and opportunities. An important effort of consultation was launched in 2003 with the filling of a *diagnostico situational* for each CEC. In addition, local accountancy mechanisms were introduced at the local level with the *Councils of Social Accountancy*, to "control and survey" the implementation of the projects within the CECs. These councils have two characteristics: they are separated from the COPLADEMUN and they report directly to the Public Function Ministry (*Secretaría de la Función Pública*).[37] This latter institution is responsible for providing the elected members of the Councils of Social Accountancy with technical support through periodical workshops.

Conclusion

Mexico counts with an explicit rural policy. The country has acknowledged the significance of the challenge that the development of rural areas represent and is acting accordingly in constituting an institutional framework that that aims at integrating the actions of the different sectoral ministries and of the different tiers of government (federal, state and municipal) in rural areas. The new institutional framework for these changes is based in the Law for Sustainable Rural Development (LDRS), approved in 2001, which mandates the establishment of a federal horizontal co-ordination body specific for rural policy (the Inter-Ministerial Commission for Sustainable Rural Development, CIDRS), the constitution of participatory bodies for civil society (Councils for Sustainable Rural Development), and the elaboration a Special Concerted Programme for Rural Development (PEC). This last has evolved into the integration of a "rural budget" appended every year to the federal budget. An analysis of this budget demonstrates that, within the federal programmes impacting rural areas, two types of policies stand out in terms of resources: social policy (which involves poverty alleviation, education and health policies) and "productive support" policies, which have mainly an agricultural focus. Other federal policies significantly impacting rural areas are the provision of basic and productive infrastructure, environmental, land and labour policies.

The two ministries with most significant impact in rural areas, the Ministry of Agriculture, Livestock, Rural Development, Fisheries and Alimentation (SAGARPA) and the Ministry of Social Development (SEDESOL), within their own areas of competence, count with policies specifically oriented to rural development. On the one hand, SAGARPA's Programme of Rural Development (PDR) is one of the most decentralised federal programmes in Mexico. It supports productive investments for agriculture, livestock and non-farm activities with a demand- and project-driven approach. Two other complementary components are technical support and organisational support. This latter component has been instrumental in the construction of the institutional architecture mandated by the LDRS. On the other hand,

SEDESOL leads Micro-Regions Strategy as an inter-ministerial programme, which specifically targets the most marginalised rural regions and is oriented to provide basic infrastructure and framework conditions for the development around selected "micro-poles of development", the so-called *Strategic Community Centres* (CECs). The specificity of its scope allows it to monitor the advances and deficits in each of the areas of support through objective and socially shared validation mechanisms called "*banderas blancas*" (white flags).

Both the PDR and the Micro-Regions Strategy include several aspects that are in line with OECD best practices: 1) they adopt a territorial and integrated perspective on rural development that extends outside sectors; 2) they do not focus on subsidies but rather on investments and, 3) they co-ordinate efforts of multiple actors, the PDR with a stronger vertical orientation (due to its decentralised character) and the Micro-Regions Strategy with a more horizontal perspective (due to its inter-ministerial character). The two programmes differ significantly in their objectives and methodology: 1) the PDR is oriented to rural areas in general, while the MR Strategy is concentrated in a subset of rural areas, those with higher marginalisation and poverty conditions; 2) the PDR is more oriented support the rural population as economic agents or producers, while the MR Strategy focuses on their rights and living conditions; 3) while the PDR is more demand driven (beneficiaries submit projects in order to obtain support), MR Strategy co-ordinates the policy supply of different ministries in specific territories.

An important part of the way towards a coherent rural policy capable of addressing the challenges and opportunities of rural areas remains still ahead. Several critical issues will be addressed in the next chapter.

Notes

1. See OECD (1997b) for further details on PRONASOL.

2. Reforma newspaper, 16 March 2001.

3. This accounting exercise is done since before the Fox administration, however, it is not published officially as an annex to the budget since 2003.

4. It is important to clarify two things about this table. First, it only includes a reduced number of programmes and institutions, because the PEC encompasses more some 267 programmes, 111 being from SAGARPA. Secondly, the categories are not necessarily mutually exclusive so no addition is provided for the amounts and percentages, since any number would be only indicative and not based in the 100%.

5. The programme identifies families in extreme poverty, and grants mothers a monthly subsidy to assure feeding of the family, grants scholarships to children, and at the same time requires that the family receive medical and nutritional information. The conditionality of the grants has been a crucial success factor of the programme, which has been labeled internationally as a "best practice". In 2005, it covered almost five million beneficiary families, of which 69.1% were living in rural zones and 17.4% in semi-urban zones.

6. Poor communities are identified according to the marginalisation index.

7. The size of the grants increases as children pass to higher grades and are higher for girls, who have lower dropout rates at that stage of education, than boys.

8. Today Oportunidades is managed by a semi-independent "sectorised" institution, which means that it has more institutionality as a strategy and cannot easily be changed or eradicated by different administrations.

9. The National Institute of Public Health (INSP) made an evaluation of Oportunidades in 2005. Its principal findings include the following: a) it increased school registration by up to 41.5% and the number of children completing at least five school grades by 64%; b) it promoted an earlier school entry age and better reading, writing and arithmetic tests; c) it reduced by 35% the probability of working of young people; d) it increased by 35% the use of public health services and reduced days of sickness for children and adults; e) it reduced among the beneficiary groups the prevalence of chronic diseases such as obesity, hypertension and diabetes; f) it generated better examinations to detect cervix cancer and increased the use of family planning methods; g) it allowed for a continuous increase of 32% in consumption in the beneficiary homes; h prolonged exposure to the programme increased household expenses in education and clothing for children, reduced expenses on alcohol and tobacco and increased investment of running water in the home; i) for each peso transferred, the beneficiaries homes consumed 75 cents and invested or saved the rest; and j) is associated with a greater probability of migrating to form a new family or to study, but the migration of heads of families is less than the average of the other members of the household.

10. www.salud.gob.mx.

11. www.sep.gob.mx.

12. It develops 16 programmes ranging from agriculture and livestock, forestry and agro-industries to management in tourist contexts (rural tourism), environmental rehabilitation, computer science and landscape architecture.

13. www.edi.gob.mx.

14. Maize, beans, rice, sorghum, soybeans, cotton, safflower and barley.

15. CONASUPO, was responsible for much of the system of distribution and storage for these crops as well. In 1989, CONASUPO stopped direct purchases from agricultural producers and distributing crops, except for maize and beans, and its role in the market was gradually reduced until CONASUPO was dismantled in 1999.

16. For a more complete assessment of agricultural support programmes please refer to OECD 2006c.

17. www.firco.gob.mx.

18. They are the National Institute for Forestry, Agricultural and Livestock Research (INIFAP), the Universidad Autónoma Chapingo, the Colegio de Post-Graduados and the Universidad Autónoma Agrícola Antonio Narro. The first two stand out for their amount of budget. INIFAP is an institute whose purpose is to generate knowledge and technological innovations that contribute to the sustainable development of the agro-industrial, forestry, agricultural and livestock chains of the country, seeking the rational use and the conservation of natural resources. It also provides the following services for the AFF industry: laboratory analysis, training and transfer of technology, trials and evaluations, advice, diagnoses and technical opinions, certifications and

the preparation and execution of service projects. The Autonomous University of Chapingo is a federal university oriented to the teaching of rural subjects. It has several programmes at the undergraduate and graduate level of education.

19. Goes back to 1978, but the latest amendments were made in 2005.

20. Although this programme belongs to SEDESOL, it was grouped under basic and productive infrastructure for its clear orientation for these matters.

21. *www.cna.gob.mx.*

22. *www.sct.gob.mx.*

23. *www.conafor.gob.mx.*

24. Instituto Nacional para el Desarrollo de Capacidades del Sector Rural A.C.

25. Available online at *www.inca.gob.mx/registro* and in *www.psp.gob.mx.*

26. Estrategia Nacional de Atención a Microrregiones.

27. (14/02/2001), available at *www.presidencia.gob.mx.*

28. Bases de Colaboración y co-ordinación Intersecretarial.

29. Ministry of Economy (SE), Ministry of Transports and Communications (SCT), Ministry of Finance (SHCP), Ministry of Agriculture, Rural Development, Fisheries and Food (SAGARPA), Ministry of Tourism (SECTUR), Ministry of Social Development (SEDESOL), Ministry of Employment (STPS), Ministry of Health (SSA), Ministry of Agrarian Reform (SRA), Ministry of Environment and Natural Resources (SEMARNAT), Ministry of Public Education (SEP). The ministry that does not belongs to the ISC but is part of the Micro-Regions Strategy Agreement for monitoring purposes is the Ministry of the Public Function (SFP).

30. Spanish Acronym for Comité para la Planeación del Desarrollo Estatal.

31. Consejo Nacional de Población (CONAPO). For the methodology used in the definition of marginalisation indicators see "Población de México en Cifras"; available at: *www.conapo.gob.mx/m_en_cifras/principal.html.*

32. A few additional municipalities have been added to integrate those territories where 40% or more of the population is indigenous (due to particularly vulnerable conditions of such localities), as well as some municipalities with "Medium" marginalisation from those states that were left out of the strategy.

33. Centros Estratégicos Comunitarios (CEC).

34. The question whether the CECs can generate an actual change in migratory patterns, attracting new residents from more dispersed rural settlements remains open. Questions related with the ownership of land certainly represent an obstacle to the achievement of this objective. Reportedly, people tend to look for a house near the CEC but then spend most of their time where they own land to cultivate. This aspect will require further reflections and policy action.

35. Geographic Identification Systems.

36. The GIS has been used also for 1) the definition of coincidence between the municipalities covered by the National Council of Arid Areas (CONAZA); and 2) the Micro-region; and the co-relation between Mountain localities and marginalisation.

37. According to the Ministry of the Public Function (SFP, former SECODAM): "The point of departure is the respect and autonomy of the population. Within this logic, provided that the Community has some type of formal organisation, such organisation will to perform social accountancy actions and the functions of Council of Social Accountancy". See Secodam (2003).

ISBN 978-92-64-01152-6
OECD Rural Policy Reviews: Mexico
© OECD 2007

Chapter 3

The Way Forward.
Critical Issues and Priorities for Action

This chapter addresses several critical issues that deserve attention in order for the novel rural policy framework in Mexico consolidate and provides a set of priorities for action. The first issues are related to the governance framework in rural policy. The second set of issues is related to the federal policies impacting in rural areas and the prior ities that they contain in relation to the challenges and opportunities of rural areas identified in Chapter 1. A last part points the most relevant trends and results from external evaluations of the two policies explicitly targeting rural development, namely the Program of Rural Development of SAGARPA and SEDESOL's Micro-regions strategy, and highlights aspects that can improve the effectiveness and efficiency of such programs.

Key points

- Mexico should consolidate the advances in framing rural policy as a multi-sectoral policy. An important challenge resides in the co-ordination mechanisms within the context of the new legal framework for rural policy and particularly between the two most relevant actors: SAGARPA and SEDESOL. The governance of rural policy could be significantly enhanced by providing the Inter-Ministerial Commission for Sustainable Rural Development with stronger leadership, exploiting synergies between SAGARPA and SEDESOL and strengthening the process of decentralisation.

- The Special Concerted Programme (PEC) constitutes an important effort to have a coherent rural policy strategy. In order to take full advantage of this innovation, efforts should be devoted to defining clear criteria for programme inclusion into the PEC, improve transparency regarding the portion of such programmes which can be considered as being directed to rural areas. This will allow identifying and strengthening synergies between programmes.

- From a policy standpoint, priorities for Mexico's rural policy include: 1) poverty alleviation; 2) provision of basic public services; 3) strengthening and diversifying the rural economy; and finally, 4) better exploiting and preserving untapped cultural, natural and energy resources. Since these policy priorities extend the scope of any individual ministry the co-ordination of actions is necessary to pursue them efficiently.

- At present, the federal resources invested in rural areas do not fully correspond with the priorities identified: one sector-based (agriculture) and one horizontal policy objective (poverty alleviation) dominate rural policy. For rural policy to fully address these priorities, the involvement of ministries that do not have a rural focus is important. Among them are the ministries of Economy, Transportation and Communications, Finance, Tourism and Energy. Their involvement could strengthen investments in human and in physical capital, the diversification of the rural economy and the development of specific sectors that might enable rural areas to exploit employment and income opportunities.

- The mobilisation of private resources is needed in addition to public investment in order to trigger development in rural areas. This should involve both attracting new resources (which implies removing current obstacles to investment such as the low property and private security, and the inflexibility of land market) and promoting a better use of the resources owned by rural dwellers (particularly land and remittances from abroad).

- There is room for improvement in the effectiveness of the policies explicitly targeting rural development (SAGARPA's PDR and SEDESOL's Micro-Regions Strategy). Despite having grown in importance and budget in the past years, these policies constitute a relatively small share of the budget of their respective ministries.

- SAGARPA's PDR should strengthen its comparative advantages which lie in the complementarities between investment and training support and grow in the direction of supporting marginalised regions, low income producers and non-agricultural activities, where it shows higher investment returns. Orienting efforts in that direction could result in a better focus of resources than the one presently in place. The achievements in terms of decentralisation and building capacity constitute an important example for other federal programmes.

- SEDESOL's Micro-Regions Strategy should build on its institutionalisation as a multi-sectoral strategy and orient its efforts to include a broader micro-regional economic strategy. Despite the advance in the completion of its targeted "banderas blancas" (close to 60%), significant variation exists among them, which argues for efforts for broader advancement. The potential impact of the strategy could be enhanced through greater integration with other social and economic strategies, with particular attention to the *Oportunidades* programme and in general with the rest of public resources transferred to the relevant states and municipalities.

Introduction

Mexico has taken in the past few years important changes with regards to Rural Policy. The steps taken are in the direction of the best practices identified among OECD countries which constitute what has been called the "new rural paradigm". Two principles characterise this "new rural paradigm": 1) a focus on *places* instead of sectors and 2) a focus on *investments* instead of subsidies.

Table 3.1. **The new rural paradigm**

	Old approach	New approach
Objectives	Equalisation, farm income, farm competitiveness	Competitiveness of rural areas, valorisation of local assets, exploitation of unused resources
Key target sector	Agriculture	Various sectors of rural economies (ex. rural tourism, manufacturing, ICT industry, etc.)
Main tools	Subsidies	Investments
Key actors	National governments, farmers	All levels of government (supra-national, national, regional and local), various local stakeholders (public, private, NGOs)

The changes that Mexico has promoted point in the direction of having a multi-sectoral and territorial perspective in rural policy in which the different ministries orient in a concerted manner their efforts for the development of rural areas. These efforts are instrumental for obtaining the best results from government actions in rural territories since, as it was evidenced in Chapter 1, these territories are lagging behind urban areas in social and economic terms and have significant specific challenges.

There are several critical issues that deserve attention in order for this novel framework to consolidate. This chapter will addresses them and providees a set of priorities for action. The first issues are related to the governance framework in rural policy. The second set of issues is related to the federal policies impacting in rural areas and the priorities that they contain in relation to the challenges and opportunities of rural areas identified in Chapter 1. A last part points the most relevant trends and results from external evaluations of the two policies explicitly targeting rural development, namely the Programme of Rural Development of SAGARPA and SEDESOL's Micro-Regions Strategy, and highlights aspects that can improve the effectiveness and efficiency of such programmes.

3.1. Governance framework

The Law for Sustainable Rural Development (LDRS) constitutes a significant and ambitious step that was taken by the Federal government to help consolidate a new perspective of what rural development should be. Although there are still adaptations to be made to the governance system, an important change has occurred in the mentality of most of the different public actors and their realisation that through co-ordination much more can be accomplished. There are four critical issues related to the governance framework, the first of them refer to the current potential for better co-ordination at the federal level, the second to the co-ordination in particular of the two institutions which dominate the rural policy environment: SAGARPA and SEDESOL, and the third refers to vertical co-ordination and the process of decentralisation.

3.1.1. Horizontal co-ordination and collaboration at the federal level

Critical issues

Leadership of the CIDRS and commitment of the ministries. *The LDRS sets a framework for collaboration and synergy among the different ministries at the federal level.* The sectoral architecture of the government and the prevalence of an "agricultural vision" of rural areas that has prevailed not only in Mexico but in general in most countries are difficult obstacles for new approaches to emerge and sustain. In Mexico, the institutional setting foreseen in the LDSR constitutes a mayor institutional innovation which puts the country ahead many others in organising its government to "think rural".

OECD RURAL POLICY REVIEWS: MEXICO – ISBN 978-92-64-01152-6 – © OECD 2007

However, in practice, SAGARPA has been much on its own leading the promotion and implementation of the LDRS. The predominant role of SAGARPA, evident in terms of budget, (since it is the largest institution in the PEC with 33%) is reinforced by the norms set by the LDRS, according to which both the Inter-secretarial Commission (CIDRS) and the Federal Council are presided by the representative of the SAGARPA (LDRS art. 17 and 21).

The fact that the CIDRS is chaired by one sector limits the multi-sectoral objective of the law. The leading role of SAGARPA is understandable from a historical perspective and from the fact that is the ministry that in terms of budget contributes the most to the "rural budget" as it is now conformed. The role of SAGARPA in leading these efforts cannot be ignored. Possibly the institutional architecture delineated in the law, which shows a significant advance, would not have been built without having a specific ministry involved and devoted to that objective.

There is evidence that SAGARPA (which chairs the commission), has had difficulties in engaging and obtaining commitment from the other ministries involved. Experience from OECD countries indicates that a horizontal commission which is chaired by one sector (in this case, agriculture) may be limited in pursuing multi-sectoral objectives and hinder the full involvement of other ministries in a national rural strategy. This is the scenario that the LDRS has set when it gave the SAGARPA the main leadership role within the new rural development policy. On the one hand SAGARPA represents a specific sector and an equal in the eyes of the other ministries; on the other hand, the fact that one sectoral ministry, and the one precisely in charge of agricultural issues, leads this efforts contradicts the multi-sectoral perspective and shift out from the rural-agriculture vision, that the law seeks to implement.

Synergies between SAGARPA and SEDESOL. Another critical issue in terms of co-ordination is the one between SEDESOL and SAGARPA, the two most important ministries with a specific mandate for rural development. The two federal entities look at rural areas from different angles but their objectives are close and their actions are the ones that have a more substantial impact in rural areas. SEDESOL's main goals are poverty alleviation and the reduction of the causes of such poverty, and SAGARPA's main goals are promoting the primary sector, as well as the economic re-conversion and transformation of rural areas. Explicitly for targeting rural development, SAGARPA has its Rural Development Programme and SEDESOL has the Micro-Regions Strategy.

The actions of the two federal entities are ruled by two different laws. Even though SAGARPA and SEDESOL have both a clear rural mandate, their actions are guided by two different logics to some extent determined by two laws that orient their respective actions: for SEDESOL the Law of Social Development and for SAGARPA the Law of Sustainable Rural Development. These two laws have several things in common and effectively orient the actions of the two ministries:

- Both laws however confer them "authority" in Inter-ministerial commissions and in councils or committees involving different ministries, one about social policy and the other about rural policy, when these two polices are strongly related.

- SAGARPA and SEDESOL are part of both inter-ministerial commissions together with almost the same group of ministries. However, SAGARPA cares mostly for what happens in the rural commission and SEDESOL for what happens in the social commission, and they both have to lead other ministries to attain sectoral objectives. In addition SEDESOL leads the Inter-Sectoral Committee for Micro-Regions which is another co-ordination body (this one chaired by the President). This situation limits the space for impacting together rural territories in a co-ordinated fashion.

- The accountability of each ministry is with regard to their own law, and the one of the other ministries is subject to their own sectoral programmes.

However, both ministries often coincide in the same territories with two parallel structures. SAGARPA and SEDESOL both acknowledge that traditional top-down approaches and sectoral subsidies to rural areas have not given the expected results and that there is a need for place-based policies which can capture the diversity of Mexican rural areas and respond timely to their new challenges. However, for the implementation of their objectives, parallel rural policy systems have been developed and are currently being applied throughout Mexico's rural areas:

- Both bet on local participation and on new mechanisms to mobilise local resources: SAGAPRA has relied fundamentally on (and constructed) the participatory architecture delineated by the LDRS: the Councils for Rural Sustainable Development at state, district and municipal level. The Micro-Regions Strategy, on its part works at state and municipal level through the Councils for Planning of State Development COPLADEs and their respective municipal counterparts, COPLADEMUNs; at micro-regional level they have the *Consejosde Microregiones* or the *Consejos* CEC. The state and municipal structure participatory bodies that SEDESOL uses are more linked to the respective territorial governments than to the structure of SEDESOL. In this sense, SEDESOL has less power of control over the COPLADEs and COPLADEMUNs than SAGARPA has over the CDRSs.

- Both rely on their own delegaciones at each of the 31 states as their counterparts for managing their own programmes and they both put emphasis on the importance of local development agents, called "*residents*" in SEDESOL and "*promotores*" in SAGARPA.

OECD RURAL POLICY REVIEWS: MEXICO – ISBN 978-92-64-01152-6 – © OECD 2007

Priorities for action

Provide CIDRS with stronger leadership. There is no one size fits all solution to co-ordinate sectoral ministries and ensure their commitment in a new policy approach to rural territories. Several OECD countries have implemented different initiatives to cope with the objective of integrating a coherent strategy that involves different ministries into rural policy. Some examples are the following:

- Canada's "rural lens" initiative ensures that rural priorities are taken into consideration in the development of government policy and that there is policy coherence over rural objectives across ministries.

- Finland's multi-year Rural Policy Programme, also seeks to draw attention to the specific needs of rural areas. "Broad" policies proactively integrate these needs into central government decision making in different sectors. "Narrow" policies specifically target rural areas.

- The United Kingdom created DEFRA (Department for Environment, Food, and Rural Affairs) in June 2001 to broaden the focus of rural policy and to eliminate policy "silos" by gathering under one department several rural functions.

The experience of the new institutions for rural policy in Mexico after five years of initiated should translate into an agreement among the different ministries to have a true operational collaboration framework. Among the alternatives that Mexico has at hand are the following:

- *Assigning a meta-ministerial leadership to the CIDRS.* The issue of leadership among equals is not a problem of SAGARPA *per se*, the same would happen if the responsibility resided in another ministry. In that sense the alternative is a meta-ministerial leadership which could be filled by the Chief of the Executive.

- *Rotated leadership of the CIDRS.* A more direct solution to engage the different ministries could be the rotation of the presidency of the CIDRS by different ministries ensuring the continuity of a shared vision. In this sense the works of the commission are not seen as monopolised by one institution, which generates incentives for the different ministries to participate.

- *The creation of an ad hoc independent institution,* in charge of rural policy with a multi-sectoral perspective, with budget and normative arrangements to enforce collaboration from the different ministries. There is evidence that this framework may gives much stronger and clearer message in the Mexican public administration and avoids the problem of combining budgets and programmes. This was for example the case of the Federal Institute for Access to Public Information (IFAI for its Spanish acronym), created within the Fox Administration (2002-2006). It is true however that in the context of budgetary restraints of the Mexican government the creation of new institutions might not seem as the best alternative, in any case, budget from different institutions and programmes could be merged for this purpose.

- *Strengthening the legal attributions of the Inter-secretarial Commission for Sustainable Rural Development (CIDRS)*. This alternative points in the direction of enhancing existing co-ordination mechanisms. ensuring its permanence over different administrations and with stronger budgetary allowances rather than the formality of presenting the "rural budget" (PEC) to the congress. With this, the CIDRS could have some specific programmes at its command, with truly integrated territorial rural policy measures and independently financed through the PEC's budget.

Enhance synergies between SAGARPA's and SEDESOL's sub-national structures. Greater dialog between these two ministries is necessary to avoid the dispersion of resources and exploit synergies. More coherence should be sought between the actions of the federal planning bodies and the local bodies involved in the implementation of the respective strategies, envisaging when appropriate:

- The collaboration of the two ministries in the construction of a common network a territorial institutional structure that serves the purpose of both ministries, significantly independent of both of them, so that it can also be regarded by other ministries as an effective structure for canalising their programmes to rural areas, and gain efficiencies by reducing the budget that today both use for maintaining parallel structures.

- Devoting efforts at state and municipal (micro-regional or district) levels locally to identify complementarities within projects and, when necessary, towards defining one common development plan, pooling both SEDESOL's and SAGARPA's resources for certain municipalities in one single fund. Of particular importance is strengthening the co-operation between SEDESOL's local *residents* and SAGARPA's *promotores* as well as of delegates of each of them at the state level.

- Analysing the territorial overlapping of the districts that SAGARPA uses and the micro-regional boundaries, trying to homologate them, in the understanding that the micro-regions already defined would be a sub-set of a larger structure of rural districts, which involves also regions with other degrees of marginalisation.

Exploiting complementarities between SAGARPA's and SEDESOL's policies. Besides solving the possible overlapping in their sub-national structures, the most relevant issue is exploiting the complementarities between SAGARPA's and SEDESOL policies. Complementarities can emerge from specialising on different types of regions and on different building blocks of the rural policy strategy.

- *Specialisation in different types of regions*. There are complementarities in the actions of the Micro-Regions Strategy and the PDR programme since the Micro-Regions Strategy reaches areas where SAGARPA's programme find difficult to penetrate. On the other hand, SAGARPA's mandate of rural development is oriented to all rural districts, independently of their economic situation, and has been actively building a structure of participation in rural areas intended to serve for the purposes of all the public administration. It would be beneficial to identify specific territories in which one ministry could take the lead and the other a more subsidiary role.

● *Specialisation in different building blocks of rural policy.* Chapter 1 identified four policy priorities for rural areas: poverty alleviation, provision of basic public services, strengthening and diversification of the rural economy and exploitation of untapped natural, cultural and energy resources. These four priorities could be considered four complementary building blocks of rural policy. SEDESOL focus on poverty alleviation and in reduction in the causes of such poverty covers a basic floor of needs of the rural population. The programmes of SEDESOL, such as the *Oportunidades* programme, bring to rural areas significant resources that, as evaluations have proved; have an impact in the start-up of economic projects. Micro-Regions Strategy covers to some extent the second priority with the provision of infrastructure. Once the basic floor is achieved, SAGARPA's interventions are more critically needed since they are oriented to economic agents, already with certain capabilities of interacting with markets. The specialisation of both ministries in the segments of population that they could better impact is important for the effectiveness of policy interventions.

3.1.2. *Vertical co-ordination and the process of decentralisation*

Critical issues

The law on sustainable rural development states that federalism and decentralisation are core criteria for the implementation of rural development programmes. In that sense, the law establishes the creation of inter-ministerial bodies at the state level in reflection of the one created at the federal level. SAGARPA has been very active in decentralising programmes to the state and municipal level. Some critics suggest that SAGARPA's decentralisation to the municipal level has gone too far, and that state or district level are a better level to assign responsibilities and still have a more coherent regional policy instead of pulverisation of resources. In this line of thinking, the World Bank recently proposed a scheme of decentralisation at state level for all rural development programmes (World Bank, 2006). On the other hand, with the municipal approach, SAGARPA has been able to some extent to avoid the previous centralised logic that delivered programme resources through intermediary producer organisations, reaching directly small producers and increasing the transparency of the process.

Despite SAGARPA's improvements in decentralisation, the broad rural policy framework involves actions of many other ministries. However, each ministry has set different criteria and strategies for the decentralisation of the respective public policies. Thus, certain decentralised programmes at the local level are ineffective because complementary policies were not decentralised. States and municipalities have already resources and responsibilities for some policies, as it is the case of Alianza programmes, however, they don't have any control over actions of complementary policies that are decided in a centralised manner. For example a local project that might need support for road construction, or for SME support, or change in use of land, has definitely to be solved in Mexico City, since policies of the ministries of communications and transportation (SCT), economy (SECON) and the agrarian registry (RAN, which is part of SRA) are decided at the federal level. Even within SAGARPA there is lack of synchronisation: agriculture, livestock and rural development are very decentralised, while decisions regarding fisheries are concentrated in Mazatlán, where the Direction General of Fisheries is located.

The decentralisation process relies on the capacities of local authorities to deliver public policies. A problem for decentralisation at municipal level is the short period of government (3 years) and the lack of continuity of policies due to the prohibition of re-election. The response to this problem have been the "institutionalisation" of bodies, involving society that would remain across administrations. However, these bodies, including the municipal councils for sustainable rural development, in which SAGARPA has invested resources and time in constituting, does not have true power of decision nor resources for implementing a local development strategy.

Priorities for action

Decentralisation should be taken to its full potential. Only with significant involvement of local authorities will rural policy respond to the heterogeneous challenges of the different regions of Mexico. For that is imperative that the federal government consider this issue as a priority and promote that the state and municipal governments assume their responsibility in the process, ensuring the participation of local rural society. Among the most relevant courses of action are the following:

● **Define the areas of policy to be decentralised**. The concurrence and multi-sectoral approach makes sense to the extent that can be operated at the local level. It is thus important that federal ministries establish criteria and shared strategies in order to synchronise the decentralisation of programmes and resources to local governments with a view of the complementarities that they can generate at the local level. Federal ministries can identify specific areas of policy in which collaboration at the local level can give good results. A good example of what has already been done is in the area of training, through the SINACATRI system, were training institutions of different ministries have worked in elaborating combined training programmes for all states tailored to their specific needs.

OECD RURAL POLICY REVIEWS: MEXICO – ISBN 978-92-64-01152-6 – © OECD 2007

- **Define clearly responsibilities and functions of the different levels of government.** Explicit agreements are needed for vertical co-ordination to be effective. The clarification of responsibilities of the different tiers of government should be the core of such an agreement, which by definition is related to funds but also to the accountability on the use of such funds. A key issue is to distinguish between the normative, design and implementation roles. The normative role could remain at the federal level, by setting standards for rules of operation of rural programmes and criteria for evaluation and auditing the use of transferred resources. The design of certain programmes could be state's responsibility, so that they assume their own rural development agenda. Implementation role could be shared by states and municipalities, ensuring co-ordination and transparency in the distribution of resources.

- **Engage civil society in the monitoring of decentralised resources.** Accountability is a crucial aspect of the decentralisation process. The lack of clear means to make states and municipalities accountable for the resources and results of their programmes is probably one of the most important inhibitors of decentralisation. Civil society could be a powerful ally to press local governments for an effective administration of rural programmes. Providing states and municipal councils with stronger instruments to enforce accountability would be beneficial for such purpose.

- **Enhance local capacity.** Efforts for decentralisation will be in vain unless there are enough local capabilities creating demand for such a process. Institutionalisation of policies and best practices at the local level is important in the context of the short terms of government at municipal level but also at the state level. Legislative and regulatory institutions are not necessarily the best way to ensure continuity. The role of civil society is again crucial for this aspect: the potential beneficiaries of the rural development efforts at local level should be actively involved in the project development process. They must be key participants of the development efforts, active in the needs identification analysis as well as in the formulation of solutions and initiatives

3.2. Federal programmes impacting rural areas

3.2.1. Taking full advantage of the PEC as a concerted plan and as a rural budget

Critical issues

The Programa Especial Concurrente para el Desarrollo Rural (PEC) is an important effort of constituting a concerted plan for rural development. The primary objective of the PEC (and what its name stands for) is to be a concerted multi-sectoral programme that addresses with specific policies the challenges of rural areas. However, several issues both on its programmatic version and in its accounting exercise, demonstrate rigidities in the accumulation of the programmes and budgets that each ministry undertakes rather than a coherent and concerted plan oriented to attaining a common vision. In order for this instrument to be useful for policymakers some issues merit attention.

Aggregation rather than synergies. The programmes of the different ministries that intervene in the rural development are included in the programme categorised in 6 areas, without a clear co-ordination and synergies among them. This is evidenced by the categorisation of programmes which correspond more to the individual ministries attributions than to large policy objectives. Besides there is an important part of the PEC that is not easily identifiable to which category it belongs. It seems that after the publication of such document, each ministry has continued with its own goals and programmes established by their sectoral programmes, which are at the end for the ones that are accountable.

Performance indicators are based on programme outputs not shared strategic outcomes.[1] The indicators of performance established for the programmes included in the PEC are more based in outputs of the main programmes than on outcomes in general of rural development. This is another evidence of the lack of synergy since the commitment to common outcomes would imply a common vision. In addition, there is no programmatic follow up of such performance indicators nor a specific monitoring system for rural development goals, determining whether the goals are the correct ones and whether they are achieved or not.

There is lack of comparability and clarity in the categorisation of programmes. The exercise of aggregating a rural budget, even if that were the only purpose of the PEC, is a significant innovation that Mexico offers to the international community. There are however, significant variations in the number of programmes from one year to the other, which implies the question of whether the PEC itself is comparable from year to year, and even more so, from administration to administration. The original category subdivision of the 2002 document does not make clear what programmes go into which category and there is no official follow up of the categories. Neither are available the criteria and formulas used to categorise such a programme or such a percentage of a programme into the PEC. The relevant question is to what extent all the relevant policies are included and if for example administrative budgets should be included, and if so in what percentages.

There is overlapping in policy actions by different ministries. The lack of coherence in a common rural policy is perceived by the fact that many different ministries have programmes in place to promote similar actions. An analysis performed on the PEC of 2002 evidences the fact that 8 ministries were providing programmes to promote economic activity ranging from the ministries of Agriculture

(SAGARPA), Economy (SECON), Environment (SEMARNAT) and Finance (SHCP) to the ministries of Social Development (SEDESOL), Agrarian Reform (SRA) and the Ministry of Interior (Gobernación). Social policies were more clearly concentrated in three ministries: SEDESOL, Health (SSA) and Education (SEP). Basic and productive infrastructure programmes were provided by SEDESOL, SAGARPA and SEMARNAT; labour conditions were attended by the Ministry of Labour (STPS), SEDESOL and SAGARPA, agrarian aspects were more clearly concentrated in SRA (CIDRS 2003). This framework has not changed much since then.

There have been various proposals of administrative reordering of programmes within the ministries involved in the PEC. One of them proposed a much simpler categorisation of programmes, merging them into 8 large economic programmes and 9 social programmes, totalling 17 programmes. This proposal estimated savings to the federal government if changes were implemented of around 725 million MXP (AT Kearney 2003). Another proposal builds more on the current 6 categories of policy of the PEC and promotes a concentration of the programmes in which several ministries intervene in the ministry which has comparative advantages for undertaking the programme (CIDRS 2003).

Priorities for action

The above issues merit an exercise of rethinking of the PEC along the following lines:

- **Increasing transparency.** There is a need for clear and transparent criteria for defining which programmes are of rural scope and which are not. Although it is understandable the larger participation of some ministries in the "rural budget", methodology issues related to the difficulty of assigning a rural character to the different programmes might be overestimating the rural component of some ministries, such as SAGARPA (whose budget is entirely assigned to the PEC) and underestimating the contribution of others. It is important to define with respect to the underrepresented ministries, whether effectively these ministries do not have more programmes oriented to rural areas, or whether the actions that these ministries have in rural areas are not properly taken into account in the PEC. Such a debate can clarify whether more programmes should be included in the PEC and whether minor issues such as a point in the political agenda of the Ministry of Interior (Gobernación) or the Congress should be included in the PEC. Important is also to define whether administrative budget should or should not be included.

- **Merging, transferring and eliminating programmes to enhance synergies.** Communication of the different ministries is crucial for achieving a coherent development plan for rural areas. This debate should result in the merging, transfer or elimination of programmes, and to the definition of measurable outcomes for which all the ministries are responsible. This is a difficult governance issue because individual ministries will be reluctant to eliminate or transfer programmes to other ministries. However, this is the precise purpose of the PEC, to have a more coherent rural policy, and this implies strengthening the comparative advantages of each ministry and allocating public resources in the best way.

● **Monitoring and evaluation.** There is a need for clearer supervision of the basic control mechanisms that exist for the different institutions involved in the implementation of rural policy. A truly external evaluation of the national rural development policy based on outputs and outcomes established in the PEC should become a continual knowledge management system. This could positively contribute to the successful development of Mexico's rural policy making and implementation process. In addition, once a framework for the restructuring and transfer of programmes is agreed and implemented, the monitoring of the process and controls for approval of new programmes should be set in place to avoid the proliferation of programmes which might significantly overlap with others being already implemented by other ministries. Finally, for the monitoring and evaluation to be more effective, the consolidation information and databases of the different ministries into a unique system that could concentrate the beneficiaries of different programmes, the regionalisation of policy impacts and the relevant outcome indicators, would certainly provide relevant information for decision making and contribute to the effectiveness of policy actions. The Institute of National Statistics, Geography and Informatics (INEGI) could be an important partner in this process, particularly by providing information of the needs and outcome indicators at different territorial levels. Although information from this source is available for many rural indicators, they are dispersed and they don't have always the necessary continuity.

3.2.2. Towards a sectoral policy mix that addresses the challenges and potential of rural areas

Critical issues

The debate on the institutional framework and governance mechanisms, while important, should not eclipse the central debate which is how Mexico is undertaking the profound challenges of rural areas and how is it taking advantage of the opportunities and untapped resources present in those territories. From a policy standpoint, priorities for Mexico's rural policy include: 1) poverty alleviation; 2) provision of basic public services; 3) strengthening and diversifying the rural economy; and finally, 4) better exploiting and preserving untapped cultural, natural and energy resources. Since these policy priorities extend the scope of any individual ministry the co-ordination of actions is necessary to pursue them efficiently.

OECD RURAL POLICY REVIEWS: MEXICO – ISBN 978-92-64-01152-6 – © OECD 2007

Figure 3.1. **Building blocks for rural policy**

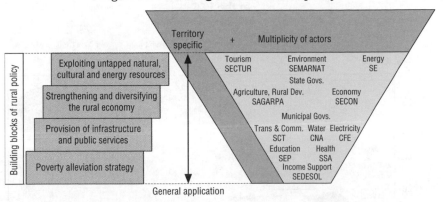

The four policy priorities identified in Chapter 1 could be considered building blocks of a comprehensive rural policy. Some of the policy priorities are much more of general application such as the poverty alleviation strategy. That means that a programme such as *Oportunidades* could be standard for all the country without making territorial differentiations and work fairly well. In fact standardisation of procedures is one of the strengths of the programme. However, as soon as we advance in the policy priorities towards provision of infrastructure and public services and particularly towards the last two priorities, each region has specific needs and policies should therefore be territory specific. Also as one goes up on the scale of building blocks, the number of institutions involved in policy delivery increases, implying greater need for co-ordination.

At present, the federal resources invested in rural areas do not fully correspond with the priorities identified: Figure 3.2 provides a grouping of ministries according to the share of their respective administrative budgets in the PEC and the share of the PEC that they represent. According to these two variables three groups of ministries can be identified: A first group labelled "entities with specific mandate of rural policy", which has more than 50% of their administrative budget in the PEC (actually all of them have more than 60%), second group which has more than 20% of their budget in the PEC or represents more than 10% of the total PEC resources, labelled "entities with significant rural policy focus/impact" and a third group of entities which have low rural focus. The criterion of selection for belonging to this third group is a share of less than 10% of the PEC individually, but actually none of them contributes with more than 5%, or less than 20% of their budget in the PEC, although the highest in the group has 12%. From this categorisation, some critical issues can be derived which reveal priorities that at least in terms of budget, the "broad rural policy" has in Mexico.

Figure 3.2. **Ministries and budget involved in rural policy according to the PEC**

2006

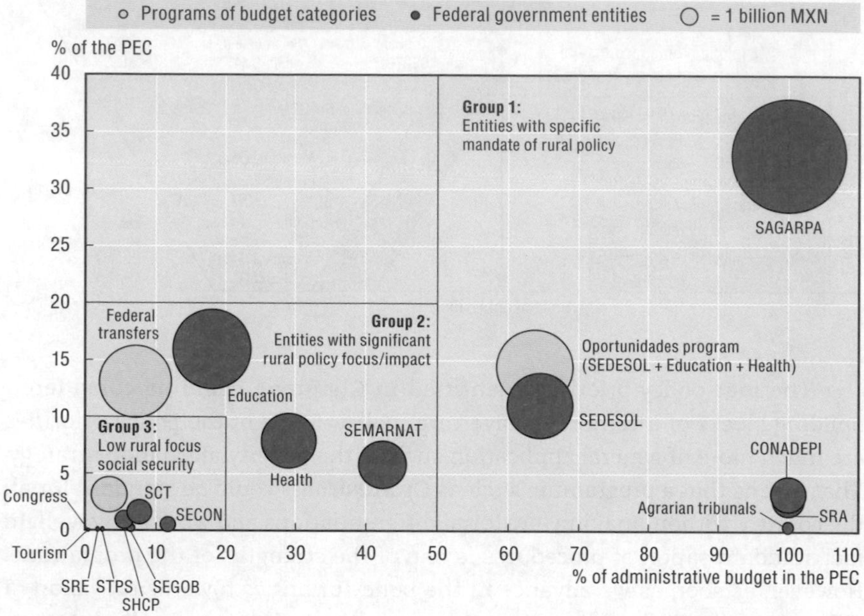

Source: PEC, 2006.

One sector-based (Agriculture) and one transversal policy (poverty alleviation) dominate rural policy. The entities with a clear mandate for rural policy are the Ministry of Agriculture (SAGARPA) and the Agrarian Reform Ministry (SRA) on the one side, and the Ministry of Social Development (SEDESOL) and the Commission for the Development of Indigenous Communities (CONADEPI) on the other. These ministries make together slightly more than 50% of the PEC and have most of their budget devoted to rural areas and indicate two clear priorities of the federal government investment in rural areas.

SAGARPA's predominance, beyond the governance issue discussed above indicates the prevalence of a clear agricultural focus of rural policy. Despite the facts, already acknowledged, that SAGARPA counts with a programme (the PDR) which goes beyond the scope of the primary sector and that the administrative budget of SAGARPA, in contrast to other ministries, is included in the PEC, the large share of resources devoted to this sector contrast with the small share of other sectors.

The other priority is indicated by the role of SEDESOL. As it was already mentioned in chapter two, adding SEDESOL budget to that of education and health, make "social policy" the most important component of the "rural policy". Individually, although SEDESOL budget is not entirely devoted to rural areas (65%) because they also have urban social programmes such as Habitat, this ministry together with SAGARPA has most of the "rural policy" responsibility, one on the "social" front and the other on the "productive" front. The graph also shows the *Oportunidades* programme, which is lead by SEDESOL but its rural budget as percentage of the PEC is higher than SEDESOL's (14% *vs.* 11%) because part of their resources come from the education and health ministries. This programme is also not entirely rural, although the 64% of its budget registered in the PEC might be underestimated.

Education, health and environmental policies are transversal policies with significant impact on rural areas. The second group is integrated by entities that does not necessarily have a rural mandate but, because of the extension of rural population and territory, an important part of their policies and resources are oriented to rural areas. Within this group are the Ministry of Public Education (SEP) and the Ministry of Health (SSA) and the Ministry of Environment (SEMARNAT) of which an important part of the budget is undertaken by the National Water Commission (CNA). Although federal transfers to states and municipalities are not an institution but a budget allowance, for its amount, which accounts for 13% of the PEC, they would be classified into this group.

Most "economic" related ministries have very low rural focus. The rest of the entities included in the PEC contribute with a much smaller portion of it. The group comprises entities clearly related to economic development issues such as the Ministry of Economy (SECON), the Ministry of Communications and Transportation (SCT), the Ministry of Labour (STPS) The Ministry of Finance (SHCP)[2] and the Ministry of Tourism, all of which would be expected to have a more significant role in rural areas. There are also entities which does not have a significant relation to rural areas such as the Ministry of Interior (*Gobernación*), the Ministry of Foreign Relations (SRE) and the Congress. Social Security budget belongs also to this category and evidences the low incidence of social security in rural areas, an issue that was already pointed out in Chapter 1.

The relative policy priorities reflected by the composition of the "rural budget" contrasts with the challenges of rural areas identified in Chapter 1. Issues of particular attention are the effectiveness of the agricultural support, which as it is evidenced, is large, but it is not clearly reflected in the performance of the sector, particularly of the poorest farmers; the quality of investment in human capital, which is also high in amount but is not necessarily providing the required economic and social returns; and, the low focus in other areas of government that could enhance a greater investment in rural areas and contribute to the diversification and strengthening of the rural economy.

Priorities for action

Poverty alleviation. The PROGRESA/*Oportunidades* programme is regarded as one of the best practices for fighting poverty in the international community. The evaluation of this programme evidences that it has been effective in increasing school registration (by up to 41.5%), augmenting the number of children completing at least five school grades (by 64%); and reducing (by 35%) the probability of working of young people. Similar results are obtained with regards to the use of public health services (35%), which has contributed to a reduction in the days of sickness for children and adults. Significant areas in which the poverty alleviation strategy could be strengthened are:

- *Improving quality of education and health services.* An important next step of the process of investment in human capital consists in warranting the quality of education and health services, now that rural children are going to school and rural population is going to health clinics. This step is as crucial or more than the first one but it is the only way in which the investment in human capital is transformed in economic and social returns for the rural population and their communities. The results of the OECD student performance evaluation (PISA, 2003) show that the difference in performance of urban students over rural students is almost the double for Mexico that for the average OECD countries (Figure 3.3). This implies a significant educational backwardness since even the urban standards are low in Mexico with respect to other OECD countries.[3]

- *Incorporating rural population to social security.* An important part of the investment in human capital besides the attention in rural clinics is the insurance of rural population against natural phenomena and illness, for which the poor are the most vulnerable. In absence of a formal social security, poor people in rural areas tend to cover themselves in safety nets. The attachment to subsistence agriculture and ejido rights of elder people instead of passing them to younger generations are examples of these safety nets. Extending the social security coverage to the "uncovered" is an important priority that will have significant spillovers to the rural economy. The *seguro popular* is an effort in that direction as well as the recently launched pension and savings provisions in *Oportunidades*. These initiatives should be continued and strengthened with steps to the integration of a universal social security policy.

- *Focalisation towards the indigenous population.* It would be important to increase the mechanisms of co-ordination and institutional concurrence for the attention of the regions and municipalities where indigenous people live which have greater indices of marginalisation. The support to these regions should involve territorial connectivity as well as economic,

OECD RURAL POLICY REVIEWS: MEXICO – ISBN 978-92-64-01152-6 – © OECD 2007

Figure 3.3. **Difference in performance of urban and rural students in PISA evaluation**

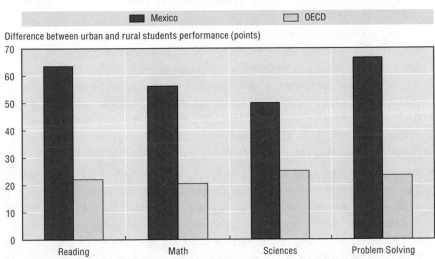

1. Rural refers to students attending school in localities of less than 15 000 inhabitants, urban refers to localities larger than that threshold.

Source: OECD PISA 2003.

environmental, social and human development, by means of the generation and management of plans of territorial development with a strong social participation

Provision of basic public services. The provision of public services is undertaken by many different ministries and institutions in Mexico. Among the most important actors are the Ministry of Communications and Transportation which provides roads and telecommunication infrastructure, the Federal Electricity Commission, in charge of the electricity network, the National Water Commission, which provides water infrastructure for sanitary and productive uses. The provision of basic and productive infrastructure took an integral approach in the case of the most marginalised regions with the Micro-Regions Strategy that SEDESOL co-ordinates (specific recommendations for the improvement of this strategy are provided in the last section of this chapter). The multi-sector nature of the strategy has proven useful for identifying the deficits of infrastructure in these regions and co-ordinating the efforts of the different ministries in the fulfilling of that deficit. Areas in which provision of public services in rural areas can be improved are:

● *Improve accessibility.* The dispersed character of rural localities is one of the major obstacles to overcome in order to open them a variety of opportunities that they don't have at reach. Accessibility is a determinant of diversification of income and higher salaries. Therefore, continuing improving the rural roads and communication network is essential. Connecting the South-eastern region to the rest of the country is an important specific target.

- *Extend productive infrastructure as engine of economic growth.* Besides the importance of public service delivery as a fulfilment of citizen's rights to have services such as electricity, water, sewage, etc., public services can be a powerful tool for economic development in rural areas. However prices of electricity and water provision for productive purposes usually have much higher costs (even than in urban areas) that inhibit the development of many economic activities. Schemes could be developed to allow small producers to attain reasonable costs for productive activities.

- *Extend the integral approach of public service delivery beyond the micro-regions.* The co-ordination of the different ministries in the provision of public services to the most marginalised regions has proven useful in the case of the Micro-Regions Strategy. The micro-regions are however just a small set of the rural territories, it might be worth evaluating whether the co-ordinated provision of public services with a territorial dimension would be more effective than it is at present, in which case it would be useful extending the micro-regional approach not only to the most marginalised municipalities but to all municipalities and therefore have marginalised micro-regions and non-marginalised micro-regions.

Strengthening and diversifying the rural economy. The participation of the ministries involved in economic policy (Economy, Transportation and Communications, Energy, Finance, Tourism) is crucial to incorporate rural regions to the competitiveness strategy of the country. Only if rural areas grow and become competitive will they leave the underdeveloped status that they have and will allow Mexico to be a more competitive country.

The productive (agricultural) support policies of SAGARPA are relevant in the context of the importance of the agricultural sector in the rural economy. The competitiveness and productivity of this sector could have a significant impact in the improvement of social conditions in rural areas.[4] It is important to distinguish between small scale agriculture and intensive agriculture. For small scale agriculture areas of improvement are:

- *Improve productivity.* Insuring that small scale agriculture and rainfall agriculture becomes more productive will have an important impact in reducing poverty, since it is closely linked to the income of the most needed. Policy should target the most needed agricultural producers and provide them with tools for performing better, financing and technical assistance.

- *Incentives to migrate to higher profit crops.* Policies that tie small scale producers to uncompetitive crops might be delaying the long-term development of these producers and their regions. Technical assistance in

OECD RURAL POLICY REVIEWS: MEXICO – ISBN 978-92-64-01152-6 – © OECD 2007

the migration to higher profit crops and support during the transition period, together with linkages to markets would be conducive to improving their productivity and long term standard of living.

Rural areas where intensive agriculture is performed deserve a different attention. Agricultural regions in the central and northern regions, mainly dependent on irrigation, have obtained significant productivity gains during the past 20 years. Recall that irrigated land produces 55% of agricultural production and 70% of agricultural exports. Policies oriented to this agricultural land should promote productivity growth but also care about two specific areas:

- *Reflect societal benefits and costs impacts on the environment.* Policy aimed to make agricultural producers pay a more adequate value for water than with the current pumping electricity subsidies, seems urgent, especially in a context where average efficiency of the use of irrigated water is estimated in 46% (PEC, 2002-2006).

- *Respond to consumer demand domestic and foreign.* Mexico has a strong comparative advantage in the production of certain fruits and vegetables. Creating a better framework for internal and external commercialisation of products can allow agricultural producers to profit from those comparative advantages.

In the context of a declining participation the agricultural in the overall economy and in the rural economy, the involvement of the other economic ministries are important for the creation of enterprises and the diversification of the rural economy. The significant increase in the non-agricultural share of rural income and of employment in non-agricultural jobs even in dispersed rural regions have undoubtedly contributed to the reduction of poverty and the relative increase of rural income with respect to urban income. It is important to highlight that while diversification from agriculture to other activities might be the solution for some regions, "diversification" *per se* into many industries might not be the most adequate way, most probably regions can take greater advantage from specialisation in certain comparative advantage. However, that comparative advantage varies from region to region therefore, involvement of local actors is needed in determining each region's priorities. Several areas for policy improvement are:

- *Promoting SME development in rural areas.* The Ministry of Economy, which has a specific Under-ministry for SME development should closely follow and support the diversification of the rural economy that is taking place in Mexico. Although it was already acknowledged in Chapter 2 the participation of this ministry in SME promotion in rural areas through FONAES, the aggregate budget oriented to this purpose is clearly low. Specific types of support are needed for the rural SMEs. The formalisation of the rural economy is a requirement that goes along with SME development in order to create a true "private sector" in rural areas, conformed by different individuals and SMEs that today are informal economic units. The experience of the Programa de Desarrollo Rural of SAGARPA and FONAES should be taken into account. These two instruments of policy are the ones that currently have had more impact in generating new enterprises in different sectors in the rural economy. In addition the conformation of co-operatives as a way for rural producers to gain scale and integrate better to markets should be explored, regulated and promoted. OECD countries have interesting experiences about SME development initiatives in rural areas (see Box 3.1).

● *Facilitate migration to non-agricultural jobs.* The transition of sector is not an easy one and even after having transited, the quality of jobs does not necessarily improve in a substantial manner the standard of living of the population. Active labour market policies and improvement of legislation might provide a better framework for the transition. In addition, secondary education should be tailored to local knowledge needs. Incentives for training should be increased both at for individuals and for enterprises. Changes in the regulatory framework might also be needed to provide tools for entrepreneurship and self-employment.

The mobilisation of private resources is needed in addition to public investment in order to trigger development in rural areas. The non-market economy that prevailed for long time in rural areas privileged the investment of the public sector. Still today, the participation of private investment in rural areas is limited. A co-ordinated effort of public and private investment in physical capital can increase economic growth in rural areas, and in turn make them contribute more substantially to the Mexican economy. This will require both investment itself and removal of obstacles that as of today provide adverse incentives that generate the low-investment trap in which rural Mexico is today. It will also require a better use of the resources owned by rural dwellers. Several actions that could be taken in this regard are:

● *Strengthening the rural financial sector.* An important source of investment in rural areas is the rural population itself. Unfortunately, rural areas have very low capitalisation in part associated with the unfortunate conditions that the agricultural sector has faced in the past decade and the decrease in credit to the rural economy. There is room for improvement in the deepening of a rural financial sector. The creation of the *Financiera Rural* and Bansefi are important steps, although the process of immersion of these two new institutions in the rural economy is still low. An important source of income to the rural economy which should not be underestimated are the direct transfers of both *Oportunidades* and *Procampo*. The former in particular has become a redistribution of income tool similar in some way a negative tax, in the

Box 3.1. **Small- and medium-sized enterprise (SME) initiatives in rural regions**

In Canada, both private and public initiatives are contributing to the development of SMEs in rural areas. In Atlantic, there exists a network of 41 Community Business Development Corporations (CBDCs) located throughout eastern Canada. Their mandate is to stimulate private sector employment in rural Atlantic Canada through business financing, counselling, and advisory services to small businesses. In Northern Ontario, the Federal Economic Development Initiative for Northern Ontario (FedNor) (*www.fednor.ic.gc.ca*) is responsible for promoting economic growth, diversification and job creation and helping to build sustainable communities in northern and rural Ontario. Although much of its support is provided through community organisations, it provides direct support to SMEs as well. Through the Northern Ontario Development Fund, FedNor provides support to SMEs in the areas of innovation and technology, business financing, trade and tourism, and human capital. It also supports community economic development through a network of Community Futures Development Corporations (CFDCs), which provide small businesses in small towns and rural communities with repayable financing, technical advice, counselling, information and referrals.

In France, the Fund for Service, Craft and Commercial Enterprises (FISAC) was created in 1989 to respond to the threats to the survival of local commercial and craft enterprises in rural and urban areas adversely affected by economic and social change, in particular the threats posed by the depopulation of certain rural areas, the development of large-scale retailers, especially on the outskirts of towns, and the difficulties of distressed urban areas. FISAC is a scheme based on financial solidarity between small commercial and craft enterprises and large-scale retailers, and is funded through a levy on the gross surplus of the proceeds of the Tax for Assistance to Commerce and Crafts (TACA) paid by large-scale retailers (companies with a sales area greater than 400 m2). Since the 2003 Finance Act, the proceeds of this tax are allocated to the general State Budget. Focus is aimed at but not restricted to individual operations aimed at enterprises in rural areas and specific collective initiatives dealing with cultural goods.

Source: OECD (2005). SME and Entrepreneurship Outlook.

context of the informality that prevails among the beneficiaries of the programme. The payment of *Oportunidades* through bank accounts is also a good way to incorporate its beneficiaries to the financial economy, although for the moment this provision is more common in urban areas.

- *Channelling remittances to investment purposes.* Another significant source of income with which rural population counts is the one of remittances from abroad. As it was pointed out in Chapter 1, remittances totalled 20 034.8 million dollars in 2005. The importance of remittances in the local economy varies by state and by municipality, but for some rural regions the percentage of homes receiving remittances as their most important source of income is higher than 40%.[5] These resources have a strong potential of generating productive results if utilised for investment in private and community projects. Policies can generate proper incentives for the channelling of these resources to the alternative that provides best returns for local development. The 3x1 programme of SEDESOL is oriented to that purpose, financial institutions can play an important role also with that aim.

● *Providing greater personal and property rights security.* Security is a necessary requirement for investment. Improved security in rural areas is needed for new investors to open sources of employment in rural areas. In addition, among the obstacles to private investment in rural areas it is important to highlight the lack of definition of property rights. A clear definition of property rights is a priority for the improvement of rural development as it will allow rural population to have economically valuable assets which is a necessary input of the market economy.

● *Providing greater flexibility to the land market.* Despite the recent reforms to the land property regime of the communal property of land (in 1992), the land market is very inflexible and is a natural inhibitor of the investment that rural regions require. The clearest beneficiaries of greater changes in this direction would be the *ejidatarios* themselves because they will be able to use their land as collateral asset for credit or sell it if the value of the land is greater than the benefit they obtain from it. Flexibility would allow the development of projects of different nature and possibly with higher rateability in current communal property, such as forest activity, rural tourism, environmental services and production of energy, among others.

Exploiting untapped natural cultural and energy resources. Rural areas in Mexico count with significant richness in terms of natural, cultural and energy resources. The policies devoted to exploiting natural, cultural and energy potential of rural areas are very limited. The potential of forestry and fisheries is very large, as well as the development of the tourism and energy sectors in rural areas. There are projects for developing eco-tourism and rural tourism were both the Ministry of Tourism and the Ministry of Environment are engaged, but this are small unfunded programmes. In addition, the share of the "rural budget" as reported by the Special Concerted Programme for Rural Development (PEC) is minimal. Energy policies does not have a rural perspective at all. The Ministry of Energy is not even included in the PEC. There are some initiatives such as the recent construction of the first wind energy project in rural Oaxaca, as an important step of the Mexican government in seeking to diversify its energy sources into renewable energy. However this project and in general energy projects are poorly linked to the rural population even when they might take place in rural areas. Priorities to consider in this regard are:

- *Building a stronger forestry and wood derivatives industry.* The large and forested land faces important troubles related to informal falling and forest fires. Reforestation efforts are well under way but they require higher efforts. Incentives, property rights and technology are key variables in defining a sustainable future for forests, which could considerably cover part of the current imports of wood. Organisation of local population into production associations that allow them to obtain better returns from this activity than from agriculture and livestock is an important part of the process.

- *Fishing and aquaculture.* The longitude of Mexican coasts and the diversity of species evidence the remarkable potential of these activities. Fishing and aquaculture industries need further organisation and linkages to local and foreign markets. Policy can be effective in aiding fishers' organisations to attain quality standards. Modernisation of ports and availability of capital to improve storing and transportation facilities are important priorities.[6]

- *Linking rural communities to mass tourism.* A greater involvement of the Ministry of Tourism in rural development seems necessary in view of the opportunities of income that this sector can provide to rural areas. Mexico has become an important destination for world tourism. In 2005, it received 21.9 million tourists, who spent close to 11 800 million dollars. Tourism has become the third foreign exchange generating activity, only after oil and remittances. However, most of the benefits of this activity are concentrated in mass-tourism destinations. Rural areas in Mexico can benefit from new mass tourism poles as well as from the linkage of these poles with adjacent rural areas. It is important to highlight that the most important destinations of beach mass tourism in Mexico, Cancun and Los Cabos are located in two states that two decades ago had predominantly rural economies based on agriculture and fisheries and that today occupy the 4th and 8th place in GDP per capita in the country. In general, 80% of the municipalities dedicated to the tourism activity fall into the category of low and very low marginalisation index according to CONAPO.[7] These arguments favour the orientation of public resources to the consolidation of the tourism activity and the integration of nearby communities to benefit from the resources that this activity generates either as product or services providers.

- *Develop rural tourism as a new niche.* Worldwide, rural tourism has grown significantly in the past years. Its estimated growth is 6% per year, which is higher than the rate of growth of world tourism.[8] This activity has great potential for providing an alternative income to rural population since it provides employment equally for women and men for youth and old people. The global changes in the behaviour of the tourist markets are clearly favourable for rural tourism as a differentiated product. Although rural tourism has been and continues being mostly of national origin, fundamentally maintained by the internal demand of each country, international tourist flows towards rural destinations has increased sensibly in the last years. In many rural destinations of Europe, the international demand is even already more important than its national market. Both OECD countries and non-OECD countries have useful experiences in the development of this niche (see Box 3.2).

Box 3.2. **Tourism and the rural economy in selected OECD and non-OECD countries**

Spain, which in the last decades has positioned itself as the second most important tourist destination country in the world has not done so without an important impulse to rural tourism: 53% of the budget of the rural programme Leader+ is oriented to rural tourism.[*] The government-owned enterprise *Paradores de Turismo de España* (*www.parador.es*) counts with more than 90 establishments which includes ancient castles, monasteries, hospitals and sites in the natural environment, restored to receive national and international tourism. They receive more than 1.5 million visits every year and generate an income of 273 million euro. Although not all of them are in rural areas, their network concept favours integration to the natural and rural environment promoting the sustainable development of these areas.

In Crete, Greece there are several initiatives oriented to link tourism to the local economy and spread the benefits of tourism revenue to parts of Crete that are at distance from the most visited areas and thereby ensure that the public goods associated with Cretan farming landscapes benefit to all. Individual hotel enterprises offer special diets or are concerned with their own positive environmental friendly image that sustainable farming can be enhanced by tourism. Grecotel has launched a pilot project (Agreco) to ensure supply of fresh high quality food for its hotels. In Rethymnon where Grecotel has 3 500 beds, this initiative includes 40 varieties of fruit and vegetables.

In Bregenzerwald, Vorlarberg, Austria, a strategic lead project for the LEADER II programme was implemented with the aim up building on a well-established local product – cheese – in ways that assured the livelihood of the rural population, reduced commuting and helped to create new jobs in tourism and trade. It was a holistic concept, with multiple and multi-sectoral beneficiaries, strong public-private partnership, and co-operation between different sectors including agriculture, dairies, accommodation providers, alpine pasturemanagers, trade and commerce. It has led to further innovative products (such as "Käsezwickel", "Käseträger" and "Käse and Design") and the establishment of a new high quality regional branding. It has helped to maintain traditional alpine farming, and hence the quality of the cultural landscapes.

Box 3.2. **Tourism and the rural economy in selected OECD and non-OECD countries** *(cont.)*

The Italian Province of Siena (Sistema dei Musei Senesi) *http://musei.provincia.siena.it/* provides a good example of valorisation of cultural heritage through it's intertwining Museum network. Items that were previously kept in a myriad of municipal and parish museums are to be exhibited in a series of 25 museums scattered over the territory. The museum system policy provides a good example of efforts to increase the experiential value of the province to tourists while also relieving the carrying capacity problem ("the Venice effect") of the most popular destinations. It does this by providing a mechanism for redirecting the 200 000 visitors of the main museums in the city to less popular areas. Each museum provides links to other museums in the network, assembling a sort of organised serendipity so that during the course of discovery in one museum one is directed to the other sites.

Costa Rica is a non-OECD country which could represent a closer example to the context of Mexico. This country has bet substantially on its natural resources as an attractor of international tourism. In 2001 the value of tourist services amounted 25% of the total exports of the country. The country has worked in the development of an image of Costa Rica as an ecotourism destination and has invested in providing infrastructure, equipment and training to rural localities rich in natural resources.

* ATKearney (2003).

Source: OECD The New Rural Paradigm (2006), Instituto Costarricense de Turismo. Plan Nacional de Desarrollo Turístico Sostenible 2002-2012.

- *Exploiting rural energy potential.* A more decisive involvement of rural areas in the energetic strategy of the country can have positive impact both on the development of rural areas and in the increase of energetic resources of the Mexican economy. Rural population has access to many potential sources of renewable energy ranging from water and air to alternative uses of their agricultural and livestock production, which could be converted into bio-energy sources. The relevance of ethanol as a bio-fuel, for example has been growing in the past decades. This product can be obtained either from agricultural products such as wheat, maize and sugar cane. International comparisons show that producers of sugar cane (such as Brazil and potentially Mexico) are much more competitive in energy production. The critical issue for policy is to find innovative ways in which rural dwellers can benefit from the energy resources that are available to them in terms of employment opportunities and income. In many OECD countries, energy has become a true "rural" issue from the fact that the quest for renewable sources of energy has unequivocally directed attention to rural areas. Germany is a good example (see Box 3.3).

Box 3.3. **Renewable energy in Germany**

The village of Jühnde, Germany in combination with The Interdisciplinary Centre for Sustainable Development (IZNE) is currently becoming the first bio-energy model village in Germany. This involves the generation of energy from domestic energy sources such as wood, straw, liquid manure, energy crops and other biomass which are particularly abundant in rural communities. The advantage to using biomass is advantageous in its storage ability and constant availability. The project instigated by IZNE choose Jühnde for it's large number of farms while the ten full-time agricultural businesses in the area supply liquid manure and garden waste for the biogas plant. The project has already involved the population of Jühnde in the planning process and has motivated the population to become involved in the implementation of the project. The primary aim of the project is to implement the use of a sustainable, renewable energy source and demonstrate that through the participation of the local rural population, it is possible to supply energy to an entire village through renewable raw material located within the rural region.

In Germany, renewable energy sources account for 170 000 in jobs, 16 billion EUR in revenue, and 4.1 billion EUR in exports. The greatest growth in renewable energy is coming from wind and biomass generation. In 2003, 8% of arable land was used to cultivate renewable raw materials. In 2005, bioenergy made the largest contribution of all renewable energy sources to final energy consumption in Germany while biogas electricity generation, and biofuel sales doubled during this year.

Source: OECD (forthcoming), Rural Policy Review, Germany.

3.3. Policies targeted to rural development: possible effectiveness and efficiency gains

This section provides an analysis of the key issues that merit attention with relation to the two integrated policies that were presented in Chapter 2: SAGARPA's Rural Development Programme and SEDESOL's Micro-Regions Strategy. The assessment and recommendations in this case can be based from the relevant trends in the evolution of these programmes as well as in the results from external evaluations publicly available.

3.3.1. Strengthening the comparative advantages of the Rural Development Programme

Critical issues

The Rural Development Programme of SAGARPA, described in detail in Section 2.3 constitutes an important policy tool in the overall rural development policy of the Mexican government. Despite the fact that it represents only 4% of the resources of the Ministry, the programme has impact beyond the scope of SAGARPA for two reasons: it has become instrumental in the construction of the institutional architecture of delineated in the LDRS, and it is the only programme in the ministry that is not circumscribed to the primary sector. Several important facts can be concluded from an analysis of the information available[9] on the programme about its resources, scope and impacts:

Decreasing participation of State funding. One of the most distinctive characteristics of *Alianza* programmes, and particularly within them, the PDR is its decentralised character. The PDR counts then with resources provided by the federation, but also by the states and the beneficiaries themselves. Although at the beginning the distribution of resources was more equilibrated (43% federal, 31% beneficiaries and 26% states in 1996), during the last decade federal resources have increased in importance with the most significant reduction in the share of states. In 2004, the distribution was 65% federal, 25% beneficiaries and 10% states (FAO, 2005).

Figure 3.4. **Total investment in the PDR by source**
MXN of 2004

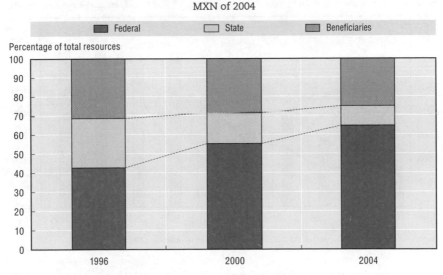

Source: FAO (2005).

The evident reduction in the participation of states is an issue that should be analysed in view of the orientation of the programme to grant greater attributions to the state and municipal level. This development might also be related to the decentralisation process which has gone to the municipal level and might be leaving states with little margin to own the programme and have interest in investing a greater share of resources in it.

Increase in the investment per beneficiary. From 1996, the total investment of the PDR has increased substantially. Its resources grew on average 16% from 1996 to 2004, the double of the growth of *Alianza* resources. The number of beneficiaries has not grown in the same proportion, it has had over the 1996 to 2002 period an erratic movement, and then after 2002, the year with the highest number of beneficiaries, it has declined considerably. However, as the FAO evaluation states the greater coverage was associated with pulverisation of resources. Therefore, since 2003, there was a policy decision to reduce the number of beneficiaries in search of having greater investment by beneficiary, and therefore greater impact. While in 2002, the average beneficiary obtained 1 200 MXP (federal plus state resources, all programmes), in 2004 the average beneficiary obtained 2 900 MXP. In fact, if only considering the PAPIR programme, the increase in the average investment per beneficiary is from 2 200 MXP in 2002 to 5 500 in 2004.

Figure 3.5. **Federal and State investment in PDR and number of beneficiaries**

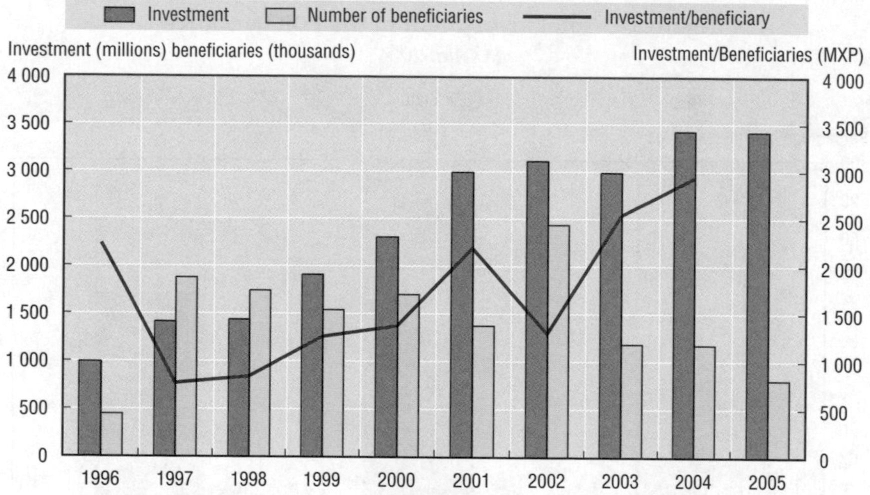

Source: OECD calculations with data from FAO (2004) and Presidencia (2005).

Focalisation of resources. The evaluation of the PDR undertaken by FAO uses two instruments to evaluate the focalisation of resources to the persons and regions that the programme is meant to attend. For classifying beneficiaries, FAO created a classification of the surveyed beneficiaries of the programme according to several indicators.[10] Producers were classified from Type I to Type V, were Type I are worse off and Type V are better off. For classifying regions uses the typology developed by CONAPO's marginalisation index. The funds and number of beneficiaries by these two classifications are depicted in Figure 3.6.

OECD RURAL POLICY REVIEWS: MEXICO – ISBN 978-92-64-01152-6 – © OECD 2007

Figure 3.6. **Beneficiaries and regional focalisation of PDR resources, 2004**

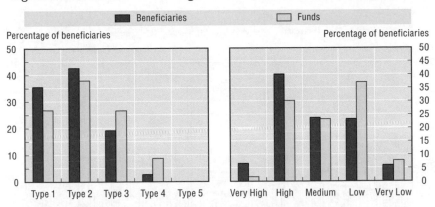

Source: OECD based on data provided in World Bank (2006).

According to the evaluation, Type II producers constitute the larger number of beneficiaries and are the ones which receive a larger share of the programme's funds, although in a smaller proportion than the share of beneficiaries. This is true also for Type I beneficiaries and opposite for Type III and Type IV beneficiaries, which implies that Type I and Type II receive lower amounts of support per beneficiary than Type III and Type IV. In terms of regional targeting, the regions with high marginalisation are the ones with higher number of beneficiaries, but the region with highest number of resources allocated are regions with low marginalisation. This means that beneficiaries in high marginalisation regions receive a lower support per beneficiary, and the opposite is true for the regions of low and very low marginalisation. Regions with very high marginalisation receive significantly lower resources and have a small number of beneficiaries. This concern is also risen by the World Bank in a recent study (2006) highlighting the fact that that resources are not focused to the states and localities where the poorest population lives. Figure 3.7 shows the total and per rural capita resources by states ordered according to their marginalisation index in 2005. Effectively, although total resources have a declining trend line, per capita resources have a positive slope, which indicate that richer states are receiving more resources per rural inhabitant.

Higher impact in non-agricultural activities. Figure 3.8 shows that despite the fact that non-farm activities receive a small share of the resources of the PDR (24% in 2004) and constitute even a smaller share of the beneficiaries (20% compared with 39% of agriculture and 40% of livestock), the impact of the programme is considerably higher in this sector than in the agricultural and livestock sectors both in terms of increase in income of beneficiaries and employment imputed to the programme. According to the external evaluation

Figure 3.7. **Total and per rural capita resources of the RDP by state**
2005

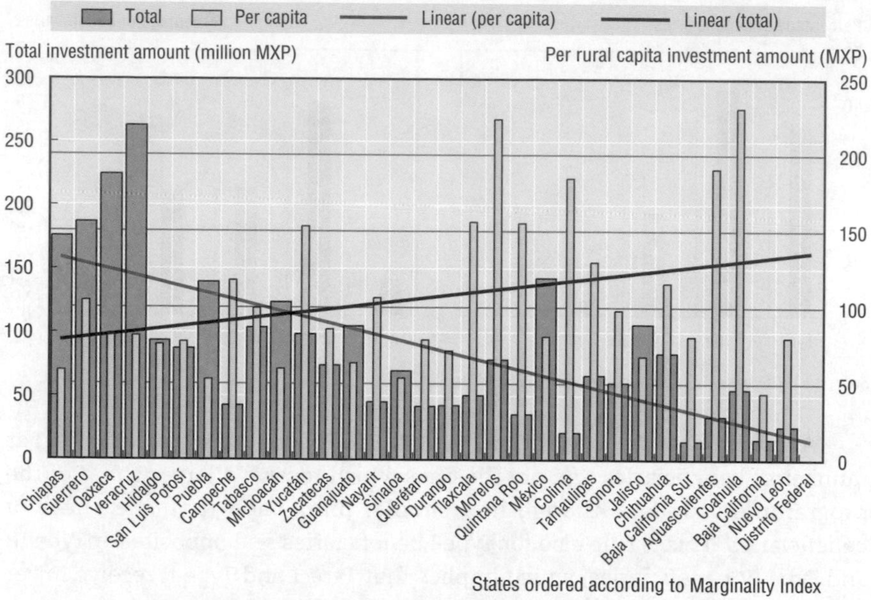

Legend: ▆ Total   ▢ Per capita   —— Linear (per capita)   —— Linear (total)

Total investment amount (million MXP)

Per rural capita investment amount (MXP)

States ordered according to Marginality Index

Source: OECD based on data provided in World Bank (2006).

from FAO, the programme contributes to a 48% increase in the income of beneficiaries dedicated to non-agricultural activities while it only contributes to a 20% increase in beneficiaries dedicated to agriculture and 27% in beneficiaries dedicated to livestock.

Within non-farm activities, the economic activity that obtained highest returns in terms of income was manufacturing, the one that obtained least was retail commerce. In terms of employment, FAO evaluation estimates that form 2002 to 2004, the PDR created 19 680 jobs, of which close to 16 000 were among family members and 3000 contracted employees. Non-farm activities are again the ones with a higher impact. It is estimated that 55% of the new jobs imputable to the programme were generated by non-farm activities, while agricultural and livestock activities contributed with 16.3% and 28.9% respectively. The performance of non-farm activities is related also to the fact that non-farm activities distinguished for being the most innovative and entrepreneurial, since 42% of the groups supported initiated a new productive experience. In general about half of non-farm activities are manufacturing (55%), markedly textile workshops and *tortillerías*.

Higher impact in most marginalised areas. In a similar way to non-farm activities, municipalities with high and very high marginalisation index, despite receiving a lower share of resources (30%) were the regions that

Figure 3.8. **Resources, beneficiaries and impact indicators by sector of support**

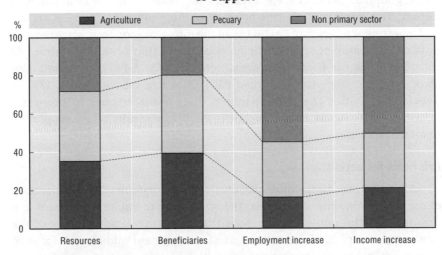

Source: OECD calculations based on FAO (2005).

contributed the most in terms of employment (59%). This is particularly true for the zones of high marginalisation which contribute with 54% of total generated employment. In contrast, the relationship resources-beneficiaries-employment generated is much lower and a matter of concern, for the regions with low and very low marginality (Figure 3.9).

Figure 3.9. **Resources, beneficiaries and impact indicators by degree of marginalisation**

2004

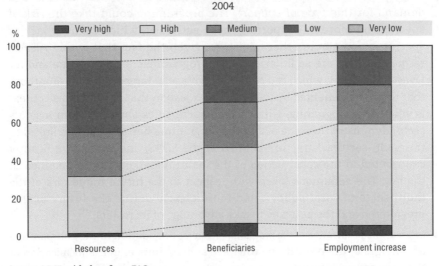

Source: OECD with data from FAO.

Complementarities matter. The complementarities of the three subprogrammes of the PDR are a relevant fact revealed in the evaluations of impact. This is particularly true between training provided from PRODESCA and investment projects of PAPIR. For all the different economic activities, the impact in income of the beneficiaries of those that obtained training is considerably higher. For those in agriculture, PRODESCA-PAPIR increased their income in 28% while those without PRODESCA saw an increase of 17%. In livestock activities the relationship is 43:22 and for those in non-farm activities 83:26. Again, it is to highlight the better results when supporting non-farm activities.

Priorities for action

Strengthen the comparative advantages of the programme. The evaluations of the programme corroborate that the orientation to vulnerable regions and persons and the non-farm focus are the comparative advantages of the programme, since the impact in terms of employment and income for each peso spent in regions with high and very high marginalisation index, in poor producers (Type I and Type II) and in non-farm activities, is higher than invested in the alternative regions, producers and activities. In the presence of such comparative advantages it is pertinent that the programme grow in focus to these objective beneficiaries. In this context, actions to improve the effectiveness of the programme include:

● *Strengthen the specialisation of the programme.* The support of non-farm activities is a characteristic that makes unique the PDR programme with respect to other programmes. The generation of higher income and employment when supporting these activities is a clear indication of the high demand for this type of support. The programme could take the risk of specialising more in supporting these activities, which seem to lack of specific support from other ministries, given the fact that within *Alianza* resources, there are additional specific programmes for Agriculture and for Livestock support, which can certainly increase in targeting and favour those that today are benefited by the PDR. The question that arises in this context is whether a programme with such characteristics should remain inside a sectoral ministry. To some extent the programme has always been linked to the multi-sectoral structure defined in the LDRS, and it has significantly contributed to the construction of the institutional architecture defined in the law. The definitions taken with respect to the future framework of the multi-sectoral rural policy could more clearly define the future of this programme and the best way to take advantage of its results.

● *Improve the focalisation of the programme.* The consolidation of the comparative advantages of the programme will have a direct impact in the focalisation of the programme. However, specific actions can be taken in order to strengthen the focalisation. One of them is limiting the amount of support by project, which as the evaluation shows is reaching average levels that might be too high. An additional resource is ensuring the application of the rule established for the distribution of resources to states and municipalities, strengthening policies that favour attention to municipalities in greater need and limiting political considerations. A greater co-ordination with SEDESOL's Micro-Region's Strategy might also enhance the focalisation since the scope of this strategy is specifically oriented to the municipalities with greater marginalisation. Finally, it is pertinent for the greater focalisation of the programme to ensure mechanisms that prevent large organisations to crowd out resources that could be better used by small groups of rural producers. This is consistent with the new approach of the programme wants to imprint in rural policy in a clear counter position to the status quo that prevailed decades ago, which still has roots in the rural organisational structure.

- *Consolidate the institutional architecture of the LDRS.* The PDR has become the living expression of the Law for Sustainable Rural Development, the constructor of its institutional infrastructure and its main beneficiary. It has even incorporated in itself, as mentioned above the multi-sectoral approach intended for the national rural policy. It is difficult therefore to dissociate the national rural policy intended by the LDRS and the programme. However, the programme is too small and under-funded for being a national rural policy and the structure and infrastructure of the law is too vast for being utilised only by this programme. It is important therefore to strengthen the ties of the programme with the different programmes that other ministries are undertaking in rural areas and let the other ministries benefit from the subsidiary building capacity effort that the PDR has undertaken within its training and building capacity programmes.

3.3.2. Consolidating the achievements of the Micro-Regions Strategy

Critical issues

The Micro-Regions Strategy, described in detail in Section 2.3 constitutes one of the most significant efforts of the Mexican government to integrate a territorial approach to rural and social policy. As it was already described, the strategy is intended as a co-ordination tool between different ministries to focalise resources and investments in selected localities (the so called *Centros Estratégicos Comunitarios,* CEC) capable of becoming development hubs within the most marginalised communities in Mexico.

Several conclusions can be drawn from an analysis of the information available on the resources and areas of investments of the strategy[11] and from the external evaluation of the Local Development Programme, which a part of the strategy specifically managed by SEDESOL.

Varied degree of advancement in the banderas blancas. The strength of the Micro-Regions Strategy is the platform it offers for co-ordinated sectoral policy interventions in the most marginalised rural areas. By July 2006, 18 687 white flags had been implemented, and 1478 were in process of being completed during the year, which means that by the end of the year, 56% of the mandatory flags would have been covered in the micro-regions. This constitutes an important advance, considering that at the beginning of the programme in 2001 only 29% of the respective basic public services were provided in these regions. This degree of advancement makes policymakers in charge of the programme affirm that in one more sexenio, 100% of the basic public services could be available at the CEC of the most lagging regions.

Figure 3.10. **Degree of advancement in the provision of basic public services "Banderas blancas"**

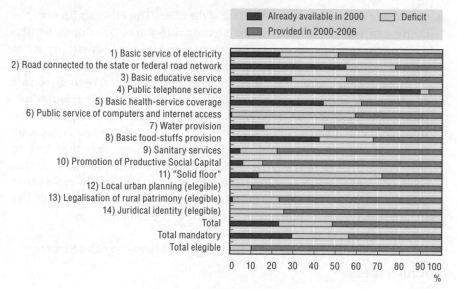

Source: OECD (2003), OECD calculations with data from SEDESOL.

Some *banderas blancas*, however have a much significant advance than others. Figure 3.10 shows the degree of advancement of each of them. The most advanced one is public telephone service which has covered the deficit in more than 90%. It is understandable then, the low priority of this area in the investment budget indicated before. The white flag that has relatively advanced the most is the "solid floor" flag which by 2001 was considered fulfilled in only 20% and in 2006 it reached more than 70%, and it is the result of the significant housing investment share of the programme. Other significant areas of advancement are the connectivity to the national network of roads (which has covered almost 80% of the deficit), the installation of public service computers and internet access, which advanced from zero to close to 60% of the deficit, as result of the significant investment in learning community centres (CCAs); as well as water and electricity provision which reached close to 50% of the deficit starting from close to 20%.

Little amount of resources. One of the most striking features when analysing the Micro-Regions Strategy not from its internal procedures or its institutional framework but within the amount of resources oriented to rural development is the low amount of resources that it receives. The Micro-Regions programme, adding the SEDESOL and the Ministry of Economy's participation, add only 0.3% of the PEC. It is true that the resources devoted to the programme does not constitute the total amount of resources of the strategy. Those funds are complemented by funds from other ministries, and from the resources transferred to states and municipalities. However, these additions allow for an increase of about 75% of the budget of the programme, which at the end is still an irrelevant figure in the total amount of resources spent in rural areas. In any case, the deficit approach of the programme allows a clear estimation of the investment needed for each of the *banderas blancas* in order to fulfil the total deficit in one more administration. The recent addition of new *banderas blancas* has increased the challenge: the total budget requirement is of 11 378 million MXP, which will imply an annual budget to the strategy of close to 1 900 million MXP, which is considerably higher than the 464 million MXP that received the LDP programme in 2006, even if complemented by an almost equal figure with other budgets.

Figure 3.11. **Deficit and cost of deficit of "Banderas blancas"**

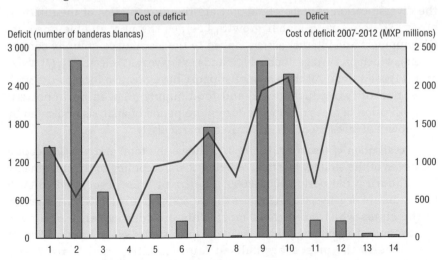

Source: OECD with information provided by SEDESOL.

The breakdown by *"banderas blancas"* of such cost brings important implications about where the resources should come from and therefore, what are the ministries or agencies which should have a protagonist role in the development of the strategy. There are three *banderas* whose deficit implies a cost of more than 2 400 million MXP (400 MXP by year): (2) Road construction, largely responsibility of the Ministry of Communications and Transportation, (9) Sanitary services, dependent on the National Commission of Water (CNA) and (10) Promotion of productive activities, dependent on the Micro-Regions Unit in SEDESOL in co ordination with the financial institutions and the Ministry of Economy. There is a second group of banderas with a cost higher than 1 200 million MXP (200 MXP by year): (1) Electricity service, dependent on the Federal Electricity Commission and (7) Water provision dependent on municipal governments and the CNA. Finally the rest of the issues represent a more manageable budget, which reaches 600 million MXP (100 million MXP by year) only for (3) Education and (5) Health infrastructure, and less than 240 million MXP (40 million MXP per year) for the rest.

Diversification areas of support. Figure 3.12 shows the distribution of the Micro-Regions Strategy funds by *"banderas blancas"* and average annual growth in funds for each area during the period 2002-2005. Several conclusions can be drawn from it: First, there is a clear preponderance of road construction as the area of support in which the strategy has invested the most (36%). This is not surprising given the costs of this type of support in comparison with other *white flags*. Second, there is a more or less equilibrated distribution of the remaining areas of support in around 10% of total investment, and some few that have very little resources ((8) food supply, (4) telephone and two eligible (14) juridical identity and (12) local urban planning)). An important signal of the diversification of areas of support are the growth rates of the different areas. The ones with higher growth, besides the new eligible ones are (6) computers and internet access, linked to the learning community centres (CCAs), which on average doubled its funds every year, (1) electricity, (7) water and (11) solid floor. All the areas of support have positive increments with exception of two: education (2) and food supply (8) been an important diversification of areas of support during the period of analysis, indicated by the growth of investment in certain areas, particularly.

Focalisation of resources. Figure 3.13 shows the total and per CEC capita resources of the strategy by state, ordering them according to the marginality index, during the period 2002-2005. The trend lines associated to both indicators are negative, which implies that at state level, resources are oriented to the states which need them most. This provides evidence of a good focalisation of resources, which is due in part to the *ex ante* orientation of resources to the most marginalised municipalities, which are vastly concentrated in the poorest states such as Chiapas, Oaxaca and Guerrero. There

OECD RURAL POLICY REVIEWS: MEXICO – ISBN 978-92-64-01152-6 – © OECD 2007

Figure 3.12. **Distribution and growth of investment by "Bandera blanca"**

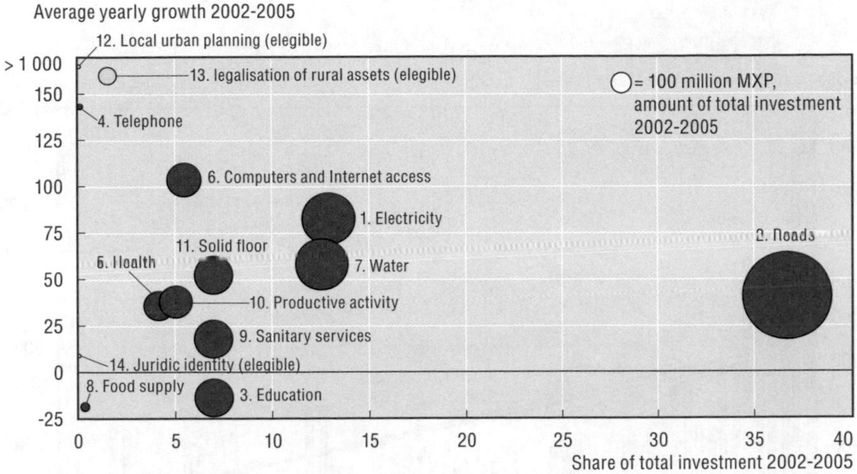

Average yearly growth 2002-2005

Source: OECD with data provided by SEDESOL.

are, however marked peaks for some states such as San Luis Potosí, Durango, Mexico, and Coahuila. However, contrasting the amount of resources to the population living in CEC localities in those states (which is not the total population of the micro-region but at least a proxy of the closest beneficiaries), the result is a surprisingly almost mirrored image of the distribution of funds, which evidences that even if those peaks are related to the marginalisation index by state, in per CEC capita terms the resources are oriented adequately.

This fact is also corroborated within the scope of the Local Development Programme in its external evaluation. (Figure 3.14) From 2002 to 2005 the total investment of this programme in municipalities of very high marginalisation was 290 million MXP, increasing in participation from 13% in 2002 to 21% in 2005. Municipalities with high marginalisation have always been the ones with higher participation (49% in 2002, 47% in 2005). They received in total 763 million MXP during the period of reference. Municipalities with medium marginalisation, received 296 million MXP during the period, increasing its participation from 14% to 19% during the period. Municipalities with low and very low marginalisation, as expected received only marginal 3.6% of the resources of the programme during the period. At locality level the focalisation of resources shows a similar pattern, during the period of reference, 17% of the resources went to very high marginalisation localities, 45% to high marginalisation, 18% to medium marginalisation and 8% to low and very low marginalisation localities. The relatively higher proportion of resources devoted to medium and lower marginalisation levels is related to a focalisation of the programme in CEC localities that will be described below.

Figure 3.13. **Focalisation of resources of the MR Strategy**
2002-2005

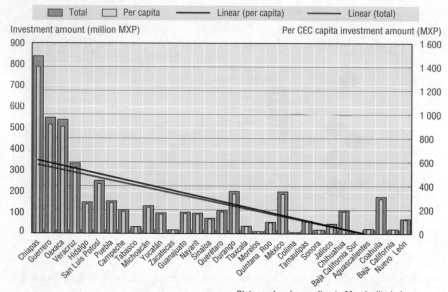

Source: OECD based on data provided by SEDESOL.

Figure 3.14. **Focalisation of LDP resources by type of municipality and locality 2002-2005**

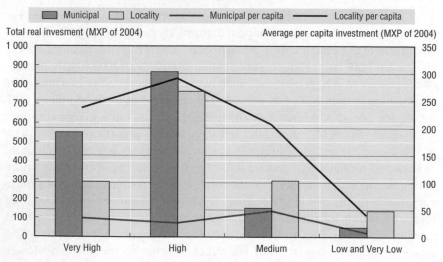

Source: Local Development Programme External Evaluation (2005).

OECD RURAL POLICY REVIEWS: MEXICO – ISBN 978-92-64-01152-6 – © OECD 2007

The external evaluation of the local development programme, which constitutes a core programme of the Micro-Regions Strategy, undertaken fully by SEDESOL, allows identifying other important results:

Greater coverage. The external evaluation of the LDP acknowledges a significant increase in the coverage of the programme. Of the 263 micro-regions, in 2002 only 113 (43%) were reached by the programme, whereas in 2005, 244 of them (92%) received attention. In the same sense, while the programme started attending 199 of the 1338 municipalities included in the micro-regions (15%), in 2005 projects fiom the programme were undertaken in 826 (62%). The number of localities attended by the programme almost tripled from 2002 to 2005, from 1 355 to 3 082. The percentage of coverage when compared to the Target is disproportionately low (of 1% in 2002 and 3% in 2005) because at locality level it is difficult to say that there is a target. Although the micro-regions include 99 891 localities, the orientation of the programme is not to attend every locality in the micro-region but to concentrate resources in the CECs. The high number of localities includes communities as small as two houses, which are not directly reached by the programme but are indirectly benefited by the development of their CEC. The same rationale could be applied for the population covered by the programme, whose figures should be considered indicative, since it is difficult to estimate the population "benefited" by the programme. One may argue that all the population living in the micro-regions to some extent is beneficiary of the strategy. The figures provided by the external evaluation show that in 2004, the year with greatest coverage in terms of population, the LDP reached almost 5 million people, 25% of the total population living in the micro-regions.

Table 3.2. **Coverage of the LDP of the MR Strategy**

	Micro-regions		Municipalities		Localities		Population	
	Number	Percentage (%)	Number	Percentage (%)	Number	Percentage (%)	Number	Percentage (%)
2002	113	43	199	15	1 355	1	2 316 582	12
2003	37	14	567	42	1 165	1	1 784 712	9
2004	183	70	875	65	2 822	3	4 995 723	25
2005	244	93	826	62	3 082	3	4 562 598	23
Target	263	100	1 338	100	99 891	100	19 900 000	100

Source: Local Development Programme External Evaluation (2005).

Concentration of budget in CEC localities. An important policy shift can be clearly identified from 2004 when investment in the localities identified as CEC was privileged over non-CEC localities. This situation that did not happen in 2002 and 2003 where resources oriented to non-CEC localities (182 million

MXP and 241 million MXP for 2002 and 2003 respectively) were higher than the amount oriented to CEC localities (68 and 111 million MXP, respectively). As Figure 3.15 shows, in 2004 this was reverted. In 2005 the amount destined for CEC localities was 326 million MXP while the amount devoted to non-CEC was 249 million. This change formalised by the introduction of a specific clause into the rules of operation of the programme, and is also reflected in the higher total and per capita amount received by localities of medium marginalisation, since by definition, the CECs are the most developed localities in a certain area and destined to be poles of development for the micro-region.

Figure 3.15. **Resources of the LDP by type of locality**

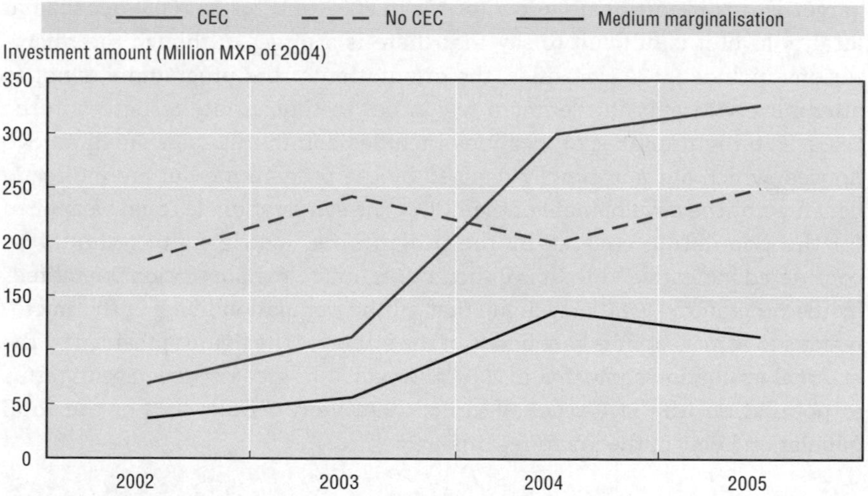

Source: Local Development Programme External Evaluation (2005).

Priorities for action

The strength of the Micro-Regions Strategy is the platform it offers for co-ordinated sectoral policy interventions in the most marginalised rural areas. In that context, the strategy would benefit from the following actions:

● **Institutionalisation of the Strategy.** In the face of a changing administration, it is important to further "institutionalise" the strategy through formal agreements that would foster co-ordination, make explicit the responsibilities and budget commitments of the ministries involved, and guarantee the continuity of a strategy. Despite its results, the strategy lacks of clear and transparent distribution of responsibilities and budgets among the ministries involved. Therefore there is a permanent effort of the co-ordination of the strategy to obtain funds for a particular micro-region project. In addition, the clarification of inputs and outputs is relevant for strengthening the strategy, both because of the increased transparency, as for the better understanding of the results. Since from a general perception, Micro-Regions is a programme of SEDESOL, the outcomes are often unjustly identified only with this ministry while, the recognition of the contribution of other ministries as well as state and municipal resources in an official manner, could strongly contribute to collaboration within the strategy, whereas the opposite might be a deterrent for investing in something from which *other* will accrue the benefit.

- *Greater resources for faster advancement* The strategy as such constitutes a best practice in terms of territorial policy. The positive advancements that the strategy has demonstrated as well as its clear focalisation of resources to the most marginalised communities, evidence the potential that a larger budget for the strategy could bring. If, as it is corroborated with the evaluations, in the four years of the strategy the focalisation of resources has allowed to close the deficit of basic infrastructure and services in the CECs, measured by the "banderas blancas" from two thirds to one third, a considerable increase in the resources of the strategy might allow to complete the remaining third in less time, to benefit more non-CEC communities or to extend the support to other investments that might have multiplier effects on the growth dynamics of those communities. However, as it was already pointed out, the addition of new *banderas* has given new dimensions and costs to the challenges. The specific ministries or agencies involved in this challenge were identified above, which leaves a concrete process of negotiation with these agencies and a concrete need for allocation of resources to the strategy either from their respective administrative budgets, from a greater specific allocation from the government to this strategy through the local development programme (LDP), or from new sources, which would imply involving private and/or international resources to a concrete development purpose.

- **Integration with other social and economic strategies.** The most valuable comparative advantage of the Micro-Regions Strategy is its territorial perspective. The actions of the strategy according to the last evaluation have enabled it to reach close to 5 million people in clearly identifiable regions. This people are recipients of a variety of policies and federal, state and local programmes outside of the specific multi-sectoral targets of the strategy. The identification of the synergies between these programmes and the strategy can certainly contribute to achieve grater outcomes. The relationship within territorial policies, and between territorial and sectoral policies is a challenge not only in Mexico but in all OECD countries. We have already pointed out the relevance of the relationship between the territorial strategy of SAGARPA and that of SEDESOL. It remains an important issue the relationship of the Micro-Regions Strategy with the overall social strategy of SEDESOL, in particular with its most important and institutional programme *Oportunidades*. Given the systematic consolidation of information of both *Oportunidades* and Micro-Regions Strategy, there is room for analysing opportunities of synergies in each of the 263 micro-regions. The resources that *Oportunidades* transfers in cash the localities within the micro-regions are substantial, given the initial focalisation of the programme. The impact of those resources in local development can be enhanced by adequate initiatives within the MR Strategy. On the other hand, for *Oportunidades* to establish in any community there is a specific need for counting with education and health services, which are already targets of the MR Strategy for all the CEC communities. The completion of the deficit in these two areas could effectively contribute to the extension of *Oportunidades* to localities that does not reach today.

- **Improve involvement of state authorities.** The top-down design of the strategy and the implied bottom-up perspective of the strategy might sometimes set aside key actors in the development of the Micro-Regions which are state governments. The evaluation of the programme shows good results in terms of the focalisation of resources to the most marginalised regions but at municipal and locality level. This is an imperative of the programme since there was an *a priori* focalisation objective in the selection of the regions to be served by the strategy. Still, at state level although the focalisation of resources is still progressive there are marked peaks for some states. This element might reflect that the engagement of the respective governments in the success of the programme might be strongly conductive to the canalisation of resources and therefore the achievement of progress.

- **Increase co-ordination with the relevant ministries and local authorities.** The final success or failure of the Micro-Regions Strategy may depend largely on the incentives actors might find to co-operate. The introduction of incentives schemes seems particularly important at the state level where it could be included in the signature of the *Convenio Annual* (annual agreement). At the level of municipalities, an important incentive to take part in the Micro-Regions Strategy is already present since it brings in the possibility to count on partnerships for investments that would otherwise be sustained by the municipality alone. A worthy experience pioneered in several OECD countries is the creation of funds to provide incentives for co-operation, but also to start a positive competition among rural areas in the quality of local initiatives.[12] An instructive example regarding the use of incentives to favour participation in space-based policies is represented by the Italian experience. In Italy, policy instruments like the Territorial Pacts (now evolving into the PIT – Integrated Territorial Planning), falling under the so-called "negotiated-planning" strategy, have made large use of performance reserves and incentives mechanisms (OECD, 2003b).

- **Monitoring of the Regional Development Outcomes.** The evaluation of the LDP evidences an important policy shift in favour of CEC localities since 2004. This shift goes in line with the objective of creating critical masses of public investment in these hubs for them to become poles of development. Two things are important to consider with this regard. First, it is important to monitor the development of the non-CEC communities and continue measuring the level of investment in these localities, because it is true that in terms of the CEC communities, important advances in reducing the deficit of basic infrastructure have been pursued, but the challenge of providing these services to all the population prevails, and it is possible that structural issues impede population from non-CEC communities to benefit from the investments made in their closest CEC. Secondly, it is important to evaluate outcomes of the strategy, and not only the outputs that represent the "banderas blancas". One of the most important outputs to be evaluated is whether the CECs themselves have become or not poles of development, and distinguish between those that have and those that don't. Several indicators such as education, income, employment, migration, monitored at CEC level could be used to obtain such a measure. The Index of Human Development and the Marginalisation Index, are too other indicators that can be measured at micro-region level.

Conclusion

The implementation of Mexico's innovative framework for organising the government to have a coherent rural policy has not been without challenges. The co-ordination framework proposed in the LDRS fails to work at its full potential and therefore would benefit from the dialog among the relevant actors to be improved. In particular, the two most relevant actors of rural policy, SAGARPA and SEDESOL have room for exploiting synergies within their own approaches. The governance of rural policy could be significantly enhanced by providing the Inter-Ministerial Commission for Sustainable Rural Development with stronger non-sectoral leadership, and by strengthening the process of decentralisation.

From a policy standpoint, priorities for Mexico's rural policy include: 1) poverty alleviation; 2) provision of basic public services; 3) strengthening and diversifying the rural economy; and finally, 4) better exploiting and preserving untapped cultural, natural and energy resources. Since these policy priorities extend the scope of any individual ministry the co-ordination of actions is necessary to pursue them efficiently. Although the Special Concerted Programme (PEC) constitutes an important effort towards the design of an integrated federal policy for rural development, it still exercised more as an inventory of programmes rather than a tool to exploit synergies between programmes impacting on rural areas. It could benefit from clear and transparent criteria for programme inclusion as well as better categorisation and organisation of the programmes oriented to generate synergies and avoid duplication of efforts. In addition, a more normative revision of the PEC and in general of "rural policy" should be made oriented to address the question of to what extent rural policy is addressing the challenges and opportunities present in rural areas, identified in Chapter 1. For rural policy to fully address these challenges and opportunities, the involvement of ministries that do not have a rural focus is important. The involvement of the ministries related to economic policy is particularly important in order to include rural areas in the competitiveness strategy of the country.

The policies specifically targeting rural development, described in Chapter 2 are analysed with greater detail in this chapter, based on external evaluations available, in search of improvements in their efficiency and effectiveness. Despite having grown in importance and budget in the past years, these policies constitute a relatively small share of the budget of their respective ministries. The evaluation of SAGARPA's Programa de Desarrollo Rural (PDR) demonstrates that its comparative advantages lie in the support to marginalised regions, low income producers and non-agricultural activities. The specialisation in these comparative advantages, and particularly in diversifying the rural economy could result in a better focalisation of resources than the one that presently has. SEDESOL's Micro-Regions Strategy, on its part should build on its institutionalisation as a multi-sectoral strategy and consolidate its advances in the completion of its targeted "banderas blancas", which reach close to 60% of the total deficit. However, the variation in the completion of such deficit urges for efforts on the advancement of the lagging ones. The strategy is at a stage in which a greater co-ordination with other social and economic strategies could generate higher impact. In particular, there is room for greater benefit from the impact of the *Oportunidades* programme and of public resources transferred to the micro-regions.

Notes

1. The difference between outputs and outcomes is widely used in the public policy discipline. Outputs refer to the results of the process of a public policy, for example the number of roads constructed. Outcomes refer to the degree in which the policy objective is achieved, that is for example the degree of connectivity achieved with the construction of roads. Significant outcomes to be considered for public policy in Mexico are reduction of poverty, degree of access and quality of public services, degree of diversification of the rural economy, etc.

2. The SHCP budget does not include the National Commission for the Development of the Indigenous Population (CONADEPI), which is circumscribed to this ministry for budgetary issues.

3. Please refer to the OECD PISA study (2003) available online at *www.oecd.org*.

4. Chapter 2 makes a quick review of agricultural policies. Specific recommendations for this sector are however beyond the scope of this review. Please refer to the OECD (2006c) for greater detail in this matter.

5. In Ajutla, 53.7% of homes received remittances, in General Franco Murguia it was 47.7%, in Chilla de la Sal, 47.2%, in Santa Ana del Valle, 45.5%, in Cuatla, 41.1%, and in Sustican, 40.7%.

6. Please refer to the OECD (2006c) which provide concrete recommendations for the fisheries sector.

7. FONATUR with information of 2000.

8. World Tourism Organisation

9. From the external evaluation of the programme, undertaken by FAO in 2004 and from a recent publication of the World Bank (2006).

10. The indicators are schooling, irrigation area that they have, scale of operation of livestock producers, assets and technology available. The following table describes the characteristics of each of them:

Average characteristics	Type of beneficiary					
	I	II	III	IV	V	Total
Beneficiaries (%)	37.8	41.9	17.8	2.5	0.0	100.0
Age (years)	45.2	45.3	45.9	53.9	43.0	45.3
Education (years)	4.8	6.3	8.9	14.3	19.0	6.5
Value of assets (MxP)	1 799	56 557	208 853	662 765	512 000	83 503
Number of equivalent cattle units	5.6	8.3	13.8	28.6	71.0	8.9
Irrigated land equivalent (hectare)	0.8	3.0	11.1	33.1	10.0	4.6
Technological level	0.2	0.3	0.5	0.6	0.8	0.3

Source: FAO (2005).

11. At the time of the writing of this report the first external evaluation of the overall strategy, comprising the work of all the ministries involved, was being elaborated. Therefore the analysis was made on information provided by the co-ordination Unit of the Micro-Regions Strategy.

12. Whether these mechanisms can be built around the conditional fund structure of the "Ramo 22" for Social Development or other resources remains to be determined.

ISBN 978-92-64-01152-6
OECD Rural Policy Reviews: Mexico
© OECD 2007

Bibliography

Alvarado, O. and K. Kemper (2001), "Water", in M. Gingale, Olivier Lafourcade and Vinh Nguyen (eds.), *Mexico: A Comprehensive Development Agenda for the New Era*, The World Bank, Washington, DC, pp. 619-643.

Attanasio, O. and M. Székely (1999), "Introducción: la pobreza en América Latina. Análisis basado en los activos", *El trimestre económico*, Vol. 66, No. 263.

AT Kearney (2003), "Reordenamiento Administrativo en Materia de Desarrollo Rural", final presentation, 23 October 2003.

Banco de México, Indicadores Económicos, *www.banxico.org.mx*.

Ceron Monroy, H. (2004), "El Rol del Empleo no Agropecuario como estrategia de Ingreso en la Reducción de la Pobreza", in *El Sector Rural De México*, El Colegio de México.

CIDRS (2003), "Comisión Intersecretarial para el Desarrollo Rural Sustentable", Reordenamiento Administrativo en Materia de Desarrollo Rural, presentation, June 2003.

CONAPO (2001a), Consejo Nacional de Población, Índices de Marginación 2000. Available online at *www.conapo.gob.mx*.

CONAPO (2001b), Consejo Nacional de Población, Índice de Desarrollo Humano Municipal 2000, in La población de México en el nuevo siglo, available online at *www.conapo.gob.mx*.

CONAPO (2004), Consejo Nacional de Población, "Distribución Territorial de los Adultos Mayores", in *Situación Demográfica de México*, note elaborated by Carlos Anzaldo, Juan Carlos Hernández and Minerva Prado, available online at *www.conapo.gob.mx*.

De Janvry, Alain; Araujo Caridad and Sadoulet Elizabeth. "El Desarrollo Rural con una Visión Territorial". Paper presented at the Seminar "Enfoque Territorial en el Desarrollo Rural" of INCA Rural, Boca del Río Veracruz, October 2000.

Díaz Cayeros, A. (1995), *Desarrollo Económico e Inequidad Regional: Hacia un Nuevo Pacto Federal en México*, Fundación Friedrich Naumann, Centro de Investigación para el Desarrollo, A. C., Miguel Ángel Porrúa, Las Ciencias Sociales, Colección.

FAO (2005), *Evaluación Nacional Alianza para el Campo 2004*, Evaluación del Programa de Desarrollo Rural.

INAFED (2000) Sistema Nacional de Información Municipal (SNIM) Versión 7.0. Instituto Nacional para el Federalismo y el Desarrollo Municipal. Secretaría de Gobernación.

INEGI (1999a), *Censos Económicos*, Instituto Nacional de Estadística Geografía e Informática.

INEGI (1999b), *Resultados del Levantamiento Censal en Área Rural*, Censos Económicos 1999, Instituto Nacional de Estadística, Geografía e Informática, pp. 9-10.

INEGI (2004a), Información Georeferenciada Espacialmente Integrada en un Sistema (IRIS) Instituto Nacional de Estadística, Geografía e Informática, Versión 3.0.

INEGI (2004b), *Censos Económicos*, Instituto Nacional de Estadística, Geografía e Informática.

INEGI (2005), *Conteo de Población y Vivienda 2005*, Instituto Nacional de Estadística, Geografía e Informática.

INEGI (2006), *Series Históricas en Gráficas*, available online at *www.inegi.gob.mx*.

Ley de Desarrollo Rural Sustentable (LDRS), México 2001.

McKenzie, D.J. (2006), "Beyond Remittances: The Effects of Migration on Mexican Households", in C. Osden and M. Schiff (eds.), *International Migration, Remittances and the Brain Drain*, The World Bank and Palgrave Macmillan, Washington, DC.

Mora, J. and J.E. Taylor (2006), "Determinants of Migration, Destination, and Sector Choice: Disentangling Individual, Household, and Community Effects", in C. Osden and M. Schiff (eds.), *International Migration, Remittances and the Brain Drain*, The World Bank and Palgrave Macmillan, Washington, DC.

OECD (1994a), *Creating Rural Indicators for Shaping Territorial Policies*, OECD Publications, Paris.

OCDE (1994b), *Tourism Strategies and Rural Development*, OECD Publications, Paris.

OECD (2003a), *OECD Territorial Reviews: Mexico*, OECD Publications, Paris.

OECD (2003b), "Horizontal Review on Multi-Level Governance and Rural Development. The Micro-Regions Strategy (Mexico)", document submitted for discussion to Working Group on Territorial Policy for Rural Areas at its 5th Session, Paris, November 2003.

OECD (2003c), *Environmental Performance Reviews: Mexico*, OECD Publications, Paris.

OECD (2005a), *Regions at a Glance*, OECD Publications, Paris.

OECD (2005b), *Trade and Structural Adjustment: Embracing Globalisation*, OECD Publications, Paris.

OECD (2006a), *The New Rural Paradigm: Policies and Governance*, OECD Publications, Paris.

OECD (2006b), *OECD Territorial Reviews: The Mesoamerican Region. South-eastern Mexico and Central America*, OECD Publications, Paris.

OECD (2006c), *Agricultural and Fisheries Policies in Mexico. Recent Achievements, Continuing the Reform Agenda*, OECD Publications, Paris.

Presidencia de la República (2004), *Evolución Reciente del Bienestar de la Población Rural*, note prepared by the Oficina de la Presidencia para las Políticas Publicas for the Comisión Intersecretarial para el Desarrollo Rural Sustentable, 23 June 2004.

Presidencia de la República (2005), *Quinto Informe de Gobierno 2005*, Anexo estadístico, available online at *http://quinto.informe.presidencia.gob.mx/*.

Ruiz Castillo, J. (2005), An Evaluation of "El ingreso rural y la producción agropecuaria en México 1989-2002", Servicio de Información Agropecuaria y Pesquera, SIAP.

Rios Piter, Armando (2006), YOUNG FARMERS: An Engine for the Rural Sector. Presentation at the OECD Rural Conference 2006 "Investment Priorities for Rural Development", Edinburgh, Scotland, October 2006.

OECD RURAL POLICY REVIEWS: MEXICO – ISBN 978-92-64-01152-6 – © OECD 2007

PEC (2002), *Programa Especial Concurrente para el Desarrollo Rural Sustentable 2002-2006*, Poder Ejecutivo Federal, Comisión Intersecretarial para el Desarrollo Rural Sustentable.

SEDESOL (2006) Instrumentos Para la Medición de la Pobreza, PowerPoint presentation.

SEMARNAT (2002), "Inventario Nacional de Suelos", México, 2002, from *Carta de uso del suelo y vegetación*, serie II del INEGI (2002).

SEMARNAT (2006), Secretaría del Medio Ambiente y Recursos Naturales, *www.semarnat.gob.mx.*

SIAP (2006), "Servicio de Información y Estadística Agroalimentaria y Pesquera", *Encuesta Nacional de Ingreso-Gasto de los Hogares* (1992-2004), elaborated by the Instituto Nacional de Estadística Geografía e Informática, INEGI, *www.siap.gob.mx.*

Sojo, E. (2004), *De la Planeación Centralista al Desarrollo Regional.*

Sojo, E. and R. Villareal (2004), "Public Policies to Promote the Productive Occupation and Increase Formality among Population in Moderate Poverty", paper presented at the EGDI-WIDER Conference on "Unlocking Human Potential: Linking the Informal and Formal Sectors", September 2004, Helsinki.

Wodon, Q., D. Angel-Urdinola, D. Revah and C. Siaens (2002), "Migration and Poverty in Mexico's Southern States", in *Development Strategy for the Mexican Southern States*, The World Bank, Washington, DC.

World Bank (2005), *A Study of Rural Poverty in Mexico*, The World Bank Report No. 32867MX, Washington, DC.

World Bank (2006), *Mexico: Programatic Poverty Study*, Part 3, Decentralisation of Rural Development Programmes, July 2006.

Yúnez-Naude, A. and E. Taylor, E., *Los determinantes de las actividades y el ingreso no agrícola de los hogares rurales de México, con énfasis en la educación*, Comisión Económica para América Latina y el Caribe CEPAL, Seminarios y conferencias, No. 35.

ISBN 978-92-64-01152-6
OECD Rural Policy Reviews: Mexico
© OECD 2007

Évaluation et recommandations (Français)

Caractéristiques du Mexique rural : enjeux et perspectives

*L'importance de la superficie et de la population
des zones rurales contraste avec leur faible
contribution au PIB*

Les régions rurales représentent plus de 80 % de la superficie du Mexique et abritent 37 millions d'habitants environ (36 % de la population du pays). Le Mexique est ainsi le pays de l'OCDE qui compte la plus forte population dans les zones essentiellement rurales. Malgré leur importance sur le plan de la superficie et de la population, les régions rurales ne prennent qu'une part modeste à l'économie. Le contraste est particulièrement saisissant si l'on adopte la définition mexicaine de la localité rurale (localité de moins de 2 500 habitants), puisque les régions rurales représentent alors près d'un quart de la population mais seulement 2 % du PIB national (voir graphique F.1).

*Les régions rurales doivent faire face
à des difficultés liées à la dispersion
des habitations...*

La population rurale du Mexique est très dispersée : 24 millions de personnes occupent en effet plus de 196 000 localités isolées et 13 millions de plus vivent dans quelque 3 000 localités rurales *semi-urbaines*. Cette dispersion est due au caractère montagneux d'une grande partie du territoire, et dans une certaine mesure au fractionnement des terres, ainsi qu'au manque de clarté des droits de propriété dans le cadre du régime des biens communaux. C'est pourquoi, depuis la redistribution des terres qui a suivi la révolution, de nombreux propriétaires terriens et leurs descendants se sentent fortement incités à rester près de leurs terres, mais loin des marchés et des services publics, ce qui limite leurs activités à une agriculture de subsistance ou de faible productivité.

... à une baisse de la population...

La croissance démographique des régions rurales se distingue de celle du reste du pays. À l'inverse de la population nationale et urbaine, en forte hausse et concentrée, la population rurale, restée relativement stable et dispersée pendant la deuxième moitié du XXe siècle, a diminué en termes relatifs.

OECD RURAL POLICY REVIEWS: MEXICO – ISBN 978-92-64-01152-6 – © OECD 2007

Graphique F.1. **Le Mexique rural**

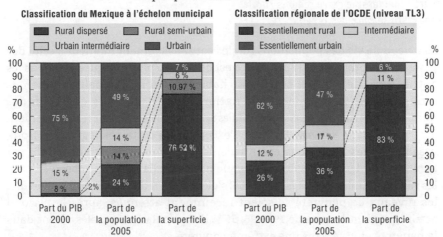

Source : *Panorama des régions de* l'OCDE, à paraître, et calculs effectués à partir de données de l'INAFED (2000) et de l'INEGI (2006).

Depuis 2000, la population des localités *rurales dispersées* baisse aussi en termes absolus. Cette évolution résulte de deux phénomènes combinés : la baisse des taux de fécondité enregistrée dans la dernière décennie, qui a beaucoup réduit le taux de dépendance des enfants et des personnes âgées, et l'exode des jeunes en direction de villes de taille moyenne et de l'étranger, qui a de nombreuses conséquences sur le plan social et économique, comme la féminisation de la population rurale, la hausse du taux de dépendance des personnes âgées, et l'accroissement de la part des envois de fonds dans les revenus.

Graphique F.2. **Population des zones urbaines et rurales**
1910-2005

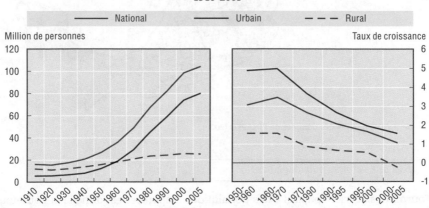

1. Le terme « rural » s'applique aux localités de moins de 2 500 habitants.
Source : INEGI (2006).

... à l'écart considérable entre régions rurales et urbaines, sur le plan des revenus....

Le niveau de vie des populations rurales est sensiblement inférieur à celui des populations urbaines et la différence est beaucoup plus marquée que dans les autres pays de l'OCDE. Le PIB par habitant des municipalités urbaines atteignait 141 % de la moyenne nationale en 2000, alors que celui des municipalités *rurales dispersées* et *rurales semi-urbaines* s'élevait respectivement à 27 % et 43 % seulement. En fait, à l'exception de certaines régions du Nord, presque toutes les régions essentiellement rurales enregistrent un PIB par habitant inférieur à 50 % de la moyenne nationale (la moyenne observée pour les régions rurales des pays de l'OCDE s'élève à 82 % du PIB national). Bien que les niveaux de pauvreté se soient récemment atténués, après le plafond atteint pendant la crise de 1995-96, 56 % des populations rurales vivent dans la pauvreté et 28 % dans une extrême pauvreté.

Graphique F.3. **PIB par habitant dans les régions essentiellement rurales en pourcentage du PIB par habitant national**

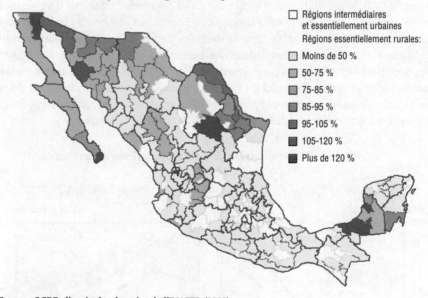

Source : OCDE, d'après des données de l'INAFED (2000).

... et de l'accès aux services publics de base.

Fournir des services publics à des populations dispersées est difficile et coûteux, et le niveau de vie des populations rurales s'en ressent. Les niveaux d'infrastructures ainsi que des services de santé et d'éducation des localités les

OECD RURAL POLICY REVIEWS: MEXICO – ISBN 978-92-64-01152-6 – © OECD 2007

moins accessibles sont faibles. Parmi les logements des populations *rurales dispersées*, 68 % seulement avaient un sol en dur, 52 % un système d'évacuation des eaux, 87 % l'électricité et 16 % une ligne de téléphone en 2000. La durée de la scolarité dans ces populations est inférieure à cinq ans, alors qu'elle est de 7.8 ans dans les zones urbaines et de 9.7 ans à Mexico. Les ménages vivant en habitat *rural dispersé*, dont 80 % seulement ont accès à des services à moins de cinq kilomètres de chez eux, ne disposent que de 22 lits d'hôpitaux et de 96 médecins pour 100 000 habitants, contre 109 lits et 179 médecins dans les zones urbaines. Cette situation influe sur l'espérance de vie, qui, dans certaines municipalités rurales, est inférieure de dix ans à celle de Mexico, et sur les taux de mortalité infantile, trois fois plus élevés que dans la capitale.

Il existe cependant de nombreuses perspectives favorables liées à « l'avantage démographique » dont bénéficient les zones rurales...

L'ampleur impressionnante des défis à relever a tendance à masquer l'hétérogénéité des zones rurales et les possibilités liées à d'abondantes ressources inexploitées. L'exploitation de ces possibilités pourrait contribuer au renforcement de l'économie rurale et soutenir la croissance nationale. Tout d'abord, la population rurale est majoritairement jeune, l'âge médian étant de 20 ans. Cette génération, qui fera partie de la population active dans une décennie, est un élément de « l'avantage démographique » dont bénéficie le Mexique par suite de la transition démographique. Elle pourrait contribuer à une amélioration de la production et de la croissance économique, comme on l'a observé dans d'autres pays de l'OCDE. En outre, bien que les indicateurs moyens de scolarisation des zones rurales restent très bas (parce qu'ils incluent aussi la population active), l'accès au cycle secondaire et le taux d'achèvement des études secondaires montrent que la jeune génération est mieux préparée que les précédentes. De nombreuses études indiquent aussi que les jeunes ruraux mexicains ont souvent un esprit d'entreprise affirmé et connaissent mieux les possibilités offertes par les marchés et les technologies nouvelles.

... aux vastes possibilités de diversification économique...

Deuxièmement, les problèmes rencontrés mais aussi les perspectives d'avenir sont liés à la transformation en cours de l'économie rurale du Mexique. La contribution de l'agriculture, de la foresterie et de la pêche au PIB a été ramenée de 8 % en 1990 à 5 % en 2004. Cependant, l'agriculture reste le secteur qui emploie le plus de main-d'œuvre dans les municipalités rurales dispersées (dont les populations travaillent à 44 % dans le secteur primaire). La part de ce secteur est plus élevée au Mexique que dans les pays de l'OCDE en moyenne, aussi bien pour les régions essentiellement rurales (30 % contre 10 %) que pour l'économie nationale (16 % contre 6 % en moyenne dans la zone de l'OCDE). Les gros exploitants agricoles ont pu pénétrer les marchés internationaux et augmenter considérablement leurs exportations, mais les petites exploitations sont pour la plupart encore peu diversifiées, limitées à des produits de faible valeur et très mal armées pour faire face aux fluctuations des prix. Le passage de l'agriculture à d'autres activités est rapide dans les zones rurales. Deux éléments en témoignent. Premièrement, la part des activités non agricoles dans le revenu a beaucoup augmenté (au point de représenter plus de 50 % des revenus, même dans les habitats ruraux dispersés). Deuxièmement, l'emploi non agricole a progressé davantage dans les régions rurales (5.2 %) que dans les régions urbaines (3.5 %) entre 1999 et 2004.

Graphique F.4. **Diversification de l'économie rurale : Taux de croissance de l'emploi rural et urbain dans les secteurs non agricoles.**

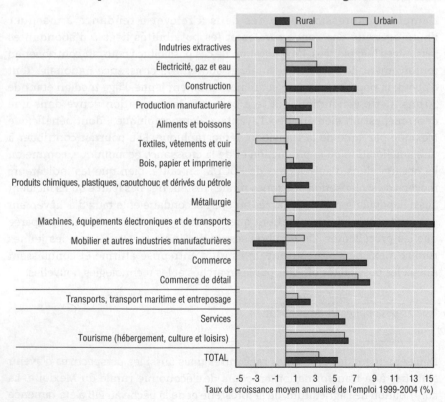

Le terme « rural » inclut les localités rurales (de moins de 2 500 habitants) et rurales semi-urbaines (de moins de 15 000 habitants).

Source : INEGI, Recensement économique 1999, 2004.

OECD RURAL POLICY REVIEWS: MEXICO – ISBN 978-92-64-01152-6 – © OECD 2007

La première activité choisie par les exploitants qui ont quitté l'agriculture est le commerce de détail. Ce secteur déjà important a connu une forte croissance pendant la période 1999-2004 (8.5 %). Les activités manufacturières ont enregistré une hausse moins nette, néanmoins supérieure à celle qu'elles ont connue dans les régions urbaines, ce qui semble indiquer un déplacement de certaines industries vers des zones moins urbanisées. Il faut signaler que les secteurs manufacturiers qui ont connu une croissance plus forte dans les zones rurales sont des secteurs de pointe comme les machines, l'électronique et les transports (15 %, voir graphique F.4) La diversification de l'économie rurale varie d'une région à l'autre. Bien que sa contribution à l'amélioration du niveau de vie ne soit pas facile à évaluer, on sait que le PIB par habitant des régions essentiellement rurales des États du Nord les plus diversifiées, comme le Nuevo León, la Basse-Californie, la Basse-Californie du Sud et Coahuila, est plus élevé que la moyenne dans les zones rurales mais aussi que la moyenne nationale.

… et à la présence de ressources naturelles, culturelles et énergétiques inexploitées.

Troisièmement, il est intéressant de souligner la croissance de secteurs comme le tourisme qui peuvent constituer une nouvelle source de revenus. De 1999 à 2004, le tourisme a fait partie des secteurs qui enregistraient les plus forts taux de croissance, qui sont là aussi légèrement plus élevés dans les zones rurales (6.3 %) que dans les zones urbaines. En 2004, 9 % des emplois du secteur touristique se situaient dans des zones rurales. Le sud-est et la péninsule de Basse-Californie comportent des zones rurales où le tourisme représente un pourcentage particulièrement élevé de l'emploi et de la valeur ajoutée brute (plus de 25 %). En particulier, dans le sud-sud-est, la partie la plus pauvre du pays, les ressources naturelles, le patrimoine culturel et les sites archéologiques et historiques d'une grande richesse pourraient devenir des facteurs essentiels de développement économique. Il existe aussi dans les zones rurales un potentiel inexploité de sources d'énergies renouvelables, solaire, éolienne, hydraulique et bio-énergie. L'expérience de nombreux pays membres et non membres de l'OCDE montre que les zones rurales peuvent apporter une contribution importante à l'approvisionnement en énergie du pays et de leur propre territoire, tout en offrant des sources nouvelles de revenus et d'emplois aux populations locales.

Il existe en fait plusieurs Mexiques ruraux, dont
les difficultés et les potentialités sont différentes

Les régions rurales présentent une grande hétérogénéité; même s'il existe des « ruraux pauvres », on ne peut généraliser en assimilant « rural » à « pauvre ». Une partie de l'économie rurale est fortement liée aux secteurs de l'agriculture, de la foresterie et de la pêche, mais il existe des zones rurales qui se sont diversifiées dans les secteurs de la production manufacturière et des services. Certaines régions rurales sont déjà devenues des destinations touristiques et d'autres comptent encore des ressources naturelles et culturelles inexploitées. Les politiques rurales du Mexique doivent donc répondre à des impératifs très divers, comme 1) la réduction de la pauvreté; 2) la mise à disposition de services publics de base; 3) le renforcement et la diversification de l'économie rurale; et enfin 4) l'amélioration de l'exploitation et de la préservation des ressources culturelles, naturelles et énergétiques inexploitées.

Comment le Mexique aborde-t-il les enjeux et les perspectives des régions rurales?

Le Mexique a pris des mesures novatrices en
se dotant d'un cadre intersectoriel à plusieurs
niveaux en faveur des politiques rurales.

La démarche mexicaine en matière de politiques rurales, autrefois centrée sur un secteur unique (l'agriculture), a évolué au cours des dernières décennies pour privilégier l'intégration des actions de différents ministères et niveaux d'administration (fédération, États et municipalités) dans les zones rurales. Le nouveau cadre institutionnel de ces changements se fonde sur la loi relative au développement rural durable, approuvée en 2001, qui prévoit l'établissement d'un organe fédéral horizontal de coordination spécialement chargé des politiques rurales (la Commission interministérielle de développement rural durable, CIDRS), la création d'organes participatifs rassemblant les organisations de la société civile (Conseils de développement rural durable), et l'élaboration d'un Programme spécial concerté en faveur du développement rural (PEC). Ce dernier a abouti à la création d'un « budget rural » annexé chaque année au budget fédéral. L'analyse du budget fédéral montre que les programmes fédéraux qui influent sur les régions rurales comportent essentiellement deux types de politiques : des politiques sociales (lutte contre la pauvreté, mesures en faveur de l'éducation et de la santé) et des politiques de « soutien productif », axées sur l'agriculture. D'autres mesures fédérales influent de façon significative sur les zones rurales, comme la création d'infrastructures de base et d'infrastructures de production ou la protection de l'environnement, les politiques foncières et de l'emploi.

Les deux acteurs les plus importants
des politiques rurales mettent en œuvre
des programmes explicitement orientés
vers le développement rural...

Les deux ministères dont l'action influe le plus sur les zones rurales, le ministère de l'agriculture, de l'élevage, du développement rural, de la pêche et de l'alimentation (SAGARPA) et le ministère du développement social (SEDESOL) mettent en œuvre, chacun dans leur domaine de compétences, des politiques spécialement axées sur le développement rural. D'une part, le Programme de développement rural (PDR) du SAGARPA, l'un des programmes fédéraux les plus décentralisés du Mexique, soutient des investissements productifs en faveur de l'agriculture, de l'élevage et d'activités non agricoles, mis en place en fonction de la demande et dans le cadre de projets. Deux composantes complémentaires s'y ajoutent, le soutien technique et le soutien organisationnel. Ce dernier a joué un rôle essentiel dans la construction de l'architecture institutionnelle imposée par la loi sur le développement rural durable. D'autre part, le SEDESOL a adopté une stratégie d'aide à des microrégions qui prévoit des actions interministérielles visant spécialement les régions rurales les plus marginalisées, auxquelles seront fournies les infrastructures de base et les conditions nécessaires au développement autour de certains « micropôles » de développement, appelés *Centres stratégiques communautaires* (CEC). La spécificité du contenu de cette stratégie permet de suivre les progrès et les insuffisances de chaque domaine d'action au moyen de mécanismes de validation objectifs et communs appelés « *banderas blancas* » (drapeaux blancs).

... qui suivent des objectifs différents selon
une démarche intégrée.

Le PDR et la stratégie d'aide aux microrégions présentent plusieurs aspects qui correspondent aux meilleures pratiques de l'OCDE : 1) ils adoptent une perspective territoriale et intégrée du développement rural qui s'étend à d'autres secteurs; 2) ils ne reposent pas sur des subventions mais plutôt sur des investissements et; 3) ils coordonnent les efforts d'acteurs multiples, le PDR par une orientation verticale plus prononcée (due à son caractère décentralisé) et la stratégie d'aide aux microrégions dans une perspective plus horizontale (en raison de son caractère interministériel). Cependant, ils diffèrent aussi beaucoup dans leurs objectifs et leurs méthodes : 1) le PDR vise les zones rurales en général, tandis que la stratégie d'aide aux microrégions est axée sur une petite partie des zones rurales, les plus marginalisées et les plus pauvres; 2) le PDR s'efforce plutôt d'aider les populations rurales en tant qu'agents économiques ou producteurs, tandis que la stratégie met l'accent sur leurs droits et leurs conditions de vie; 3) les actions du PDR sont plutôt conçues en fonction de la demande (les bénéficiaires soumettent des projets pour obtenir un soutien), tandis que la stratégie coordonne les politiques de différents ministères dans des zones spécifiques.

Enjeux essentiels et priorités de l'action

Le cadre de gouvernance en faveur
du développement rural pourrait être amélioré
par une direction plus forte…

La *coordination horizontale* au niveau fédéral pose deux types essentiels de problèmes. Le premier concerne la coordination des 14 ministères représentés à la CIDRS. Le SAGARPA (qui la préside) a manifestement rencontré des difficultés pour obtenir la participation et l'engagement des autres ministères. D'après l'expérience acquise dans d'autres pays de l'OCDE, le fait de confier la présidence d'une commission horizontale à l'un des secteurs participants (l'agriculture dans le cas de la CIDRS) risque de limiter la réalisation de ses objectifs plurisectoriels et d'empêcher les autres ministères de participer pleinement à la mise en place d'une stratégie rurale nationale. La gestion des politiques rurales et l'engagement des différents participants pourraient être considérablement améliorés si la CIDRS avait une direction « méta-ministérielle » plus forte. On pourrait par exemple en confier la présidence au chef de l'exécutif, ou créer un organe *ad hoc*, ou prévoir une rotation des différents ministères à la tête de la Commission.

… une meilleure coordination horizontale entre
les principaux ministères…

Le deuxième problème concerne la coordination entre le SAGARPA et le SEDESOL, les deux ministères qui interviennent le plus dans les affaires rurales. Tous deux sont en effet guidés par des logiques différentes et s'appuient sur des lois différentes. Chacune de ces lois leur confère une « autorité » dans les commissions interministérielles (l'une sur les politiques sociales et l'autre sur les politiques rurales) auxquelles prennent habituellement part les mêmes ministères. En outre, le SEDESOL coordonne la stratégie d'aide aux microrégions qui repose aussi sur un organe interministériel. Ce problème institutionnel se prolonge aux niveaux infranationaux, où les deux ministères ont des structures administratives parallèles qui agissent souvent sur les mêmes territoires : le SAGARPA s'appuie pour l'essentiel sur les Conseils de développement rural (qu'il a créés) dans le cadre de la loi relative au développement rural durable, tandis que le SEDESOL se sert davantage des organes locaux de planification déjà en place (COPLADE et COPLADEMUN). Aux délégations dont ils disposent dans les 31 États du Mexique s'ajoutent les structures décentralisées dont se servent les deux ministères pour la mise en œuvre de leurs programmes au niveau local, comme les « résidents » dans le cas de la stratégie des microrégions du SEDESOL et les « promoteurs » du SAGARPA. Il devrait être possible de trouver une meilleure organisation qui exploite les synergies des politiques rurales et sociales et de constituer un réseau commun d'institutions garantissant l'efficacité des politiques des deux ministères au niveau local. De telles modifications permettraient de définir les complémentarités de leurs démarches respectives : les politiques du SEDESOL visent à fournir aux habitants des zones rurales une plate-forme de base pour le développement tandis que la politique rurale du SAGARPA, polyvalente et orientée vers le développement économique, peut intervenir efficacement une fois que cette plate-forme est en place.

... et une définition plus claire des responsabilités des différents niveaux d'administration.

D'après la loi sur le développement rural, le fédéralisme et la décentralisation sont les critères de base de la mise en œuvre du programme de développement rural. Cependant, chaque ministère a défini des critères et des stratégies différents de décentralisation de ses propres politiques. C'est pourquoi certains programmes décentralisés au niveau local sont inefficaces, parce que des politiques complémentaires n'ont pas été décentralisées. Pour renforcer la décentralisation des politiques de développement rural, il faut : 1) trouver un accord sur les domaines d'action à décentraliser dans chaque ministère, axé sur les complémentarités qui existent entre eux, 2) définir les responsabilités (en termes de budget et de reddition des comptes) et les fonctions (élaboration, conception, mise en œuvre et évaluation des règles applicables) des différents niveaux d'administration, et 3) renforcer les capacités locales, en particulier au niveau municipal, et assurer la continuité des capacités en place, tâche difficile compte tenu de la brièveté des mandats municipaux.

S'il offrait une cohérence et une transparence
plus grandes, le Programme spécial concerté pourrait
renforcer l'efficience des budgets consacrés aux zones
rurales…

Sur le plan de l'action publique, les priorités des politiques de développement rural du Mexique portent sur : 1) la réduction de la pauvreté; 2) la mise à disposition de services publics de base; 3) le renforcement et la diversification de l'économie rurale; et enfin 4) l'amélioration de l'exploitation et de la préservation des ressources culturelles, naturelles et énergétiques inexploitées. Ces priorités correspondent aux attributions de plusieurs ministères, de sorte qu'il est nécessaire de coordonner les actions pour qu'elles soient efficaces. Le Programme spécial concerté (PEC) constitue un progrès important vers la conception d'une politique fédérale intégrée de développement rural, mais il s'apparente davantage à un inventaire de programmes qu'à un outil d'exploitation des synergies entre les activités qui influent sur les zones rurales. Il inclut en fait des programmes et des institutions qui ne sont pas tournées vers le développement rural. L'image de la stratégie fédérale dans le domaine rural reste donc floue et les données de dépenses rurales ne correspondent pas complètement à la réalité. Pour tirer pleinement avantage de cette innovation, il faudrait s'efforcer : 1) d'accroître la transparence des critères d'intégration des programmes au PEC et la part des programmes qui peut être considérée comme orientée vers les zones rurales, 2) d'engager un dialogue qui puisse aboutir à la fusion, au transfert et à l'élimination de certains programmes, pour obtenir un ensemble d'instruments cohérents et efficaces de soutien aux zones rurales. Des efforts ont été accomplis dans ce sens mais il faut que les différents ministères fassent preuve d'une volonté politique plus forte et que la CIDRS assure une direction de qualité; 3) de mettre en place des mécanismes de suivi et d'évaluation des produits et des résultats des politiques rurales du PEC en fonction des objectifs approuvés.

… et orienter les ressources publiques vers
les priorités du développement rural,…

À l'heure actuelle, les ressources fédérales investies dans les régions rurales ne correspondent pas bien aux priorités définies : un objectif sectoriel (l'agriculture) et un objectif horizontal (la réduction de la pauvreté) dominent les politiques rurales. Les nombreux investissements effectués dans ces deux domaines contribuent à atténuer la pauvreté et à renforcer l'économie rurale, mais il serait possible de créer des synergies si les ressources investies dans la mise à disposition de services publics, le développement d'activités non agricoles et l'exploitation durable des ressources naturelles, culturelles et

OECD RURAL POLICY REVIEWS: MEXICO – ISBN 978-92-64-01152-6 – © OECD 2007

énergétiques étaient plus importantes. Alors que les ministères de l'éducation, de la santé et de l'environnement ont une action importante sur le développement rural, d'autres ministères chargés des politiques économiques, comme ceux de l'économie (SECON), des transports et des communications (SCT), des finances (SHCP), du tourisme, du travail (STPS) et de l'énergie, accordent très peu d'importance à cet aspect du développement (voir graphique F.5). Leur intervention dans les zones rurales, par le soutien des PME, le développement du secteur financier et l'amélioration des infrastructures économiques, pourrait apporter beaucoup à l'économie rurale. Elle contribuerait aussi à la diversification économique des zones rurales, en facilitant l'expansion de secteurs particuliers comme le tourisme et l'énergie.

Graphique F.5. **Ministères et budgets intervenant dans les politiques rurales**

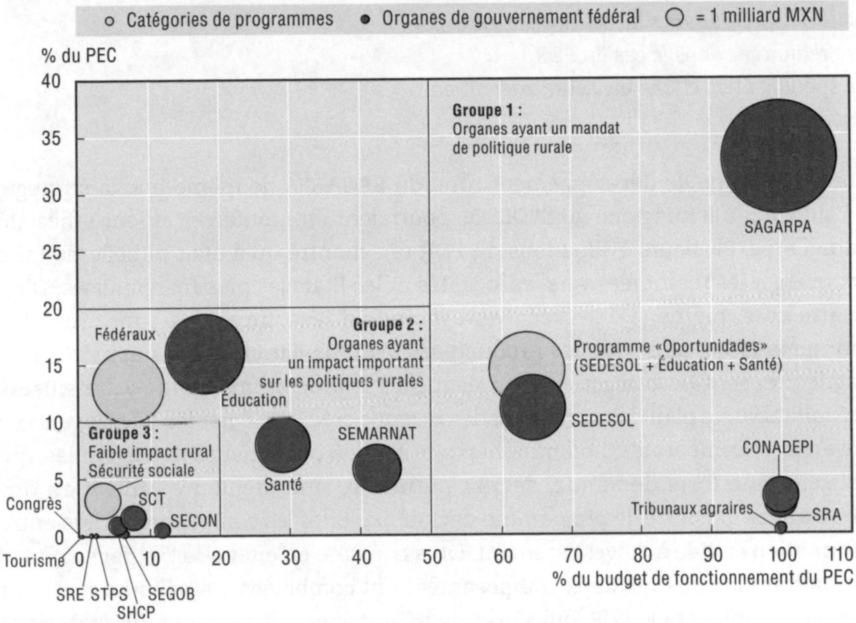

Source : PEC 2006.

---

*... en les complétant par des investissements privés
et une meilleure utilisation des fonds envoyés
par les émigrés.*

La mobilisation de ressources privées venant compléter les investissements publics est nécessaire pour déclencher la croissance économique des zones rurales. Il s'agit à la fois d'attirer des ressources nouvelles et de promouvoir une meilleure utilisation des ressources détenues par les populations rurales.

L'obtention de ressources nouvelles nécessite une plus grande souplesse des marchés, en particulier des marchés fonciers, ainsi qu'une sécurité plus grande sur le plan personnel et des droits de propriété. Pour mieux exploiter les ressources qui existent déjà dans les zones rurales, principalement sous forme de terres et de fonds envoyés par les travailleurs émigrés, les populations rurales doivent pouvoir convertir leurs droits de propriété en atouts économiques, et accéder plus facilement à des solutions de crédit, d'épargne et d'investissement. Les envois de fonds des travailleurs émigrés, qui servent surtout pour l'instant à l'achat de biens de consommation, pourraient servir à des investissements productifs, si un portefeuille d'investissements était proposé aux émigrés. Ainsi, le programme 3x1 pourrait être mieux rattaché au PDR et à la stratégie d'aide aux microrégions pour que les envois de fonds soient utilisés de façon stratégique.

L'efficacité des programmes de développement rural
peut être renforcée : dans le cas du PDR,
par une spécialisation et une meilleure orientation
des ressources…

Le programme de développement rural du SAGARPA de même que la stratégie d'aide aux microrégions du SEDESOL pourraient être renforcés et leur efficacité améliorée. Plusieurs évaluations du PDR ont montré qu'il était difficile de faire converger les ressources vers les localités et les États les plus marginalisés. D'un autre côté, même si elles reçoivent moins de ressources, les zones les plus marginalisées, ainsi que les producteurs les plus pauvres et les activités non agricoles, sont les catégories dans lesquelles le programme donne les meilleurs résultats sur le plan des emplois et des revenus créés. Orienter les efforts vers ces avantages comparatifs, notamment par le soutien des activités non agricoles, qui suscite une forte demande, devrait permettre une meilleure utilisation des ressources. En outre, le programme devrait exploiter les complémentarités entre formation et aide à l'investissement. On a constaté en effet que l'impact est plus important lorsque ces deux composantes sont combinées. L'amélioration de ces aspects renforcera le PDR, qui s'inscrira mieux dans la structure multisectorielle définie par la loi sur le développement rural durable.

… et, dans le cas de la stratégie d'aide
aux microrégions, par l'institutionnalisation
et une intégration accrue avec d'autres
programmes sociaux et économiques.

La force de la stratégie d'aide aux microrégions vient de ce qu'elle offre une plate-forme pour des actions sectorielles coordonnées dans les zones rurales les plus marginalisées. La stratégie a notamment permis de mettre en œuvre

OECD RURAL POLICY REVIEWS: MEXICO – ISBN 978-92-64-01152-6 – © OECD 2007

près de 60 % des « *banderas blancas* » nécessaires pour équiper complètement chacune des communautés visées des infrastructures et des services de base dont elle a besoin. Cependant, les progrès enregistrés varient beaucoup selon les domaines de soutien, et l'adoption récente de nouvelles « *banderas blancas* » a encore élargi les objectifs et les tâches du programme. Il faut par conséquent accroître les ressources et renforcer la coordination entre les ministères, en particulier dans les domaines de la construction de routes, des services sanitaires, de la promotion des activités productives, de la fourniture d'électricité et d'eau. Dans ce contexte, il est important de continuer « d'institutionnaliser » par des accords officiels qui favorisent la coordination, définissent explicitement les responsabilités et les budgets des ministères concernés, et garantissent la continuité de la démarche. L'incidence potentielle de la stratégie pourrait aussi être renforcée par une intégration plus grande avec d'autres programmes de développement économique et social qui acheminent déjà des ressources importantes vers les zones les plus marginalisées, comme le programme *Oportunidades*, et par d'autres transferts de ressources vers les États et les municipalités.

Résumé.

Les zones rurales du Mexique doivent faire face à d'importantes difficultés. Elles abritent une forte population (plus élevée que la population totale de nombreux pays de l'OCDE), très dispersée et majoritairement pauvre. Ces régions présentent de nombreuses potentialités, à condition que leurs ressources humaines abondantes (et jeunes), et leurs atouts naturels, culturels et physiques soient exploités dans le cadre d'une économie plus diversifiée, pour contribuer au développement national et s'intégrer à la dynamique de la mondialisation. L'analyse a montré que les enjeux et les potentialités des zones rurales sont différents selon les endroits, et requièrent par conséquent une approche fondée sur le contexte local. Le gouvernement mexicain a bien progressé en créant un cadre en faveur d'une politique rurale multisectorielle. Certains des résultats obtenus peuvent servir d'exemple à d'autres pays de l'OCDE. La continuité et l'institutionnalisation de ces progrès sont une priorité. En outre, il faut s'efforcer d'améliorer l'efficacité et l'efficience des programmes de développement rural et de garantir leur cohérence avec les autres grandes politiques sectorielles. Une telle démarche permettra de tenir compte des principales inégalités territoriales et individuelles et de faire des régions rurales une source de développement national.

ISBN 978-92-64-01152-6
OECD Rural Policy Reviews: Mexico
© OECD 2007

Conclusiones y recomendaciones (Español)

Perfil del México Rural: retos y oportunidades

La amplitud del territorio y la población rural
contrastan con su contribución al PIB.

Las regiones rurales abarcan más del 80 % del territorio mexicano y en ellas habita, utilizando una definición amplia, 37 millones de personas, es decir le 36 % de la población mexicana. Estas cifras hacen de México el país con mayor población en áreas predominantemente rurales entre los miembros de la OCDE. A pesar de su importancia en términos de territorio y población, las regiones rurales contribuyen con una pequeña parte de la economía. El contraste es particularmente visible cuando se considera la definición oficial de rural en México (localidades de menos de 2 500 habitantes), pues teniendo casi a un cuarto de la población del país, su participación en el PIB se estima en 2 % (ver Figura E.1).

Los retos de las áreas rurales están ligados
a la dispersión,...

La población rural se encuentra altamente dispersa: 24 millones de personas viven en más de 196 000 localidades remotas y 13 millones adicionales viven en cerca de 3 000 localidades rurales semiurbanas. Causas de esta dispersión son el carácter montañoso de una gran parte del territorio mexicano, y en alguna forma también la atomización de la tierra y la poco clara definición de derechos de propiedad asociada al régimen de propiedad comunal. En consecuencia, desde la distribución de tierras que siguió a la Revolución Mexicana, muchos propietarios de tierra y sus descendientes tenían fuertes incentivos a permanecer cerca de su tierra pero lejos de los mercados y servicios públicos, quedando restringidos a la agricultura de subsistencia o de baja productividad.

... a una población decreciente,...

La evolución demográfica de las áreas rurales ha sido significativamente distinta a la del resto del país. En comparación al crecimiento rápido y concentración de la población nacional y urbana, la población rural, permaneció relativamente estable y dispersa durante la segunda parte del siglo XX, y por tanto disminuyendo en términos relativos. A partir de 2000, la

OECD RURAL POLICY REVIEWS: MEXICO – ISBN 978-92-64-01152-6 – © OECD 2007

Figura E.1. **El México rural definido**

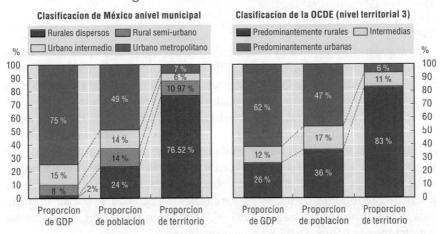

Fuente: OECD Regions at a Glance (por publicarse) y cálculos con información de INAFED (2000) e INEGI (2006).

población en localidades rurales dispersas se redujo también en términos absolutos. Esta reducción es resultado de dos efectos combinados: las menores tasas de fertilidad durante la última década, que ha reducido significativamente la tasa de dependencia de niños y adultos mayores; y la migración de jóvenes a ciudades medianas y al extranjero, que a su vez ha traído múltiples efectos económicos y sociales, incluyendo la feminización de la población rural, un aumento en la tasa de dependenciade adultos mayores y el incremento de las remesas como fuente de ingreso.

Figura E.2. **Población en areas rurales y urbanas**
1910-2005

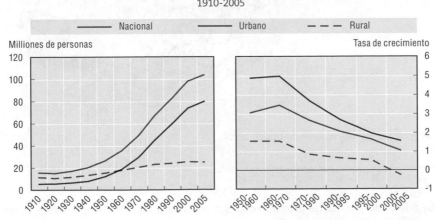

1. Rural se refiere a las localidades rurales dispersas (menos de 2 500 habitantes).
Fuente: INEGI (2006).

*… a una marcada división rural-urbana
en términos de estándares de vida….*

Los estándares de vida de la población rural son significativamente menores que los de la población urbana y la diferencia entre ellos es mayor que en el resto de los países de la OCDE. Mientras que el PIB per cápita promedio en áreas urbanas es 41 % mayor que el promedio nacional, en los municipios rurales dispersos y rurales semi-urbanos, es 73 % y 57 % menor que el promedio nacional respectivamente. De hecho, con excepción de ciertas áreas del norte, casi todas las regiones predominantemente rurales tienen PIB per cápita menor a 50 % del promedio nacional, cuando en general el promedio entre los países de la OCDE para estas áreas es 82 % del promedio nacional. A pesar de reducciones recientes en los niveles de pobreza desde su máximo alcanzado durante la crisis de 1995-96, 56 % de la población rural vive en condiciones de pobreza y 28 % en pobreza extrema.

Figura E.3. **PIB per capita en Regiones «Predominantemente Rurales» (PR) como porcentaje del promedio nacional**

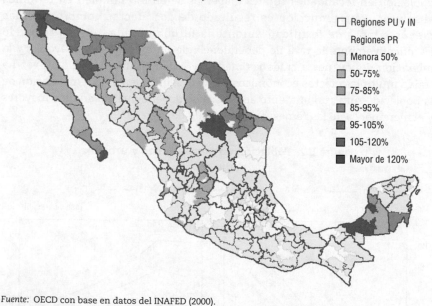

Fuente: OECD con base en datos del INAFED (2000).

… y en términos de acceso a servicios públicos.

La dificultad y costo de proveer servicios públicos a localidades dispersas tiene implicaciones en los estándares de vida de la población rural. Las localidades menos accesibles enfrentan bajos niveles de infraestructura y servicios de

OECD RURAL POLICY REVIEWS: MEXICO – ISBN 978-92-64-01152-6 – © OECD 2007

educación y salud. Solamente 68 % de los hogares en municipios rurales dispersos contaba con piso firme, solo 52 % con drenaje, 87 % con electricidad y 16 % con servicio telefónico en 2000. La escolaridad promedio es menor a 5 años en municipios rurales en contraste con 7.8 en áreas urbanas y 9.7 en la Ciudad de México. Solo cerca del 80 % de los hogares en localidades rurales dispersas tiene acceso a servicios de salud a una distancia menor a 5 km, los cuales cuentan con 22 camas de hospital y 96 médicos por cada 100 000 habitantes, en contraste con las 109 camas y 179 médicos en áreas urbanas. Estos hechos se reflejan en la esperanza de vida, que en ciertas localidades rurales es 10 años menor que en la Ciudad de México y la tasa de mortalidad infantil que llegan a ser tres veces mayor que en la capital.

Hay sin embargo oportunidades significativas ligadas al «bono demográfico»...

La dimensión abrumadora de los retos frecuentemente difumina la percepción de la heterogeneidad de las áreas rurales y las oportunidades relacionadas con recursos abundantes escasamente explotados. El aprovechamiento de estas oportunidades podrá contribuir al fortalecimiento de la economía rural y al sostenimiento del crecimiento nacional. Primero, la población rural es predominantemente joven; la edad mediana es 20 años. Esta generación, que formará parte de la fuerza laboral durante la próxima década, forma parte del bono demográfico que México está experimentando como resultado de su transición demográfica. Ella podría contribuir al incremento de la producción y al crecimiento económico como ha sido el caso en el caso de otros países de la OECD. Además, aunque el promedio de los indicadores de escolaridad de las áreas rurales permanecen bajos (ya que incluyen también a la población adulta), las tasas de acceso y finalización de educación secundaria muestran que la actual generación de jóvenes está mejor preparada que las generaciones precedentes. Numerosos estudios también resaltan que la juventud rural mexicana es frecuentemente emprendedora y más familiarizada con las oportunidades de mercado y los avances tecnológicos.

... al amplio potencial de diversificación económica,...

Segundo, retos pero también oportunidades están ligadas a la transformación actual de la economía rural en México. La contribución de las actividades agropecuarias, pesqueras y forestales al PIB se ha reducido de 8 % en 1990 a 5 % en 2004. En términos de empleo, sin embargo, la agricultura sigue siendo la actividad preponderante en los municipios rurales dispersos (con 44 % de su población ocupada en el sector primario). La proporción de empleo en este sector en México es aún mayor que en el promedio de la OECD tanto para las regiones predominantemente rurales (30 % contra 10 %) como para la economía nacional (16 % vs 6 % promedio de la OCDE). Mientras que los productores agropecuarios grandes han podido integrarse a los mercados internacionales y han incrementado considerablemente las exportaciones agropecuarias, la gran mayoría de los productores pequeños aún se encuentran concentrados en cultivos de bajo valor agregado y con alta vulnerabilidad a cambios en precios. La transición de agricultura a otras actividades tiene lugar con gran rapidez en las áreas rurales. Dos hechos son evidencia de este fenómeno. Primero, la proporción del ingreso no-agropecuario que ha crecido sustancialmente, hasta el punto de representar más del 50 % del ingreso familiar aún en las áreas rurales dispersas.Segundo, el empleo no-agropecuario que creció más en áreas rurales (5.2 % anual) que en áreas urbanas (3.5 %) entre 1999 y 2004.

Figura E.4. **Diversificación de la economía rural: Crecimiento en el empleo rural y urbano en actividades no agropecuarias**

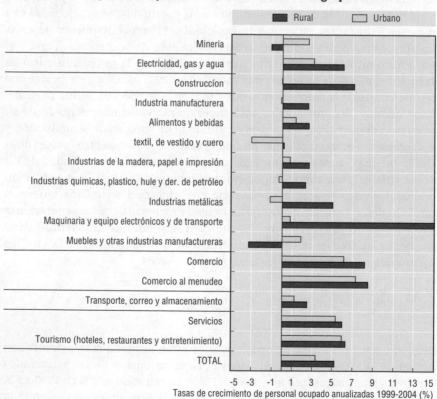

Rural incluye a las localidades rurales dispersas (de menos de 2,500 habitantes) y rurales semi-urbanas (de menos de 15 000).

Fuente: INEGI Censos Económicos 1999, 2004.

OECD RURAL POLICY REVIEWS: MEXICO – ISBN 978-92-64-01152-6 – © OECD 2007

El primer refugio fuera de la agricultura es el comercio al menudeo. A pesar de ser un sector grande, tuvo un crecimiento importante (8.5 % anual) en el período 1999-2004. El crecimiento de las actividades manufactureras no fue tan fuerte, sin embargo, fue también mayor que en el contexto urbano. Destaca el hecho de que los sectores manufactureros que crecieron más en áreas rurales fueron sectores avanzados como la fabricación de maquinaria, equipo electrónico y de transporte (15 % anual). La diversificación creciente de la economía rural varía de región a región. Aunque la contribución de la diversificación al mejoramiento de los estándares de vida no es fácilmente cuantificable, la evidencia demuestra que el PIB per cápita en las regiones predominantemente rurales más diversificadas (los estados del norte como Nuevo León, Baja California, Baja California Sur y Coahuila) es mayor que no solo en el resto de las áreas rurales sino que el promedio nacional.

... y a la presencia de recursos naturales, culturales
y energéticos subutilizados.

Tercero, el crecimiento de sectores como el turismo como alternativa de ingreso en áreas rurales digno de ser destacado. De 1999 a 2004 el sector turismo fue uno de los sectores con mayor crecimiento, nuevamente ligeramente superior en áreas rurales (6.3 %) que en áreas urbanas. En 2004, 9 % del empleo turístico se encontraba concentrado en áreas rurales. Las regiones Sur-Sureste y la Península de Baja California contienen las áreas rurales donde el turismo representa una proporción significativa del empleo y del valor agregado (más de 25 %). En particular, en la región Sur Sureste, que es la región más pobre del país, su riqueza en recursos naturales, herencia cultural y arqueológica y sitios históricos, podría convertirse en una de las llaves de su desarrollo económico. Adicionalmente, hay un potencial no utilizado en términos de fuentes de energía renovable presentes en áreas rurales incluyendo energía solar, eólica, hidráulica y bio-energía. La experiencia de varios países miembros y no miembros de la OECD indica que las áreas rurales pueden contribuir significativamente a la provisión de energía para consumo propio y del país en su conjunto, a la vez que proveen alternativas de ingreso y oportunidades de empleo a la población local.

En suma, hay diferentes «Mexicos rurales» con
retos y potenciales distintos.

Las áreas rurales presentan una alta heterogeneidad: existen definitivamente las áreas rurales pobres, pero no puede generalizarse que «rural» implica «pobreza». Hay una parte de la economía rural que esta fuertemente ligada a la agricultura, la pesca y la actividad forestal, mientras que hay áreas rurales que han diversificado su economía hacia las manufacturas y los servicios. Hay áreas rurales que se han desarrollado como destinos turísticos y otras tantas que contienen recursos naturales, y culturales no utilizados. Hay por lo tanto diversos retos para la política rural en México. Estos incluyen: 1) la reducción de la pobreza rural, 2) la provisión de servicios públicos básicos, 3) el fortalecimiento y diversificación de la economía rural y finalmente 4) la mejor explotación y preservación de los recursos culturales, naturales y energéticos subutilizados

Como ha enfrentado México los retos y oportunidades?

*México ha tomado pasos innovadores hacia
un esquema intersectorial y multinivel
de política rural.*

La política rural en México ha venido evolucionando en las últimas décadas de una política de un solo sector (agricultura) hacia una política que busca la integración de las acciones de los diferentes secretarías y de los diversos niveles de gobierno (federal, estatal y municipal) en las áreas rurales. El nuevo entorno institucional de estos cambios se basa en la Ley de Desarrollo Rural Sustentable (LDRS) aprobada en 2001 que plantea el establecimiento de un órgano específico para la coordinación horizontal a nivel federal en materia de política rural (la Comisión Intersecretarial para el Desarrollo Rural Sustentable, CIDRS), la constitución de órganos participativos para la sociedad civil (Consejos para el Desarrollo Rural Sustentable) y la elaboración de un Programa Especial Concurrente (PEC). Este último ha evolucionado hacia la integración de un «presupuesto rural» que figura anualmente como anexo del presupuesto federal. Un análisis de este presupuesto demuestra que de entre los programas federales destinados a las áreas rurales, dos políticas sobresalen en términos de recursos: la política social (que involucra políticas de combate a la pobreza, educación y salud) y las políticas de «soporte productivo», que fundamentalmente tienen un enfoque agropecuario. Otras políticas federales con impacto significativo en las áreas rurales son la provisión de infraestructura básica y productiva y las política ambiental, agraria y laboral.

*Los dos actores más relevantes de la política rural
tienen programas explícitamente orientados
al desarrollo rural…*

Las dos secretarías con mayor impacto en áreas rurales, la Secretaría de Agricultura, Ganadería, Desarrollo Rural, Pesca y Alimentación (SAGARPA) y la

OECD RURAL POLICY REVIEWS: MEXICO – ISBN 978-92-64-01152-6 – © OECD 2007

Secretaría de Desarrollo Social (SEDESOL), dentro de sus propias áreas de competencia, cuentan con programas específicamente orientados al desarrollo rural. Por un lado el Programa de Desarrollo Rural (PDR) de SAGARPA es uno de los programas federales más descentralizados. Está orientado al fomento de inversiones productivas en agricultura, ganadería y actividades no agropecuarias con un enfoque de demanda y de proyecto. Dos componentes complementarios son asistencia técnica y apoyo organizacional. Este último componente ha sido instrumental en la construcción de la arquitectura institucional planteada en la LDRS. Por otro lado, SEDESOL coordina la Estrategia Micro-Regiones que es una estrategia multisectorial específicamente enfocada a las regiones rurales más marginalizadas con el objeto de proveer infraestructura básica y mejores condiciones para el desarrollo creando «micro polos de desarrollo», los llamados Centros Estratégicos Comunitarios (CECs). La especificidad de su ámbito de acción permite monitorear los avances y el déficit en cada una de las áreas de apoyo a través de mecanismos de validación objetivos y socialmente compartidos a través del sistema de «banderas blancas».

... que atienden distintos objetivos con un enfoque integrado.

Tanto el PDR como la Estrategia Micro-Regiones incluyen diversos aspectos que están en línea con las mejores practicas entre los países de la OECD: 1) tienen una perspectiva territorial e integral del desarrollo rural que se extiende de las fronteras sectoriales; 2) no se enfocan en subsidios sino en inversiones, y 3) coordinan esfuerzos de distintos actores, el PDR con una mayor orientación vertical (dado su carácter descentralizado) y la estrategia Microrregiones con una perspectiva más horizontal (dado su carácter Intersecretarial). Los dos programas, sin embargo difieren en sus objetivos y metodologías: 1) el PDR esta orientado a las áreas rurales en general, mientras que la Estrategia Microrregiones se enfoca en un subconjunto de áreas rurales, aquellas con mayor marginación y condiciones de pobreza; 2) el PDR está mas orientado al apoyo a la población rural en tanto agentes económicos o productores, mientras que la estrategia Microrregiones se enfoca en sus derechos y condiciones de vida; 3) mientras que el PDR tiene un enfoque de demanda (los beneficiarios proponen proyectos para obtener apoyo), la estrategia Microrregiones coordina la oferta de políticas públicas de diversas secretarías en territorios específicos.

Aspectos críticos y prioridades de acción

*La governanza del desarrollo rural podría
mejorarse con mayor liderazgo...*

Hay dos aspectos críticos con respecto a la coordinación horizontal a nivel federal. El primero tiene que ver con la coordinación de las 14 secretarías que integran la CIDRS. Hay evidencia de que SAGARPA, que dirige la comisión, ha tenido dificultades en involucrar y obtener compromiso por parte de las otras secretarías. La experiencia de diversos países de la OECD indica que una comisión horizontal presidida por un sector (en este caso agricultura) puede encontrarse limitada para llevar a cabo objetivos multisectoriales e inhibir el involucramiento completo de otras secretarías en la estrategia nacional rural. La governanza de la política rural y la participación de los distintos actores podría mejorarse proveyendo a la CIDRS con un liderazgo fuerte meta-secretarial. Esto podría obtenerse por ejemplo asignando la presidencia al Jefe del Ejecutivo o vía la creación de una institución *ad hoc* o la rotación de las distintas secretarías al frente de la comisión.

*... mejor coordinación horizontal coordination entre
secretarías clave...*

Un Segundo aspecto es relacionado a la coordinación entre SAGARPA y SEDESOL, que son las dos secretarías más involucradas en asuntos rurales. Por un lado, la cooperación entre ellas es limitada por el hecho de que se guían por lógicas distintas y responden a ordenamientos legales distintos (La ley de Desarrollo Rural Sustentable y la Ley de Desarrollo Social). Cada una de estas leyes les confiere «autoridad» en comisiones intersecretariales (una sobre desarrollo rural, otra sobre desarrollo social) que involucran frecuentemente a las mismas secretarías. Además, SEDESOL coordina la Estrategia Microrregiones, que a su vez, cuenta con un organismo intersecretarial. Este problema institucional se traslada posteriormente al nivel subnacional donde las dos secretarías tienen estructuras administrativas a menudo actuando en los mismos territorios: SAGARPA utiliza fundamentalmente (y ha conformado) los consejos de desarrollo rural sustentable propuestos por la LDRS mientras SEDESOL utiliza las instituciones de planeación local preexistentes (COPLADEs y COPLADEMUNs). Además de sus propias delegaciones en cada uno de los 31 estados, ambas secretarías tienen estructuras descentralizadas para operar sus programas a nivel local, tales como los llamador «residentes» en el caso de la estrategia Microrregiones y los «promotores» de SAGARPA. Hay condiciones para encontrar mejores arreglos institucionales que permitan a la política rural y social explotar

OECD RURAL POLICY REVIEWS: MEXICO – ISBN 978-92-64-01152-6 – © OECD 2007

sinergias y construir una red común de instituciones que permita a las dos secretarías llevar a cabo sus políticas eficientemente en el ámbito local. Dichos cambios podrían ayudar a encontrar complementariedades en sus enfoques de política: las políticas de SEDESOL están orientadas a proveer una plataforma básica para el desarrollo de los habitantes rurales, particularmente en las zonas de mayor marginación mientras que las de SAGARPA, con un enfoque universal en cobertura y una orientación productiva, puede embonar eficazmente una vez que dicha plataforma está constituida.

... y una definición clara de responsabilidades entre distintos niveles de gobierno.

La LDRS establece que el federalismo y la descentralización son criterios fundamentales de la implementación de la agenda de desarrollo rural. Sin embargo, cada secretaría tiene distintos criterios y estrategias de descentralización de sus respectivas políticas públicas. Por tanto, algunos programas descentralizados en el ámbito local son poco efectivos por la falta de políticas complementarias que no están descentralizadas. El fortalecimiento del proceso de descentralización de las políticas de desarrollo rural requiere 1) un acuerdo de las áreas de política a ser descentralizadas por cada secretaría relevante con enfoque en las complementariedades entre ellas. 2) La definición clara de responsabilidades (en términos de presupuesto y rendición de cuentas) así como de funciones (establecimiento de estándares, diseño, implementación y evaluación de las políticas) que llevará a cabo cada nivel de gobierno. 3) Fortalecimiento de la capacidad local, particularmente a nivel municipal y el aseguramiento de la continuidad de la capacidad existente, lo cual es un reto en el contexto de los cortos períodos de gobierno de las autoridades municipales.

Un Programa Especial Concurrente más transparente y coherente podría mejorar la eficiencia del gasto rural...

Desde el punto de vista de políticas públicas, las prioridades de la política rural en México incluyen: 1) la reducción de la pobreza, 2) la provisión de servicios públicos básicos 3) el fortalecimiento y diversificación de la economía rural y finalmente 4) la explotación y preservación de los recursos naturales culturales y energéticos. Dado que estas prioridades sobrepasan el ámbito de acción de una secretaría individual, la coordinación de las acciones es necesaria para llevarlas a cabo eficientemente. Si bien el Programa Especial Concurrente (PEC) constituye un esfuerzo importante hacia el diseño de una política federal integral para el desarrollo rural, en su condición actual es un inventario de programas más que una herramienta para explotar sinergias entre los programas con impacto en áreas rurales. El resultado es la inclusión de programas e instituciones que no están necesariamente orientados al desarrollo rural. Esto produce una imagen distorsionada de la estrategia de política rural e información sobre el gasto rural que no corresponde completamente con la realidad. Con el objeto de sacar provecho del propósito de esta innovación, se deberían enfocar esfuerzos en 1) mejorar la transparencia con respecto a los criterios de inclusión de programas en el PEC y la proporción de dichos programas que sea considerada con impacto en áreas rurales; 2) establecer un diálogo que pueda resultar en la fusión, transferencia y eliminación de programas con el objeto de obtener un conjunto de herramientas de política para las áreas rurales coherente y efectivo; 3) Introducir mecanismos de monitoreo y evaluación de los resultados y objetivos de política alcanzados con base en metas acordadas.

... y orientar los recursos públicos hacia las prioridades de política para el desarrollo rural...

Actualmente los recursos federales invertidos en áreas rurales no corresponden completamente con las prioridades identificadas: un sector (agricultura) y un objetivo horizontal (reducción de la pobreza) dominante el ámbito de la política rural. Si bien la inversión significativa en estas dos áreas contribuye a las prioridades de reducción de la pobreza y al fortalecimiento de la economía rural, importantes sinergias podrían obtenerse de invertir mayores recursos en la distribución de servicios públicos, el desarrollo de negocios en actividades no agropecuarias y la explotación sustentable de recursos naturales, culturales y energéticos. Mientras que las secretarías de educación pública, salud y medio ambiente tienen un impacto significativo en el desarrollo rural, otras secretarías como las de economía, transportes y comunicaciones, hacienda, turismo, trabajo y energía tienen muy poco enfoque rural (ver Figura 5). El involucramiento de estas secretarías en las áreas rurales podría contribuir significativamente al fortalecimiento de la economía rural a través de la promoción de PYMEs, el desarrollo del sector financiero rural y mejor infraestructura. Asimismo, contribuiría a la diversificación de las áreas rurales facilitando la expansión de sectores específicos con oportunidades como el de turismo y energía.

OECD RURAL POLICY REVIEWS: MEXICO – ISBN 978-92-64-01152-6 – © OECD 2007

Figura E.5. **Secretarías y presupuesto asignado a la política rural**

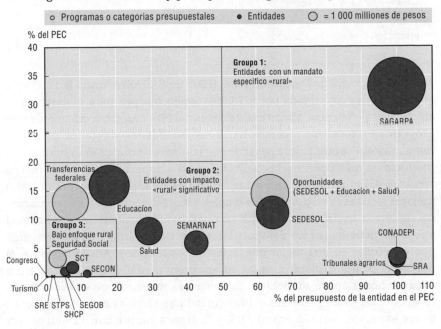

Fuente: PEC 2006.

... complementados por inversión privada
y un mejor uso de las remesas.

La movilización de recursos privados es necesaria además de la inversión pública para generar desarrollo económico en las áreas rurales. Esto involucra tanto la atracción de nuevos recursos como la promoción de un mejor uso de los recursos que los pobladores rurales poseen. Para atraer nuevos recursos, se requiere de mayor flexibilidad en los mercados, particularmente en el de la tierra, así como mayor seguridad personal y de los derechos de propiedad. Para la mejor utilización de los recursos que residen actualmente en las áreas rurales, principalmente en forma de tierras y de remesas, los habitantes rurales deberían poder transformar fácilmente sus derechos de propiedad en activos económicos y tener mayor acceso a alternativas de crédito, ahorro e inversión. Las remesas, que tienen un sesgo actualmente hacia el consumo, podrían ser invertidas de forma productiva si se les propusiera un portafolio de inversiones a los que las envían. Por ejemplo, el programa 3x1 podría estar mejor ligado con el PDR y con la estrategia Microrregiones para que una proporción de las remesas se utilizaran en forma estratégica para el desarrollo rural.

Los programas enfocados al desarrollo rural pueden
aumentar su efectividad, en el caso del PDR
con especialisación y mejor focalización
de recursos…

Tanto el Programa de Desarrollo Rural (PDR) de SAGARPA como la Estrategia Microrregiones coordinada por SEDESOL tienen margen para mejorar en su efectividad y eficiencia. Varias evaluaciones del PDR muestran dificultades del programa en focalizar recursos hacia las localidades y estados de mayor marginación. Por otro lado, a pesar de que las áreas de mayor marginación, los productores más pobres y las actividades no agropecuarias reciben menos recursos del programa, es en estas categorías donde el programa muestra mejores resultados en términos de empleo e ingreso generados. La orientación de esfuerzos hacia estas ventajas comparativas, particularmente hacia el apoyo de actividades no agropecuarias que tienen una amplia demanda podría resultar en una mejor utilización de los recursos. Adicionalmente, el programa podría explotar más las complementariedades que existen entre capacitación y apoyo monetario. La evidencia muestra que cuando ambos componentes están presentes el impacto del programa es mayor. Avanzar en estos aspectos fortalecerá al PDR y lo ligará mejor con la estructura multisectorial definida por la LDRS.

… en el caso de la estrategia Microrregiones
con institucionalización y una mejor integración
con otros programas económicos y sociales.

La fortaleza de la Estrategia Microrregiones reside en la plataforma que ofrece para la coordinación de las intervenciones de política sectorial en las áreas de mayor marginalización. Un resultado relevante de la estrategia es la cobertura de cerca del 60 % del déficit de «banderas blancas» que son requeridas para equipar completamente a los Centros Estratégicos Comunitarios (CEC) con la infraestructura y servicios necesarios. Sin embargo, los avances son considerablemente más lentos en algunas áreas de apoyo que en otras y la adición de nuevas banderas blancas ha incrementado el ámbito de acción del programa y sus retos. Esto implica la necesidad de mayores recursos y mejor coordinación con las secretarías relevantes, en particular en las áreas de construcción de caminos, servicios sanitarios, promoción de actividades productivas, provisión de electricidad y agua. En este contexto es importante la mayor «institucionalización» de la estrategia mediante acuerdos formales que fomenten la coordinación, establezcan explícitamente las responsabilidades y recursos comprometidos por cada una de las instituciones involucradas y garantizar la continuidad de la estrategia. El impacto potencial de la estrategia podría ser aumentado mediante la integración con otros programas sociales y económicos que ya canalizan recursos a las áreas más marginal izadas, con particular atención al programa Oportunidades y a las transferencias a estados y municipios.

En resumen.

Las áreas rurales en México tienen retos significativos. En ellas reside una amplia población (más que la población total de muchos países de la OECD), altamente dispersa y mayoritariamente en condiciones de pobreza. El potencial de estas áreas es también amplio, en tanto se den las condiciones para permitir que sus vastos recursos humanos (preponderantemente jóvenes), así como sus activos naturales, culturales y físicos contribuyan, a través de una economía más diversificada, al desarrollo nacional y se integren mejor a la dinámica de la globalización. El potencial y los retos de las áreas rurales son varían para cada región y por lo tanto requieren de enfoques de política territoriales. Hay avances significativos del gobierno mexicano en darle un enfoque multisectorial a la política rural. Algunos de estos avances representan mejores prácticas para otros países de la OECD. La continuidad e institucionalización de estos avances constituye una prioridad. Adicionalmente, deben orientarse esfuerzos para mejorar la eficiencia y efectividad de los programas de desarrollo rural y garantizar su coherencia con las políticas sectoriales. Esto contribuirá a la mejor atención de las disparidades entre individuos y entre regiones y a transformar las áreas rurales en una fuente del desarrollo nacional.

OECD PUBLICATIONS, 2, rue André-Pascal, 75775 PARIS CEDEX 16
PRINTED IN FRANCE
(04 2007 03 1 P) ISBN 978-92-64-01152-6 – No. 55493 2007